Torture
in the
Age of Fear

Torture
in the
Age of Fear

Ezat Mossallanejed

Seraphim Editions

Copyright © Ezat Mossallanejed 2005
Chapter 5 copyright © Monireh Baradaran 2005

All rights reserved. No part of this publication may be reproduced or transmitted in any form or by any means – electronic or mechanical, including photocopying, recording or any information storage and retrieval system – without written permission from the Publisher, except by a reviewer who wishes to quote brief passages for inclusion in a review.

The publisher gratefully acknowledges the financial assistance of the Canada Council for the Arts and the Ontario Arts Council.

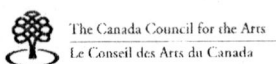

Published in 2005 by
Seraphim Editions
238 Emerald St. N.
Hamilton, ON
Canada L8L 5K8

Library and Archives Canada Cataloguing in Publication

Mossallanejed, Ezat, 1945-
  Torture in the age of fear / Ezat Mossallanejed.

Includes bibliographical references and index.
ISBN 0-9734588-6-0

1. Torture. 2. Torture victims. 3. Torture (International law). I. Title.

HV8593.M68 2005   323.4'9   C2005-905062-4

Editor: Tanya Nanavati
Cover art: Reza Sepahdari
Design: Perkolator {Kommunikation}

Printed and bound in Canada

Contents

Foreword 7

Introduction 11

1 On the Ruins of Nineveh 15
2 The Era of Fear: Torture and Terror 29
3 Legal Instruments Against Torture 51
4 A Glimpse into the Global Picture of Torture Against Children 67
5 Children of Prison 99
6 With My Child in Jail 113
7 Surviving Torture Through Self-Rehabilitation and Love 133
8 Impunity 147
9 Canada Against Torture 175
10 Limbo as a Technique of Torture 193
11 Limbo in Paradise 223
12 All is Limbo: No Paradise on Earth 257

Conclusion 289

Acronyms 293

Acknowledgements 295

Index 296

To my unforgettable friend and jail-mate Dr. Nezam Rashidiyoon, who courageously resisted severe torture and more than six years of imprisonment under the Shah of Iran. He was released following the popular uprising of 1978, rearrested by the Islamic Republican regime and executed in the early 1980s. I will forever remember his contributions towards the pursuit of freedom, social justice and human rights, as well as his generous medical services.

Foreword

MOST PEOPLE RARELY think about torture and other human rights abuses. When the Canadian Centre for Victims of Torture (CCVT) was initially established as the first rehabilitation centre for torture victims in North America, many were sceptical about the need for such a facility. There was general resistance to thinking about torture and its consequences.

Now, 27 years later, the work of the centre has garnered much attention and respect in Canada and abroad and is called upon to provide training, and to share its expertise nationally and internationally.

The CCVT is a community-based agency that believes refugee survivors of torture and war can be assisted most effectively through a partnership between original cultural communities and the new Canadian community. To this end CCVT's mandate states two organizational aims: direct service and public education. Public education is necessary to increase awareness and develop support for survivors of torture within service-providing agencies and community groups, government organizations, and the general public. *Torture in the Age of Fear* will add to this knowledge base and facilitate the work required in the provision of services. As well, the book will raise awareness on the scourge of torture and hopefully generate solidarity in the effort to stop this evil form of repression.

As I have stated above, we at the Canadian Centre for Victims of Torture (CCVT) see ourselves as a community. We have a paid core staff of less than fifteen, approximately fifty professionals (lawyers and medical personnel) working voluntarily, and 250 volunteers who assist in every aspect of the organization and act as a link to the community at large. This network serves over one thousand new clients per year. The CCVT community provides a bridge for the individual to move from isolation to contact with others. It is a place where network relationships can develop and families can find support in re-establishing themselves. It also serves to connect exile communities and the host community.

Mr. Ezat Mossallanejed has been involved in community work in Canada for the last 20 years. He is one of the key staff at CCVT where he has served as a volunteer and full-time staff member for the past 14 years. He wears two hats: as a CCVT Counsellor and as a Policy Analyst and Researcher. His work, *Torture in the Age of Fear,* is a comprehensive study that will contribute to creating a greater awareness of torture and its prevalence in the 21st century. He draws upon his professional expertise to speak about torture and the need for its prevention and eradication. He has creatively combined theory and practice by doing analytical research on the one hand and sharing his experiences and the experiences of others, especially clients of the CCVT, on the other.

He has networked with the Inter-Church Committee for Refugees, the Canadian Centre for International Justice (CCIJ), Amnesty International, the Canadian Network for the Health of Survivors of Torture, and other agencies. For their generous contributions, he has consistently expressed gratitude to all.

In *Torture in the Age of Fear,* Ezat has given voice to the voiceless who have endured horrifying experiences and to others who mourn in silence. He has highlighted the traumas, hopes, and fears of torture survivors and their families to a larger audience. This book will hopefully build understanding within the general public and facilitate the rehabilitation of victims with the support of the community. I sincerely hope that the holistic approach of *Torture in the Age of Fear* contributes towards the efforts of organizations like the CCVT and many others around the globe.

Torture and organized violence radically transforms and sometimes destroys families, social networks and communities, and the patterns of relationships within them. In our work with survivors, we focus not just on the torture and its impact on the individual but how the individual's relationships have been changed. We consider how torture survivors understand themselves as members of society. We are aware that it is this relationship which they need to reconstitute. Our task is therefore to provide a context in which previous systems of meaning can be recovered and new ones developed. *Torture in the Age of Fear* is a consistent endeavour to address these issues.

FOREWORD

We strive to provide new relationships in which trust and empathy can be re-established and new meaning generated to make sense of the experiences of survivors. We are further aware, not only of the value of scientific theories, generalized categories and conceptual frameworks, but also of their limitations. We see our role not so much as directors and organizers of the process of reconstitution, but as participants in it. This calls for us to engage in the process not only at a professional level, but also at a human one. We must be prepared to subordinate our scientific theories and professional defenses to the dialectic of an encounter between fellow human beings, cooperatively engaged in a struggle to preserve human rights and human values.

Mulugeta Abai
Executive Director
The Canadian Centre for Victims of Torture

Ezat Mossallanejed holds a Ph.D. in Political Economy. A victim of torture in Iran, he escaped to Canada in 1985. In Montreal, he was a founding member of the Iranian Cultural and Community Centre, Institut Éducatif pour les Jeunes Iraniens, and the Montreal Democratic Forum. In Toronto, he worked as a Youth Counsellor with St. Christopher House and as a Refugee Policy Analyst, and later was the Director of the Jesuit Refugee Service – Canada. At present, Ezat is a full-time Counsellor and Policy Analyst with the Canadian Centre for Victims of Torture (CCVT). He is a member of the Editorial Board of *Refugee Update,* a journal of refugee protection and advocacy in Canada. Sleeping Giant Productions has made a documentary about Ezat's experience of torture which has frequently been broadcast by Vision TV. Ezat is presently the Chair of the Board of Culturelink and is on the Board of the Canadian Centre for International Justice. He is the author of four books in Persian and one in English.

Introduction

THE END OF the Cold War did not usher in an era of peace and prosperity for the human race as expected. On the contrary, it brought with it ethnic conflicts and genocide. The forces of globalization, including the failure of Western secularism in resolving man-made problems, resulted in fanaticism of all kinds – religious, nationalistic and other. Terrorism of the worst type showed its ugly face as a manifestation of total despair. For all intents and purposes, we are living in an age of horror.

Torture in the Age of Fear is a modest attempt to create a comprehensive depiction of torture in the present-day world. The first chapter, "On the Ruins of Nineveh," is a study of the forces of evil that are ruining human life today: state and non-state terrorism. These two faces of terror nourish and complement each other. Both use abhorrent means, including torture, to achieve their main goal of power. The main victims are the common people, faceless and powerless, who work from dawn to dusk to keep their bodies and souls together.

Immediately following the tragedy of September 11, 2001, George W. Bush proclaimed that the world would never be the same. Since then, we have witnessed the rise of racism and xenophobia, official justification of torture, further erosion of the right to asylum, and the outright practice of torture by some Western democratic governments. In Canada, the US, the UK, and other countries, new anti-terrorist legislation has been implemented with the negative outcome of the violation of civil and political rights.

The authoritarian nature of modern states and their lack of accountability have given *carte blanche* to the scourge of torture to become common practice. It is difficult to tackle this evil due to the silence maintained by both victims and perpetrators.

The second chapter of the book, "The Era of Fear: Torture and Terror," deals with the root causes of torture, methods used, victims, victimizers, and its absolute prohibition under international law. Remarks are made about the holistic method of rehabilitation of torture survivors and the need for doctors, nurses and social workers to be wary of over-involvement with the trauma so as not to burn themselves out.

Chapter 3 presents a brief study of the legal instruments against torture and the shortcomings of existing international laws and institutions that deal with this ugly offspring of our barbaric antiquity.

Torture is an evil that does not spare children. They are tortured because of the political activities of their parents or close relatives. They also suffer due to their own vulnerability as easy targets for warlords. There are approximately 300,000 child soldiers around the world, half of whom are girls. Children are also subject to torture in war zones and in countries with gross human rights violations. They can be indirect victims of the scourge of torture by witnessing their families being destroyed or uprooted. These issues are examined in Chapter 4, "A Glimpse into the Global Picture of Torture Against Children."

Chapters 5 and 6 are the contributions of two courageous women survivors of torture. Both of them have spent years in Iranian jails. The first contributor, in "Children of Prison," shares her experiences in jail with many children and their mothers. The second is my client at the Canadian Centre for Victims of Torture (CCVT), who spent five years in jail with her baby as chronicled in the chapter "With My Child in Jail."

In Chapter 7, "Surviving Torture Through Self-Rehabilitation and Love," I share my own personal techniques in overcoming the after-effects of torture. I hope survivors of war and torture will utilize my experiences creatively and come up with their own methods of coping. This chapter could also be beneficial to doctors, nurses, lawyers and social workers who work with survivors.

It is unfortunate that like war crimes and other crimes against humanity, torture remains a crime without punishment. According to international law, there is no safe haven for torturers anywhere in the world. Nevertheless, torturers enjoy impunity everywhere. Impunity gives a sense of powerlessness to survivors of torture, their families, and the human population in general. Chapter 8, "Impunity," deals with this global barrier to the prevention of torture. Issues including problems of transitional justice, truth and reconciliation commissions and the International Criminal Court (ICC) are studied at length. A modest attempt is made to examine the irresolvable difficulties of the prosecution of torturers, war criminals, and those who have committed crimes against humanity.

Chapter 9, "Canada Against Torture," highlights the positive contributions of Canada in making torture an issue at the global level. It also deals with the government's failure to fully utilize its capacity to stem this human plague. Canada still has a long way to go in order to achieve an effective strategy to protect its citizens against torture in other countries, as the world witnessed in the cases of Maher Arar, William Sampson, and Zahara Kazemi.

Although there is no record of systemic torture in Canada as a means of political repression, Canadian immigration and enforcement officials have used other cruel, inhuman and degrading treatment *vis-à-vis* non-citizens in detention or in the process of removal. Canada has used violence against First Nations people and, like many other countries, is not free from police arbitrariness and violence, particularly against visible minorities and non-citizens.

Keeping victims in a state of total oblivion and uncertainty is an infamous method of torture. Throughout history, the torture of limbo has traumatized and retraumatized millions of decent people. It has also been used against non-citizens in Canada. Thousands of people are living in Canada today with no status. Thousands more have fallen between the cracks of immigration legislation due to their lack of identity documents, security suspicion, or criminal convictions. It is unfortunate that in a country regarded as a paradise on earth, the majority of non-citizens have continued to experience the torture of limbo for years. Limbo has led to the retraumatization of survivors of torture. In the last three chapters of the book, I present a study of the religious and historical roots of limbo, its use as a technique of torture, and the apathy of the Canadian immigration system.

In the final chapter, "All is Limbo: No Paradise on Earth," I share the cases of 16 CCVT clients.

In writing *Torture in the Age of Fear,* I have referred to both classical and contemporary literature. I have consulted with dozens of colleagues who provide medical, legal, community and other services to survivors of torture and trauma. I have also benefited from the knowledge and expertise of human rights advocates and academics in Canada and elsewhere. I have attempted to share my experiences as a political refugee and a survivor of torture under the Shah of Iran. My involvement with the CCVT as a volunteer, counsellor, policy analyst, and researcher has provided me with first-hand practical experiences of helping survivors of war and torture. This book, above all, has benefited from the tragic stories of scores of my decent and dignified clients who have come to Canada from across the globe. I find it my duty to give voice to these silent survivors who have lost everything in the painful attempt to make this planet a better place to live.

Although I consider myself a humble citizen of the world, I could not avoid paying special attention to Iran and Canada throughout the book. Some readers may find this an unbalanced approach to social research. However, I cannot avoid it. This is what I am. I owe any wisdom that I have today specifically to three countries: Iran, my homeland; India, where I received my education; and Canada, my home.

I hope that *Torture in the Age of Fear* will contribute towards the global efforts to expose and eradicate torture on the one hand, and the need to rehabilitate its survivors on the other. I cherish the hope that, sooner rather than later, torture will be eliminated from the globe. Then, and only then, will I retire to a small farm in a remote corner of the world and breed donkeys, whom I love as happy, stubborn, and intelligent animals.

Ezat Mossallanejed
Friday, July 29, 2005

1

On the Ruins of Nineveh

Over thy wounds now do I prophesy, –
A curse shall light upon the limbs of men;
Domestic fury and fierce civil strife
Shall cumber all the parts of Italy,
Blood and destruction shall be so in use,
And dreadful objects so familiar,
That mother shall but smile when they behold
Their infants quartered with the hands of war,
All pity choked with custom of fell deeds;
Cry "Havoc!" and let slip the dogs of war,
That this foul deed shall smell above the earth
With carrion men, groaning for burial.[1]
— William Shakespeare

NINEVEH WAS THE cradle of an ancient civilization that flourished for more than 5,000 years. It was located on the east bank of the Tigris River in what is now Iraq. It was the last capital of the fierce and ruthless Assyrian Empire that ruled half the world with an iron fist. Its walls were 100 feet high, broad enough for three chariots, and furnished with 15 main gates and 1,500 towers, each about 200 feet in height. The city comprised official buildings, a trade centre, temples and a botanical garden of global reputation. Ashurbanipal, the last great king of Assyria, built himself a palace with a library that contained more than 22,000 books.

In the summer of 612 BC, Nabopolassar, the Chaldean leader, aided by Medes and the northern nomads, invaded Nineveh. To avoid falling into the enemy's hands alive, the King placed his precious jewels and royal garments on the funeral pyre of his palace. "With cries of woe I bring my days to an end," he whispered.[2] He then had himself restrained, along with his family, in a cabin built in the centre of the pyre, and they perished in the flames.

Nineveh opened its gates to the besiegers and was plundered and burned. Defenceless civilians were enslaved or massacred, and Ashurbanipal's palace and library were reduced to ashes. With one blow, the glorious "Assyria disappeared from history."[3] Even Ashur, the eternal God, was dead.

The destruction of Nineveh established the foundations for the Neo-Babylonian Empire. It was to be the beginning of a new world order that resulted in more misery and enslavement for humankind.

And today, after more than 26 centuries, it seems that history repeats itself in a tragic way with the destruction of Nineveh by the US, British, and other coalition forces. Since the invasion of Iraq on March 20, 2003, according to conservative figures, more than 22,838 Iraqi civilians have lost their lives. Eighteen percent of the civilians killed have been women and children. Another 42,500 civilians have been maimed or injured.[4] The number of coalition casualties is estimated at 6,087, of whom 5,898 were Americans. If we consider the number of people who will yet die from the consequences of the occupation we will better understand the depths of this human tragedy.[5] The casualties, chaos, and destruction may continue for many years to come.

American journalist Derrick Jackson made a meaningful comparison:

> "Americans were outraged when 3,000 people were killed in the terrorist attacks of September 11, 2001. Now, between Afghanistan and Iraq, our vengeance has killed way more than that. We rightly demanded that the world care about our innocent dead. Now we wrongly ignore the people we killed. We not only bombed innocent people, we bombed our own innocence."[6]

Following the terrorist attacks of September 11, 2001 against the World Trade Center in New York, US President George W. Bush, in an address to the Joint Session of Congress and to the American people, declared his "War on Terror." "Every nation, in every region, now has a decision to make. Either you are with us, or you are with the terrorists."[7] He claimed that the world would never be the same. Since then, we have witnessed the rise of racism and xenophobia, official justification of torture, further erosion of the right to asylum and the outright practice of torture by some Western democratic governments. Politics have become more hypercritical, and more than at any other time, have become detached from the most basic principles of morality. Governments justify their repressions in the name of combating terrorism.

ON THE RUINS of Nineveh, humanity has had to tolerate the extra burden of military expenditure. World military expenditure in 2004 was close to $1 trillion (only 6 percent lower than the 1987-88 figures at the peak of the Cold War). It was $162 per capita and 2.6 percent of world GDP. There was an annual average increase of about 6 percent over the three-year period of 2002-2004. The US military expenditure (47 percent of the world total) has increased rapidly during this period with the supplementary allocation of $238 billion for operations in Afghanistan and Iraq for the financial years 2003-2005.[8]

Almost all governments have allocated already scarce resources for military purposes. Terrorists rejoice with the further militarization of the world and the proliferation of weapons. War has shown itself to be a kind of "state terrorism, which feeds and is fed by private terrorism."[9]

The destruction of Nineveh, if it continues, will lead to the irreversible destruction of the US economy. Ever-increasing military expenditure has already contributed to the growing fiscal deficit and devaluation of the US dollar. The impact on the developing world will also be disastrous. They have to sacrifice their socio-economic and cultural programs and be content with a meager amount of foreign assistance attached to security-related projects. Development aids "could even result in Cold War-style assistance with the strategic interests of donors dictating."[10]

The destruction of Nineveh will put new burdens, new shackles and new miseries on the working people all over the globe. Hatred and bitterness will be passed down through generations – even after the termination of the armed conflicts. The trauma and psychological damage will continue with devastating effects on the people of Iraq and Afghanistan, on the coalition soldiers and their families and on people in every corner of the globe.

Fear is haunting everybody's mind. Uncertainty is running rampant. People do not know what will happen to them next. George W. Bush was re-elected amidst widespread panic and anxiety at the possibility of more terror attacks. He has, in turn, masterminded mass fear amongst the American people. There is a systemic erosion of human and civil rights by almost all states. The process of the increased militarism of the world has been continuing at an accelerated pace. States, in countries of both the North and the South, have become more tyrannical and more authoritarian. The gap between the haves and have-nots is ever-widening, as capital has become freer and more unbridled in its movement, while, paradoxically, the freedom of human movement has become more and more restricted.

ON THE RUINS of Nineveh "governments have shamelessly used the fear of terrorism to maximize their powers and stifle public debate."[11] European countries, the United States, Australia, South Africa, Malaysia, and many others have implemented anti-terrorism legislation that disproportionately limits the scope of civil liberties. These legislations are mostly against non-citizens, and will unfortunately remain in place for decades.

The destruction of Nineveh has had a devastating impact on the prospect for peace in the Middle East. Prior to invading Iraq, President George W. Bush promised to work towards a lasting peace between Palestinians and Israelis. Bush's revamped version of the Road Map envisioned two states,[12] side by side, and called for the immediate "freeze of all settlement activity."[13]

In March 2004, President Bush exchanged letters with Mr. Sharon, in which he wrote the Israeli leader that the "US recognized that the Israeli population centres (the large settlements) in the West Bank would remain Israeli and would not become part of a Palestinian state." This unilateral redrawing of Israel's existing settlements and expansion was, according to one European diplomat, a "huge shift" in the US position and is more allied to Sharon's initiatives for the division of the West Bank.[14]

IN THE RUINS of Nineveh we are left with a weak United Nations and a divided Europe. Following the invasion of Iraq, the Secretary General of the United Nations, Mr. Kofi Annan, quietly raised his concerns about "precedents that resulted in a proliferation of the unilateral and lawless use of force."[15] The UN is becoming more and more an inefficient organization in resolving man-made and natural catastrophes. According to an observer, it is "philosophically redundant, structurally irrelevant and bureaucratically ossified."[16]

The escalating bloodshed and destruction resulting from the occupation of Iraq and Afghanistan have reopened wounds between the East and West, and the North and South, as well as the New World and the Old. The destruction of Nineveh has widened the division in US society itself. The worst forces of barbarism are at work in the name of defending Western civilization or Islamic values.

AMONG THE VARIOUS evils that ruin human lives today, two sinister forces are most conspicuous: state and non-state terrorism. These two faces of terror nourish each other and complement one another; both advocate violence and spread the culture of death; both are hypocritical and justify their actions in the name of defending their ideologies and values; both act in the name of good against evil; both disdain popular will; both use abhorrent means – including torture – to achieve their main goal of power. The main losers are average people, faceless and powerless, who work from dawn to dusk to keep their bodies and souls together.

The world witnessed both faces of terror in Beslan, Russia. The capture of a school in Beslan, by Chechen guerrillas, on September 1, 2004 serves as a constant reminder of the extent to which humanity has become alienated from itself. The takeover occurred during the welcome ceremony on the children's first day back at school. The terrorists captured more than 1,300 hostages, confining them in the overcrowded school gym, which was armoured with bombs, floor mines, and multiple armed terrorists. Russian troops have battled separatist guerrillas from Chechnya since 1994, and this act was one of many vengeful attempts at achieving independence.

The hostage-takers threatened to kill the children if the Russian government did not release prisoners taken by the Russian army in a June raid. They also demanded the complete withdrawal of all Russian forces in Chechnya. The children, ranging in age from infants to 17-year-olds, teachers, and some guardians were left without food or water for 53 hours. Many were wired to bombs. Several of the hostages became dehydrated because of the heat and lost consciousness. They had to listen all the while to their captors tell them that their lives were worthless. Children had to bear witness to the pain of their peers. Then with hardly a care for the safety and security of the children and the other hostages, the Russian government lost its patience and acted hastily with an "iron first." Within an instant the school erupted in a blaze of horror.

Due to the extent of the destruction the exact number of those who were lost is difficult to substantiate. According to official data, 344 civilians were killed, at least 172 of them children, and hundreds more were wounded. However, the actual number of deaths is suggested to be three times higher.[17] The one-sided reaction of the global media was upsetting. There was barely any condemnation of the terrorism committed by the Russian government and army in storming the school.

There is an ominous duality in terrorism in that it comes in two forms: as a state-consecrated crime and as a non-state-consecrated crime. The event in Beslan is a horrific reminder of the destruction that occurs when these two forces challenge each other's authority and power. This constant battle for power and control between the state and terrorists most affects those who reside in between, vulnerable civilians. The argument is not whether one side is more deadly than the other, but the devastation that occurs when these two forces meet, and the lack of concern for humanity that ensues in the process.

ON THE RUINS of Nineveh, the state and non-state terrorists are engaged in a fatal competition for the glorification of death – one in the name of patriotism and the other in the name of religion. According to Eduardo Galeano:

> "Home grown terrorism and high level technology terrorism are very much alike, that of the religious fundamentalists and that of market fundamentalists, that of the desperate and that of the powerful, that of madmen on the loose and that of uniformed professionals. All of them share the same contempt for human life."[18]

The culture of death has produced more and more suicide bombers. Suicide attacks that were relatively rare and limited to specific regions before are now becoming a frequent method of assault at the global level. It should be noted that the suicide attack is neither a new nor a Middle Eastern phenomenon. It has always been a component of all wars and hostilities. Both western prophetic and eastern religions have glorified martyrdom, which is a converted form of suicide.

The sinister by-products of the continuing destruction of Nineveh such as abject poverty, deprivation, occupation, humiliation and the insecurity of life have provided terrorist leaders with a rare opportunity to recruit youth for suicide missions. Suicide attacks are daily events in Iraq, and in Palestine they have replaced the non-violent Intifada with the consequence of recurrent Israeli retaliations. Where human life loses its value, death emerges as an unquestionable demonstration of honour, courage, loyalty, and moral character. It intensifies the circle of violence, as it is virtually impossible to prevent suicide attacks and one who does not care for his or her life is capable of killing people indiscriminately, including children and elders.

ON THE RUINS of Nineveh, state and non-state terrorists have joined hands to contribute towards the destruction of our system of values. According to the Irish writer, William Butler Yeats:

> Things fall apart; the centre cannot hold;
> Mere anarchy is loosed upon the world,
> the blood-dimmed tide is loosed, and everywhere
> The ceremony of innocence is drowned;
> The best lack all conviction, while the worst
> Are full of passionate intensity.[19]

With the passage of time, it might be possible to reconstruct war-ravaged areas or compensate for the war's human and material damages. It is, however, impossible to repair the universal values that once united us. The most vital asset that the human family can lose is the system of values that distinguishes between the things that are acceptable and those that are unacceptable. Nineveh has been reduced to a gigantic slaughterhouse devoid of all recognizable human values.

The ongoing massacre of vulnerable civilians, women, children and elders alike, and the destruction of houses, crops and livestock are justified by both sides as "collateral damage," or the inevitable price that must be paid for "freedom." Humanity has lost ground in the process of the dehumanization of Westerners (especially Americans) on the one hand, and Muslims on the other. Torture, war crimes, and various crimes against humanity are sanctioned and justified as necessary evils with almost no respect for customary international law.

IT IS DIFFICULT to draw a demarcation line between terrorists and freedom fighters. Both groups wear no uniforms and hide themselves among ordinary people. Like terrorists, freedom fighters may also resort to violence to reach their goals. Some observers distinguish them by emphasizing their justified or unjustified goals. I disagree. In my opinion the main difference between a terrorist and a freedom fighter comes from the means that they choose to achieve their goals. While the former uses dirty means to achieve the so-called sacred goal, in the latter's approach, the means and goals are intrinsically mingled.

In their struggle for emancipation, freedom fighters never strike non-military targets; they try their best to minimize casualties; they rely on grassroots people and are always concerned about protecting civilians; they avoid assassinations and unnecessary destruction. Operations that result in the decapitation of hostages in Iraq, the massacre of 55 innocent civilians in London (July 7, 2005), the killing of 26 children in Baghdad (July 13, 2005), and the suicide attacks that target Israeli children are outright terrorism, regardless of the goals they intend to achieve. It is upsetting that the intensification of authoritarianism and the growing desperation resulting from the destruction of Nineveh have replaced the struggle for freedom with unscrupulous acts of terror.

State and non-state terrorism have their own similarities and dissimilarities. The former is offensive while the latter is normally defensive; state terrorism is all powerful, while non-state terrorism is relatively powerless; one justifies its actions in the name of the law or by passing new legislations, while the other does not care about the law. They are, however, two sides of the same coin. Both perpetuate a climate of fear, and like a coin, can present themselves to be either face on any given day. A state terrorist may become a non-state one by losing power and a non-state terrorist becomes a state terrorist by gaining power. This is well depicted by Eduardo Galeano:

> "It is not only the religious fanatics who need enemies in order to justify their madness. The arms industry and the huge military apparatus of the United States also need enemies in order to justify their existence. Good and evil, evil and good: the actors change masks, heroes become monsters, and the monsters heroes, as those writing the drama demand."[20]

There is scarcely any attempt to address the root causes of the frustrations that foster terrorism. As the contemporary novelist and historian Andrew Sinclair puts it, "a little learning is the nipple of the militant, when the mother's milk is hatred and revenge."[21] It is absurd to expect the states that are systematically engaged in acts of terror to pacify hatred and revenge by non-violent means.

Days after the terrorist attack in New York, Simon Jenkins, a correspondent for the *London Times,* warned that a massive military retaliation would be exactly what the terrorists want:

> "Military retaliation would elevate their cause, idolize their leader, devalue moderation and validate fanaticism. If ever history needed a catalyst for a new and awful conflict between Arabs and the West, this could be it."[22]

Noam Chomsky issued much the same warning:

> "They recognize, as does everyone with close knowledge of the region, that a massive assault on a Muslim population would be the answer to the prayers of bin Laden and his associates, and would lead the US and its allies into a diabolical trap."[23]

The bad dream of Mr. Jenkins and Dr. Chomsky has become a recurrent nightmare. Religious fanaticism is on the rise in almost all Islamic countries, from Egypt to Pakistan and Turkey. Muslim terrorist groups such as the Taliban, Islamic Jihad, and Hezbollah have emerged as national saviours. Criminals like Saddam Hussein, Osama bin Laden, and Abu Mussa Al-Zakawi, who have committed multiple heinous crimes against humanity, have become public heroes. Mr. Jenkins shed bitter tears following the US and British occupation of Iraq. He had not, however, lost hope. He wrote in the *London Times*:

> "Hope now pleads for a quick victory. Hope pleads for no gratuitous bombing. Hope craves a swift rebuilding of Iraq. Hope prays for the Palestine 'road map' to be sincere. Hope longs for the UN to pick itself up and play a full role in a reconstructed Middle East. Hope wants this war to purge once and for all America's September 11 trauma and for America to rejoin the world community. Hope believes in America as a force for good in the world. Hope wants this war turned to good account. Hope hates the sound of bin Laden laughing."[24]

TODAY ON THE ruins of Nineveh, the monster of war has forced the angel of hope to disappear. The world is standing on its head. Hope has been lost in everything dreamed above. She is a seriously wounded fugitive now. Since September 11, 2001, the world has gone through recurrent vengeance and chaos. The tendency towards retribution has reduced our planet to an inferno. An "eye for an eye" attitude is going to make the entire world blind.

The lack of alternatives today is reminiscent of the story of medieval knights on a journey who suddenly came upon a road split into two paths and a large plaque with the following inscription: "the right path leads to an endless desert and the left one reaches the abode of cannibalistic monsters." We live under a devilish, unscrupulous, and highly cruel system all-powerful in the destruction it wreaks. It has no pity to spare even its own creators. Individuality has lost its meaning. Average people feel helpless more than at any other time. Philosophical pessimism, the feeling that no one can make a difference, has reached an alarming point allowing darkness to prevail.

The "War on Terrorism" has proved once again that there is no military solution to the evil of international terrorism. Let me quote an analogy by an unknown friend who has written a long letter to the fellowship of human beings:

> "Using militaries for the war on terrorism is like chasing a bicycle with the heaviest transportation vehicle. The cyclist would maneuver through narrow passages, and the heavy transportation vehicle would destroy all residential areas and kill any pedestrians who happen to be in its way. Despite all the financial losses and killings it causes on its way, it cannot do any significant harm to the cyclist."[25]

In its *2005 Annual Report,* Amnesty International also remarked on the failure of military solutions in resolving the plague of terrorism:

> "The so-called 'war on terror' appeared more effective in eroding the international framework of human rights principles than in countering the threat of international 'terrorism.' The security of women facing gender-based violence in the home, in the community or in situations of conflict barely received attention. The economic, social and cultural rights of marginalized communities continued to be largely ignored."[26]

Will hope be able to bring light amidst the darkness? Before the US invasion of Iraq, grassroots people manifested their solidarity through their anti-war demonstrations. Some states – including Russia, France, Germany, Canada, and Syria – demonstrated their opposition to the war, while others joined the coalition with little attention to the strong anti-war sentiment of their people. The government of Spain joined the US coalition despite huge anti-war demonstrations by the Spanish people. The change of government in Spain by popular vote and the subsequent pullout of Spanish troops from Iraq provide us with the hope that the power of the people may yet emerge as the ultimate determining factor.

THE POLARIZATION OF the US population during the recent presidential election is a reflection of the disagreement of millions of citizens with Mr. Bush's policies. Although the global anti-war enthusiasm has died down, international solidarity has manifested itself in other ways: youth demonstrations against G-8 summits, solidarity concerts, the internet and its positive potential, etc.

Opposition to war, torture, tyranny, and global injustice has been shown by many NGOs everywhere in both countries of the North and the South. US-based Organizations such as the Center for Constitutional Rights and Lawyers for Human Rights have started litigations against torture and other gross human rights violations in Abu Ghraib prison and in Guantánamo Bay. Exposure of torture and other international crimes has even come from elements within the ruling parties. The US Supreme Court has challenged the practice of the US administration of keeping suspected terrorists in prolonged detention with no access to US courts. On June 28, 2004, the Supreme Court ruled 6-3 in favour of a suit by the New York based Center for Constitutional Rights (CCR) and declared that the Guantánamo detainees should have access to US courts to challenge their detention.[27] The Supreme Court of Israel has ruled against torture as a means of interrogation.

AN UNPRECEDENTED SPIRIT of humanity was shown during the tsunami disaster. On December 26, 2004, a powerful earthquake in the ocean off Indonesia sent a series of fatal waves to Indonesia, Sri Lanka, India, Thailand, Malaysia, Myanmar, and East Africa. Over 300,000 people lost their lives with 100,000 missing. The tsunami demonstrated our "interconnectedness and shared vulnerability." The disaster "highlighted how the most devastating threats to security arise from a much greater range of forces than the suicide bomber."[28]

The level of global empathy and solidarity towards the victims of the tsunami proved once again that humanity is not dead. The editor of *The Wall Street Journal Europe* remarked during the catastrophe that "across the world the reaction to the tsunami is bringing out the best in human nature."[29] An outpouring of worldwide generosity influenced the governments of the industrialized nations to increase their assistance to the survivors. The former US Presidents, Bill Clinton and George Bush Sr., travelled to the most affected regions. Despite the human toll and unparalleled destruction, the tsunami ushered in a new era of global citizenship.

We may claim that ours is the most ominous era in human history. This is, however, by no means a new claim. If we examine past literature, we observe that those who care for the destiny of humankind have made similar claims in different periods of human history. Forces of light and darkness have always co-existed in constant conflict. The course of the future depends on the way the family of nations responds to today's problems.

TODAY WE ALL suffer at the hands of blood-sucking philistines who rule the world. They have, unfortunately, existed throughout history. Prophets of darkness, blood and destruction such as Nabopolassar, Nero, Genghis Khan, Timur, Hitler, Mussolini, Stalin, Khomeini and their entourages have felt omnipotent during different periods of history. Today, however, history has damned them and their ideologies as destroyers of human life and human dignity. Humanity has historically faced the dilemma of the ease with which forces of destruction are let loose and the complexity involved in leading people towards peace and prosperity. Can we resolve this dilemma in the age of information? It depends on our collective will. I like to remain optimistic and reiterate what the French novelist Victor Hugo said over a hundred years ago: "Above the cloud with its shadow is the star with its light."

Notes

1. William Shakespeare, *Julius Caesar*, Act III, scene 1, lines 255-275.
2. Will Durant, *The History of Civilization 1: Our Oriental Heritage*, Simon and Schuster, New York, 1963, p. 282.
3. Ibid. p. 283.
4. Alissa J. Rubin, "Civilian casualties tallied July 20, 2005, in Iraq War," *Los Angeles Times*, July 20, 2005.
5. Internet sources: www.icasualities.org, and www.antiwar.com/casualities.
6. Derrick Z. Jackson, "Burying the Number of Civilian Deaths in Iraq," *Chicago Tribune*, June 16, 2003.
7. George W. Bush, "Address to the Joint Session of Congress and the American People," Washington D.C., September 21, 2001.
8. Elisabeth Sköns, Wuyi Omitoogun, Catalina Perdomo and Petter Stålenheim, "Military Expenditure," *SIPRI Year Book 2005, Armaments, Disarmament and International Security*, Stockholm, Chapter 8.
9. Eduardo Galeano, "Superducks and Underducks," *Le Monde Diplomatique*, August 2004, http://mondediplo.com/2004/08/16galeano.
10. Footnote 8.
11. Tom Brown, "Civil Liberties in an Age of Terror and Information Abundance," p. 17.
12. Edward Walker Jr., "President Bush Reinvents the Road Map and US Policy," *Middle East Institute*, April 21, 2004.
13. Conal Urquhart, "US deal wrecks Middle East peace," *The Guardian*, August 23, 2004, and Edward Walker Jr., "President Bush Reinvents the Road Map and US Policy," *Middle East Institute*, April 21, 2004.

14. Footnote 13. Conal Urquhart, "US deal wrecks Middle East peace," *The Guardian*, August 23, 2004.
15. Kofi Annan, "The Secretary General's Address to the General Assembly of the United Nations," September 23, 2003.
16. Tim Hames, "Tsunami Disaster: The UN is roundly reproved after its comments on US donations," *The Times*, excerpt found in *The Guardian*, January 3, 2005, p. 20.
17. *The Moscow Times*, October 13, 2004.
18. Eduardo Galeano, "On Good and Evil," Originally published in Spanish by La Jornada. Translated by Irlandesa under the title of "Theatre of Good and Evil," Friday, September 21, 2001.
19. William Butler Yeats, "The Second Coming," The Literature Network: www.online-literature.com/yeats.
20. Footnote 18.
21. Andrew Sinclair, *An Anatomy of Terror: A History of Terrorism*, Palgrave Macmillan, December 2004.
22. Simon Jenkins, *London Times*, September 14, 2001.
23. Noam Chomsky, *9-11*, Seven Stories Press, New York, 2001. p. 17.
24. Simon Jenkins, "Bin Laden's laughter echoes across the West," on-line source: http://www.warmwell.com/2mar19jenkins.html.
25. Author unknown, "Dear Fellow Human Beings," http://www.geocities.com/mhziari/. I would like to extend my sincere thanks to my friend, Giti Hedayat, in Denmark, who sent me the full text.
26. Amnesty International, *Annual Report 2005*, p. 2.
27. The US Supreme Court ruling dated June 28, 2004. For a full background on the case see http://www.ccr-ny.org/rasul/.
28. Footnote 26.
29. Wall Street Europe Editorial, "Tsunami Disaster: The UN is roundly reproved after its comments on US donations," *The Guardian*, January 3, 2005, p. 20.

2

The Era of Fear: Torture and Terror

Introduction

IN THE EARLY 16th century, Erasmus of Rotterdam wrote his masterpiece *The Praise of Folly*. In this magnum opus, Erasmus reveals the inherent and unavoidable stupidities of the mortal race. He goes beyond accepted norms and values to explore the very essence of humankind. He condemns war by using his peculiar satire: "war is so savage a thing that it rather befits beasts than men, so outrageous that the very poets feigned it came from the Furies, so pestilent that it corrupts all men's manners."[1] He neglects, however, to deal adequately with the practice of torture as one of the cruelest absurdities of human life, a crime committed in many different societies, both democratic and tyrannical, throughout most of history.

When John Swain published his *Book of Torture* in 1968, he cherished the hope that there would not be torture in the "millennium of civilization." He even went so far as to suggest that "torture as a means to confession has disappeared."[2] It is unfortunate that today torture is being practiced in two-thirds of the countries in the world. According to Amnesty International, torture is practiced in a systemic way in 80 countries and in 50 countries it is being practiced against children systematically. In the duration of one year, CCVT accepted 798 clients from 81 different countries; 300 of these were men, 276 women and 222 were children.[3] These statistics are a vivid reflection of the widespread use of torture around the world.

What is Torture?

IN DAY-TO-DAY life, people use the term "torture" to describe all sorts of annoyances. Wives are "tortured" by their bothersome husbands, husbands by their wives, and both by their teenaged children. People sometimes even use the word "torture" for trivialities like hot or cold weather. In contrast, tyrannical regimes and their professional torturers use gentle words when they refer to their horrendous acts of torture and human butchery. In Greece, under the military rule, severe torture was called "tea-party." SAVAK, the notorious secret police of the Shah of Iran, used the term "caressing" or *navazesh* in Farsi, instead of "torture." SAVAK members used "preparation room" instead of "torture chamber." Under the present clerical regime of Iran, "torture" is replaced by such terms as "guiding punishment" or "divine penalty" (*Ta'azir*). Other dictatorial governments used terms like "dance" or "football games."

To avoid confusion, it is useful to examine what constitutes torture. Before proceeding further, it should be noted that there is a difference between the aim of torture in the past and in today's world. In ancient Greece and Rome, and in many Oriental and Western countries, torture was used as an extreme punishment up to a century ago. Today, it is used, firstly, as a means of extracting information or confession, and secondly, as a tool of political repression. In ancient Egypt, there were two types of verdicts: simple death or death by torture.

In the masterpiece *The Bridge on the Drina*, written by Ivo Andric, a Bosnian peasant, forced into labour to build a bridge proposed by the Ottomans, is sentenced to death for his rebellious actions. The Turkish foreman ordered that he must die gradually under abhorrent tortures:

> "The criminal should continue to be interrogated, but he should not be tortured beyond endurance lest he die. Everything must be made ready so that at noon that same day he should be impaled alive on the outermost part of the construction work at its highest point, so that the whole town and all the workers should be able to see him from the banks of the river … so that midday all the people might see what happened to those who hindered the building of the bridge, and that the whole male population, both Turks and rayah, from children to old men, must gather on one or other of the banks to witness it."[4]

As can be seen from the above, torture is used both as an extreme punishment and a deterrent measure.

Article 1 of the *UN Convention Against Torture and Other Cruel, Inhuman or Degrading Treatment or Punishment* defines torture as:

> "Any act by which severe pain or suffering, whether physical or mental, is intentionally inflicted on a person for such purposes as obtaining from him or a third person information or a confession, punishing him for an act he or a third person has committed or is suspected of having committed, or intimidating or coercing him or a third person, for any reasons based on discrimination of any kind, when such pain or suffering is inflicted by or at the instigation of, or with the consent or acquiescence of a public official or other person acting in a public capacity. It does not include pain or suffering arising only from, inherent in or incidental to lawful sanctions."

Thus, we cannot refer to any act of violence as torture. Torture has four clear components according to the above article:
- It is severe pain or suffering, physical or psychological, which is purposefully inflicted on a person
- It has a goal: obtaining or extracting information or a confession, meting out punishment, and so on
- It is perpetrated by a public official
- It is not sanctioned by law

Despite its usefulness, the above definition is far from adequate. It does not address state and religiously sanctioned tortures, which are prevalent in many parts of the world. In Iran, Saudi Arabia, Sudan, Nigeria, Pakistan, Mauritania, Bangladesh, and some other countries, the law permits flogging people who drink alcohol or do not observe the dress code of the government. Men and women, especially women, are stoned to death for the crime of adultery. Here, governments turn ordinary people into torturers by inciting them to throw stones at the victims. They are told to bury men up to their bellies and women up to their breasts and start throwing stones; they are instructed to choose stones which are neither too small nor too large, in order to prolong the victims' agony. This type of torture is a part of the criminal code of some fundamentalist countries.

Another religiously sanctioned form of torture is the act of suttee: the burning alive of a widow on a funeral pyre alongside the dead body of her husband. With the rise of Hindu fundamentalism in India, there have been reports of the revival of suttee. Although this extreme form of torture can be a voluntary sacrifice on the part of the widow, most of the time women are forced by the community or priests and/or tricked into believing they will not feel pain. Although suttee is illegal in India, in practice there is hardly any prosecution against people who are involved in this monstrous act and who reap profit out of the ashes of these women. What is perhaps even worse is the total silence of the international community.

Another serious deficiency with the definition of torture under Article 1 is the invisibility of women. While women are tortured for the same reasons as men, they are also subject to gender-related forms of torture like female genital mutilation, dowry murder, rape, domestic violence, childhood marriage, and so on.

It should not be forgotten that torture is not only committed by people in positions of authority. Today, specifically with the end of the Cold War and the rise of ethnic conflicts, we have systematic torture perpetrated by paramilitary groups and members of death squads. Article 1 of the *Convention Against Torture* does not address the lack of government protection for victims at the mercy of paramilitary groups (who are accountable to no one and who can therefore act with impunity).

Methods of Torture

IT IS A TRAGEDY that in our 21st century there is no shortage of torturers and human butchers across the globe. Methods of torture have become more and more sophisticated and now involve a combination of both physical and psychological techniques. Torturers are capable of inventing new methods tailored to the physical and psychological make-up of each victim. Some of the most common methods of torture are:

- Beatings (with fists, kicks, slaps, etc.)
- Mutilations (amputations or cutting of body parts, extraction of nails and teeth, and breaking of bones)
- Water immersion (frequent submersion in dirty or cold water)
- Hangings (with both hands attached to a bar, or hangings by one leg, or handcuffing both hands from behind. In the latter case they attach a chair to the handcuffs and push the chair down. Victims usually become unconscious after half an hour. The torturers usually call in a

doctor, revive the victims and repeat the torture.)
- Whippings (on the soles of the feet, hands and back with instruments such as cables, batons, whips, and sticks; this is the most common and preferred method of torture because it can be initiated at any time or place and under any conditions)
- Electric shock (normally applied to the sensitive organs such as genitals, rectum, and nipples)
- Rape (which is committed against both women and men but usually women, for a variety of purposes. Its effects on the victim are very complex; indeed, rape constitutes a category of torture in its own right.)

Other methods include exposure to physical hazards and food, water and sleep deprivation. Burning is usually used when the torturers want to extract "urgent" information from the victim. They strip the victim and tie his or her hands and legs to the bars of a steel bed frame. They push the victim's abdomen in a way that his or her buttocks touch an open flame set beneath the bed. The burning continues for two or three seconds. It is one of the most dangerous forms of torture and has resulted in the deaths of many victims.

Apart from physical torture one should not forget about psychological forms of torture like:
- Kidnapping and execution of members of the victim's family
- Forcing the victim to witness the torture, rape and murder of friends, family and fellow prisoners
- Leaving the victim in a state of limbo (keeping the victim in a state of readiness for torture and prolonging their waiting time)
- Subjecting the victim to sham executions (while blindfolded, the victims are taken to the execution site, all pre-execution formalities are carried out, and shots are aimed into the air)
- Systematic harassment with taunts and threats
- Solitary confinement with poor sanitation
- Forced ingestion of noxious substances

Torturers normally use a combination of physical and psychological techniques against their victims: for example yelling at, insulting and threatening their victims throughout the course of beatings and so on. As well, torturers will sometimes play pleasant music, animal sounds, or recite popular verses from the Holy Scripture (like *Allah Akbar*, "God is Great") while inflicting severe physical torture. This could lead to the retraumatization of victims throughout their lives, each time they hear the same piece of music or verse.

It should be borne in mind that methods of torture are not limited to the above. Torture has a fingerprint specific to each country and culture. In India, for example, victims are tied (sometimes upside down) to a ceiling fan. Torturers switch on the fan and the victims rotate with the fan. In Turkey, and some other countries, foot tortures called *Falaka, Falanga* (and *bastinado*) are common: victims are bound with their feet raised and their soles beaten with sticks, bamboo, clubs, whips or cables.[5] Syrian torturers have invented a method called "The Black Slave:" a metal chair with a hole in the middle. They tie the naked victims to the chair and then, through the hole, a heated metal skewer enters the rectum, slowly entering the intestines. In Rwanda, prisoners are kept incommunicado in dark, stinking dungeons (*cachots noirs*). Russian torturers are notorious for their use of pain-causing drugs. In Tibet, torturers used a combination of techniques, including forced sexual acts and brainwashing. Genocide is being carried out in many regions including Sudan and Sierra Leone, where mutilation is also used as a technique of torture.[6]

Capital Punishment as a Form of Torture

CAPITAL PUNISHMENT IS the legal implementation of the death penalty. The whole process is torturous – from the pronouncement of the penalty to the waiting period for the implementation of the punishment to the very act of execution. It leaves traumatizing scars on the innocent members of the family of the executed persons as well.

The methods of implementation of capital punishment (lethal injections, firing squads, hanging, stoning, beheading, etc.) are all cruel and inhuman.[7] Implementation of the death penalty in public is extremely demeaning. It spreads a culture of revenge among the grassroots population and can make them feel intimidated and impotent. The law-sanctioned violence resulting from capital punishment perpetuates the culture of violence itself.

Execution of the death penalty requires an administrative apparatus – hangman, firing squad, gallows, execution site, etc. – all reminiscent of our barbarous antiquity. It takes away our compassion and degrades enactors to the rank of death pawns. No decent human being wishes to be an executioner in any circumstances and for any cause whatsoever.

Capital punishment does remove the main witness to ghoulish tortures perpetrated against condemned persons before death. In cases of political prisoners, it is often preceded by such tortures as rape, mutilations, extracting victims' blood, etc. Under tyrannical regimes, the death penalty can be used as an excuse to get rid of "undesirable" persons.[8] Those who decide to take the life of another human being are positioning themselves on the same level as that of the person whom they sentence to death.

Apart from the infliction of physical pain, capital punishment is combined with mental, psychological and emotional torment. Prolonged suffering of a prisoner under the cruel and inhuman condition of death row is nothing less than severe torture. The phenomenon of death row may drag the victims to the point of paranoia and make them irreversibly incompetent to face the death sentence. The execution of an incompetent condemned person is an act of cruelty.[9]

Article 6 of the *International Covenant on Civil and Political Rights* has failed to go to the extent of abolishing the death penalty. It has, however, placed its use under certain conditions and has prohibited its use against children. The death penalty is prohibited under the *Second Optional Protocol* to the above Covenant and is outlawed in Europe, according to the *European Convention on Human Rights*. The number of countries that have abolished the death penalty is on the rise and international law is gradually moving towards complete abolition.[10] There is an urgent need today for all of us to raise our voices against this medieval practice.

Purpose of Torture

TORTURE SHOULD NOT be approached in isolation. It is actually part and parcel of a strategy of political repression. Governments sanction torture as a part of state terrorism in order to paralyze the whole population and to convince it of the omnipotence of the regime.

Indeed, torture is one of the most extreme components of the apparatus of tyranny. It acts as a sinister short cut to maintaining power that has not been derived from the cross-section of the populace.

Fear is the hotbed of repression and torture. According to a famous dictum, tyranny is the by-product of cowardice because it is only cowardice that activates tyranny. Just before getting the verdict to be burned alive at the stake, the Italian scientist and philosopher Giordano Bruno (1550-1600) told his inquisitors: "perhaps it is with greater fear that you pass the sentence upon me than I receive it."[11]

In a state of war or ethnic conflict, where certain people are regarded as enemies, torture can be justified and even sanctioned by both the government and extremist groups. Torture is sanctioned as a result of demonizing the enemy, or not considering them to be human beings. According to Ignacio Martin-Baro:

> "War implies social polarization, the displacement of groups toward opposite extremes. A critical split is produced in the framework of coexistence, leading to a radical differentiation between 'them' and 'us' ... People, actions and things are no longer valued in and of themselves ... Thus the basis for daily interaction disappears."[12]

In countries that suffer from religious fanaticism, torture is justified in the name of God. Torturers consider it their religious duty to torture nonbelievers. It is ironic that in today's Iran, for example, torturers and executioners start their ghoulish action by reciting a verse that is repeated in every section of the Holy Quran: "in the name of God the most compassionate, the most merciful!" The God all merciful becomes a God all revengeful and empowers torturers to continue with their "holy" action. In the course of flogging victims, sometimes with every blow, the torturers use a holy term *Allah-o Akbar* (God is the greatest).

In war zones, as well as torture chambers, torture is justified under the guise of social Darwinism: the extension of Darwin's theory of "struggle for survival" to human society. I will never forget one night I spent in Iran's infamous Evin jail, in May 1973, when a guard took me out of my cell for interrogation. The notorious torturer Mr. Rasouli, with the help of three junior torturers, was interrogating a group of political prisoners. In an apparent attempt to demoralize the victims and promote the morale of his colleagues, Mr. Rasouli shouted repeatedly, "This is a struggle for survival; kill them not to be killed."

Torture can act as a means of intimidation against the whole population. It is practiced by tyrannical regimes as a preventative measure against the masses' dissent. It can go to the extent of being used as a punitive action against third parties or even a particular community.

On an individual basis, the aim of torture is to destroy the will and personality of its victims. It dehumanizes and destroys individuals without killing them physically. Torture is always combined with degradation. The issue is not only the severe pain or suffering inflicted upon the person. It is also the prolonged psychological tension that victims experience between resisting and the possibility of betraying their country, community, family and friends. This makes torture totally different from other types of trauma. The scars, especially the psychological ones, last a lifetime.

In some countries, torture is used in such a systematic way that a kind of torture "mentality" or culture develops in jails and detention centers; prisoners are tortured for trivial issues and even for no reason, as a kind of hobby for torturers. As a political prisoner under the Shah of Iran, I have witnessed prisoners being tortured for fun. Torturers curious to see their victims' reactions brought them to torture chambers, tortured them and laughed. They even went as far as to bet on the reactions of their victims. In closed societies with gross human rights violations, where there is no accountability for interrogators or prison guards, the tendency toward torturing inmates gets accentuated. Under judicial systems where confession plays an important role in the outcome of the final verdict, the prison authorities are prone to torture people indiscriminately.

On Torturers

TORTURERS ARE NOT sent to us as alien monsters from outer space. They are by-products of cultures of violence, tyranny, repression and authoritarianism. I have seen victims turned victimizers as a result of torture and systemic brainwash. According to the Iranian writer and ex-political prisoner Ms. Monireh Baradaran:

> "It is simplistic to think that torturers are a bunch of sadists. There might be quite a few sadistic people among them, but experience has shown that quite ordinary people could become the cruelest torturers. Anybody is capable of torturing others if he stops seeing them in their human caliber. What provides a torturer with the capability of committing the crime of torture is his unquestionable power as well as his closed ideological world outlook."[13]

Torture is closely connected to the idea of subordination. As is well known, in hierarchical institutions like the army, police, and specifically

Intelligence, subordination is bestowed with the highest merit. Torturers are recruited from among the most fanatical elements in the rank and file – especially those with a strong tendency for subordination.

Torturers go through regular training and systemic indoctrination in the ideology of torture: chauvinism, social Darwinism, absolute loyalty, sacredness of performing duty, significance of their jobs, etc. During their trials, in transitional periods, torturers have frequently justified their crimes by mentioning that they had no choice but to obey orders and perform their duties: "and if I didn't do that someone else would have done it."

It is not usually possible to torture a fellow human being without the perpetrator carrying a level of philistinism: shallowness, narrow-mindedness, and lack of understanding of the humanitarian culture and philosophy. Torturers usually lead a double life: a caring person at home and a human butcher in the torture chambers.

My friend and jail-mate, Mr. Taghi Tam, told me that one day the guard took him for interrogation. The chief interrogator, Mr. Azodi, started his infamous tortures against him: a mixture of whipping, kicking, slapping, shouting and insulting. In the middle of the torture, the telephone rang. Mr. Azodi stopped his torture and began his conversation. "By the tone of his conversation," Mr. Tam told me, "I came to know that he was talking to his young daughter. He spoke with his child in such a delicate, caring and loving manner that for a moment I doubted that he was the same cruel torturer."

What follows is taken from Eduardo Galeano's masterpiece *The Book of Embraces*:

> "… he and he are not the same person … after all, he is an official who goes to work on time and does his job. When the exhausting day's work is done, the torturer washes his hands. Ahmadou Gherab, who fought for the independence of Algeria, told me this. Ahmadou was tortured by a French official for several months. Every day, promptly at 6:00 p.m., the torturer would wipe the sweat from his brow, unplug the electric cattle prod and put away the other tools of the trade. Then he would sit beside the tortured man and speak to him of his family problems and of the promotion that didn't come and of how expensive life is. The torturer would speak of his insufferable wife and their newborn child who had not permitted him a wink of sleep all night; he railed against Orán, that shitty city, and against the son of a bitch of a colonel who … Ahmadou, bathed in blood, trembling with pain, burning with fever would say nothing."[14]

There is a tremendous lack of literature on the mentality of torturers. Torturers, war criminals and those who have committed crimes against humanity do not feel compunction even in their old age. It is next to impossible to recover their lost conscience.

A Dilemma

IN EARLY 2000, I raised the following dilemma as an educational example in my work towards the prevention and eradication of torture. I never imagined in those days that after September 11, 2001, my imaginary example would be used by politicians and even academicians to justify the crime of torture:

> "Imagine a scenario where terrorists have hijacked a plane with 350 passengers, among them many women and children. Having forced a landing at a nearby airport, they send one member of their group outside as a delegate. He is captured by the police, to whom he delivers a dire message: the government has exactly 3 hours in which to comply with the group's demands, or else the plane, and its passengers, will be blown up. As the minister in charge of national security you have a weighty decision to make: the chief of police has told you that the group is serious about its threat and has been known to sacrifice lives in the past. He also tells you that he knows exactly how to extract information from the delegate about the location of the bomb. This will require rather "extreme methods" (which is his euphemism for torture). Among the passengers are your closest relatives. What do you do? Do you sanction torture under such exceptional circumstances, in which the lives of innocent people are jeopardized?"[15]

When I raised the above dilemma at different national and international educational meetings before September 11, 2001, many members of the audience preferred to remain silent and evade answering the question. A few, concerned about the lives of their family members, sanctioned torture. I have rarely raised the issue since then, as politicians and advocates of torture have given similar examples:

> "Suppose you are the president of the United States. You have hard intelligence that a dirty bomb is set to explode somewhere in Chicago within the next 12 hours. The Department of Defense is holding an

enemy combatant connected with the terrorist group that placed the bomb. You have every reason to believe he knows the location of the bomb, but he refuses to talk. 'Mr. President,' the Secretary of Defense says to you, 'with your approval, we can make this man talk, thereby saving hundreds, maybe thousands, of American lives. But the interrogation won't be pretty, and the prisoner may never recover. Shall we do whatever's necessary?' Some of those who pose this question say the answer is a slam dunk. Of course the prisoner should be softened up, by any means necessary. What's one dirty terrorist compared to thousands of innocent Americans?"[16]

A closer look at the above scenarios reveals that, first of all, we are dealing with illusory situations that rarely happen in real life. Torture-oriented governments turn illusions of this type into a reality, reduce them to life-or-death issues, and sanction torture. Secondly, there is another illusion that torture is an effective means to obtaining information. Even from the utilitarian point of view of the perpetrator, torture may lead to more defiance and intransigence on the part of the victim, who comes to view his or her suffering as a virtue. Thirdly, people may sanction torture to save their relatives. This is, again, a wrong approach. Such an important decision should be free of personal considerations and rather look toward long-term public welfare. Fourthly, there is a false assumption that the chief of police or president of the US could resort to torture in order to deal with emergency cases. This could happen under tyrannical regimes where there is no rule of law.

In liberal democracies, even in exceptional cases, no official can violate the law of the country and find him or herself beyond the law. Let us not forget that enjoying human rights and living in peace and harmony have a price. If we resort to violence to fight violence, it may entangle the whole society in a vicious circle. If we permit torture in exceptional situations it may become a rule. A government committed to human rights cannot set good versus evil and sanction torture against terrorists without losing its integrity and reducing itself to their ranks. It is impossible to defend democracy by destroying its very foundation.

There is no legal, moral or even utilitarian basis for the use of torture. It is outlawed unequivocally by the customary international law under any circumstances. This rule is an absolute.[17]

Circles of Silence

TORTURE IS BEING practiced in a very disguised and invisible manner and results in what Ignacio Martin-Baro calls "circles of silence." Governments and their torturers do their best to hide the practice of torture from the international community. Denial at various levels is an obstacle in the struggle against torture and in the treatment of the after-effects of torture. It operates on at least three levels:

On an individual level, victims are normally reluctant to talk about their bitter experiences in an attempt to protect themselves or others from further arrest and torture. They are also not sure that they will be understood or believed by the community. Most of the victims prefer not to speak about their torture in order to prevent further retraumatization. In this case, forgetfulness acts as a defense mechanism. Some victims try to avoid sharing their experiences of torture and its traumatic consequences because they view this as conceding power to the torturer. They dislike frightening people by adding to their government's propaganda about its omnipotence.

On a family level, people deny torture in an attempt to protect their loved ones who are vulnerable *vis-à-vis* their torturers and the government. While in jail, they can be subjected to torture again and again, while outside they can be rearrested, kidnapped and murdered. Besides, victims of torture are sometimes isolated or forcefully separated from their relatives, friends and communities.

On a social level, ordinary people feel frightened about speaking out against torture, let alone intervening against it. Autocratic systems create a culture of silence, referred to sometimes by the grassroots population as a "graveyard silence." In this atmosphere, people feel powerless to challenge the status quo or to change their circumstances. Most of the time, they blame the victims and do not go beyond addressing their personal daily affairs. Even in Canada, people do not want to get upset by listening to stories about torture. It has happened in our own educational meetings, where a member of the audience has stopped and asked us not to explain the various techniques of torture. Even human rights workers are reluctant to go deep inside the hell and investigate the crime of torture. I have heard from some advocates that while reading about torture, they skip the sections on methods and techniques. All these contribute to the perpetuation of torture.

It should be mentioned that denial of torture is not an absolute and cannot continue for long. Torturers themselves sometimes expose their crimes as a boasting gesture and at other times as a means of demoralizing their new victims. In the course of their sordid crime, they may explain in great detail the way they murdered celebrated political prisoners and warn the new ones: "if you don't give your information, we will kill you in the same way."

News about torture spreads rapidly in jails among political prisoners. Families come to know sooner or later, as no censorship can fully silence the human voice. During their short visits, prisoners and their families can exchange information by using a language not known to the guards.[18]

It is possible to overcome the circles of silence and denial and convert them to circles of solidarity against torture. At the individual level, there is a need for torture survivors to find understanding and support. The first step is learning to acquire coping skills to safeguard against the traumatic impacts of torture. It is a must for survivors of torture to construct "meaning" in their lives and be positively acknowledged by family and society. At the family level, it is essential that survivors of torture be understood and obtain adequate support from their dear and near ones especially in connection with their traumatic experiences. This is the first step towards establishing vital links with the community. At the social level, survivors should be provided with opportunities for justice and recognition. Appropriate coping training as well as health and social services should be available and accessible to them. Survivors who have sacrificed their lives for social justice should enjoy social recognition. It is incumbent upon society to establish commemorative practices to appreciate living survivors as well as those victims who had no chance of surviving.[19]

Helping Torture Survivors

SURVIVORS OF TORTURE and war mostly suffer from what is known as Post-Traumatic Stress Disorder (PTSD). The American Psychiatric Association introduced the term in the year 1980 and expanded its definition in 1987.[20] According to an author, PTSD "is a psychiatric condition that can occur in individuals who experience extremely stressful or traumatic life events."[21] It may develop in people who have experienced a tragedy that is beyond the range of normal human experience.[22]

Let me briefly mention tragedies faced by some of our clients at CCVT: an Afghan client told me that just before reaching his home, a warplane bombarded his house with all his family members inside. He now has no relatives at all in the world. A woman from Sri Lanka was forced to remain in solitary confinement with her husband's corpse. A woman from Angola was gang-raped in front of her brother and husband who were later murdered. Torturers killed the mother of an Iranian client, before his eyes, in an attempt to demoralize him. A client told me the story of his frequent mock executions during his three-and-a-half years of imprisonment. He is paranoid today. Torturers massacred the entire family of a CCVT client, covering their bodies and telling him to "collect your junk!"

The impact of such traumatic experiences on survivors is horrible. On the rare occasion, I have seen survivors of unexpected and uncontrollable traumas with a strong passion for life and with success stories of developing their own alternatives to live a normal life. But, in the majority of cases, PTSD has left negative effects upon survivors' consciousness, values, feelings and the way they relate to others. A major problem is the clients' tendency to relive their initial trauma through nightmares and flashbacks. I have found insomnia a common problem of almost all survivors of severe torture. The impact of PTSD may be such that it impairs the person's daily life. Symptoms of PTSD may disappear in the course of time or develop into a chronic mental disorder.

Psychiatrists usually focus on intrusion, avoidance, and hyperarousal as three major characteristics of PTSD. By intrusion, they mean unexpected reoccurrences of the trauma through frequent "flashbacks" that intrude into the daily lives of survivors. People with PTSD may become emotionally dead. They may avoid people and places – even their immediate family members. They may avoid matters or situations that are associated with the original traumatic incident. People with PTSD show constant hyperarousal symptoms such as sleep disorders, irritability, hypervigilance and lack of concentration. They feel persistently threatened by their initial traumatic event.[23]

PTSD is normally associated with (or results in) other psychiatric conditions such as depression. In an attempt to alleviate their suffering, people with PTSD often indulge in alcohol or narcotic drugs. They may involve themselves in criminal offences like assaults and shoplifting. PTSD, according to one report, "is a serious condition with significant morbidity and a high suicide rate."[24]

There are hundreds of institutions around the world working to rehabilitate survivors of torture, especially those who suffer from P.TSD. The two most widely used modes of rehabilitation are: 1) a clinical approach, which draws upon various types of medical and psychological therapies, and 2) a holistic approach, which combines clinical treatments with other social services such as befriending, language instruction, art therapy, appropriate housing, ongoing counselling, legal and immigration services, employment skills training, etc. The goal of the holistic approach is to enhance the coping capacity of torture survivors and to facilitate their participation in social life.

The holistic approach was developed in the United States in the course of the careful research and documentation of PTSD following the Vietnam War. Doctors who were involved in the treatment of survivors of war and torture from South East Asia found the clinical method of treatment necessary, but inadequate. Everything in the society could act as a trigger and lead to their retraumatization. Doctors gradually developed a comprehensive method of treatment with the aim of empowering survivors to withstand the after-effects of torture and traumatic incidents and become agents of their own rehabilitation. I have found this method most appropriate for the rehabilitation of our clients, as those who rely solely on medication have had to face negative side-effects and make a habit of using their drugs and increasing the doses with the passage of time.

In Canada, many agencies offer direct services to survivors of torture. They have organized a national network for joint advocacy, information sharing and research. The Canadian Centre for Victims of Torture (CCVT) is one of the leading members of this network. Working with the community, the Centre supports survivors in the process of successful integration into Canadian society, advocates for their protection and raises awareness of the continuing effects of torture and war on survivors and their families. The CCVT's mandate is to provide its clients with "hope after the horror."

Since its inception in 1977, the CCVT has provided services to over 15,000 survivors of torture, war and generalized violence from 130 countries. The Centre offers survivors and their families such services as the Volunteer Befriending Program, Mutual Support Groups, Art Therapy, a children's program, a drop-in counselling program, and English as a Second Language (ESL) classes. It also offers Coordinated Professional Services, including specialized medical and legal support. These programs are currently being enhanced by the assistance of over 250 volunteers, most of whom act as personal befrienders to survivors of torture. The CCVT also conducts an extensive public education program to teach service providers and the general community about torture, its effects and ways to provide an appropriate response.

Collective Trauma

REHABILITATION BECOMES extremely difficult when an entire nation has experienced such severe traumas as war, genocide, torture, massacre, etc. Treatment is hardly effective when everybody is traumatized. Trauma remains chronic and reproduces itself as long as social causes are not addressed and perpetrators continue to enjoy impunity. The whole of society may suffer from an everlasting culture of pain.

During the liberation war in Algeria, the Algerian Psychiatrist Frantz Omar Fanon found his practice of treatment of native Algerians ineffective due to the continuation of the horror of a colonial war. He emphasized the social origin of traumas, joined the liberation movement and urged the oppressed to purge themselves of their degrading traumas through their collective liberation struggle. He made the following remarks in his letter of resignation as the Head of the Psychiatry Department at the Blida-Joinville Hospital in Algeria:

> "If psychiatry is the medical technique that aims to enable man no longer to be a stranger to his environment, I owe it to myself to affirm that the Arab, permanently an alien in his own country, lives in a state of absolute depersonalization."[25]

Inculcation of horror and anxiety through widespread torture, massacre, genocide and similar coercive measures has happened frequently in human history. There are plenty of examples in our modern history. Tyrants have always used their technique of "psychological artillery" in an attempt to cause havoc and confusion in the minds of people and hypnotize them with intimidation and cynicism. The result is a collective trauma that will pass through generations. There is no magic formula of rehabilitation. Collective trauma can be alleviated through cohesive and collective efforts such as recognition, remembrance, solidarity, communal therapy and massive cooperation.

Vicarious Traumatization

DOCTORS, LAWYERS, nurses, social workers and other caregivers who serve survivors of torture and traumatic events are at risk of suffering from the vicarious effects of trauma. Their close contact with human survivors of torture and war may eliminate any level of separation through which non-victims relate themselves to a world full of trauma and horror.

It is not easy to hear stories of torture on an ongoing basis and remain unaffected. To help victims, one has to own their problems. Owning multiple traumas all the time may lead a professional to become burned out. It has been observed that personnel of mental health asylums have developed symptoms of trauma after a few years of serving traumatized people. I will never forget a colleague who used to go far beyond to assist rejected refugee claimants at the Canada-US border. After seven years of service, she burned out. She could not take it any more and became an accountant.

It is important for those professionals who assist survivors of torture to continue with their services without being afflicted by vicarious traumatization. In the chapter on "Surviving Torture Through Self-Rehabilitation and Love," I will share my personal techniques of overcoming the after-effects of torture.

There is a theory that service providers should keep a distance from survivors of trauma in order to serve them better. While I admit that service providers should be cautious not to over-identify themselves with their clients, I have found friendship with survivors highly beneficial. In my opinion, as caregivers, it is important to constantly remind ourselves and our clients about human limitations. There is a need for having a fresh outlook into the traumas resulting from torture with a global and philosophical perspective. Our clients have not been alone, historically. They have shared and are sharing their trauma with millions of survivors around the globe.

In serving survivors of torture, it has happened many times that I have accepted defeat and surrendered to the harsh reality. In such cases, I have invited myself and my clients to be patient and stoic. At CCVT, we have frequently re-energized ourselves by celebrating our small victories. In a nutshell, caregivers should not only care for their patients, clients and befrienders, but also for themselves. There is also a need for the community to understand the complexity of serving survivors of trauma and to develop a viable strategy of providing care to the caregivers.

Conclusion

WE COME TO the end of our account of a seemingly endless tragedy of human suffering. The scientific and technological revolution at the beginning of the new millennium should have hailed a decline in the use of torture and other degrading treatment. Instead, medieval methods of torture, far from vanishing from the face of the earth, have become more sophisticated. The first task before us is to break the circle of silence, reveal torture in all its colours and forms, and educate ourselves and the public about the burning need for the prevention and eradication of torture and the rehabilitation of its survivors.

The greatest danger to the foundation of civil society is public apathy towards torture, war crimes and crimes against humanity. It would be highly dangerous if the grassroots population gets deterred by their government's intimidation or constant indoctrinations and close their eyes to hideous truths. "The first person," said Eduardo Galeano, "killed by torture triggered a national scandal in Brazil in 1964. The tenth person to die of torture barely made the papers. Number fifty was accepted as 'normal.'"[26]

It is essential to challenge the atmosphere of hate, terror and violence that is ruling our fragile civilization and is the source of all sorts of torture, cruelty and atrocities. According to Mr. Irwin Colter, the Attorney General of Canada:

> "Nazism almost succeeded not only because of the industry of death and technology of terror, but because of the ideology – the pathology of hate. Indeed, it is this state-sanctioned teaching of contempt, this demonizing of others, this standing assault on human security; this is where it all begins."[27]

There is a need for the strengthening of both the instruments against torture and the institutions that work against this social evil. The death penalty must be abolished, as it is the most extreme method of torture. If the world intends to live without torture, a culture of peace and non-violence needs to be fostered at a grassroots level. This will be impossible without the termination of the present gap between haves and have-nots at the national and global levels. Peace will be an illusion without global justice. It is not enough to call upon tyrannical governments to stop torture and other human rights violations. Practical steps should be taken in this direction. Advanced industrial nations should stop supporting dictatorial regimes due to their economic and other vested interests. The practice of rendition should be stopped immediately and the West must terminate exporting instruments of torture, weapons of death and the technology of violence. As relevant today as they were more than half a century ago are the words of Mahatma Gandhi: "Absolute immorality has to be pacified by the rule of absolute morality."

Notes

1. See Desiderius Erasmus, *In Praise of Folly*, translated by John Wilson, 1688, in www.ccel.org/e/erasmus/folly.html, 2 Apr 2005.
2. John Swain, *The Book of Torture*, Worldwide Copyright Ltd., 1968, p. 244.
3. For more details see Canadian Centre for Victims of Torture (CCVT), *Annual Report 2003-2004*, Toronto, pp. 24-30.
4. Ivo Andric, *The Bridge on the Drina*, The University of Chicago Press, Chicago, 1977, p. 46.
5. For the historical roots of this torture see Cameron Kippen, *The History of Foot Torture*, Curtin University of Technology, Perth WA, 2001.
6. For more details see the *Encyclopedia of Human Cruelty* CD-ROM, Felicity Press, www.felicity.com.au.
7. For more information see William A. Schabas, *The Death Penalty as Cruel Treatment and Torture*, Boston, Northeastern University Press, 1996.
8. There was a long-standing tradition in the Iranian judicial system about the exemption of the death penalty against women that was maintained up to 1970. In the early 1970s, execution of women activists was put on the agenda of the government due to their involvement in oppositional political activities. This was preceded by the execution of Ms. Iran Sharifi – a woman accused of murdering her two stepchildren – and its vast coverage by the media. Following this break with tradition, the regime imposed the death penalty against scores of intellectual girls.
9. This is consistent with the personal observations of a senior mental health consultant at the Louisiana State Penitentiary at Angola. See Howard J. Osofsky, *JAMA*, June 26, 2002, Vol. 287, No. 24, p. 3181.
10. Prof. William A. Schabas, Director of the Irish Centre for Human Rights at the National University of Ireland, is looking to the day that the death penalty will be prohibited by customary international law. See his book *The Abolition of the Death Penalty in International Law*, Cambridge, Cambridge University Press, 2002.
11. See Dorothea Waley Singer, *Giordano Bruno, His Life and Thought*, Schuman, 1950.

12. See Ignacio Martin-Baro, *Writings for a Liberation Psychology*. A. Aron and S. Caron, eds., Cambridge, MA: Harvard University Press, 1994. Ignacio Martin-Baro was a Jesuit priest and psychologist who was born in Spain and lived among poor peasants in El Salvador. In November 1989, he was brutally murdered along with five other Jesuit priests and their housekeeper and her daughter by a special unit of the Salvadoran army. As the executions of the Jesuits began, Martin-Baro's voice was heard over the staccato reports of automatic weapons: "This is an injustice!" As a brilliant scholar, Martin-Baro carried out pioneering studies on the impact of war and tyranny on the human psyche.
13. Monireh Baradaran, Ravanshenassi-e Shekanjeh, *The Psychology of Torture*, Baran Publications, 2001, pp. 31-32.
14. Eduardo Galeano, *The Book of Embraces*, translated by Cedric Belfrage with Mark Schafer, published by W.W. Norton & Company, 1992, pp. 106-107.
15. Ezat Mossallanejed, "Torture at the Threshold of the New Millennium," *Torture*, Vol. 10, No. 2, 2000, published by International Rehabilitation Council for Torture Victims (IRCT), Copenhagen, Denmark.
16. Quoted from Rob Elder, "Bomb is ticking; do you OK torture?" August 24, 2004 in the Opinion section of the *San Jose Mercury News*. The term "we" in the quotation is self-explanatory: it is the civilized West that is suffering at the hands of others. The Harvard University professor Michael Ignatieff is also in favour of "coercive interrogations" against suspected terrorists. See his recent book *The Lesser Evil: Political Ethics in an Age of Terror* (Edinburgh University Press, Edinburgh 2004).
17. See M. Abai & E. Mossallanejed, "A Day for the Absolute Prohibition of Torture," *Human Rights Tribune*, Vol. 9, No.11, Spring 2002.
18. During a jail visit with my brother we exchanged important information in the presence of a prison guard. We simply referred to figures known to both as uncle A, cousin B, auntie C, etc. We used terms like "have gone for pilgrimage" or "is in village" for those who had escaped to other countries or who were in jail.
19. Canadian Centre for Victims of Torture, *Coming to Terms with Torture and Organized Violence: An Interactive Workshop Manual for Service Providers*, Toronto, Ontario, p. 52.
20. See *Diagnostic & Statistical Manual of Mental Disorders*, 3rd Edition (DSM-III, American Psychiatric Association, 1980) and 3rd Edition Revised (DSM-III-R, American Psychiatric Association, 1987).
21. Philip D. Harvey and Rachel Yehuda, *Risk Factors for Posttraumatic Stress Disorder*, American Psychiatric Pub, Inc., July 1999.

22. For more information on PTSD see John F. Sommer, Jr. and Mary Beth Williams, editors, *Handbook of Post-Traumatic Therapy,* Greenwood Press, Westport, CT, 1994.
23. For detailed information on PTSD, interested readers may refer to the following website: www.ptsdalliance.org.
24. Abbas Azadian, MD, Peter Stenn, MD, Ph.D., FRCPC, and Anita Gupta, BSc, "Aftermath of Trauma: Posttraumatic Stress Disorder," *The Canadian Journal of Diagnosis,* February 1997, p. 163.
25. Frantz Fanon, *Toward the African Revolution,* New York, 1967. Reprint of *Pour la Révolution Africaine,* Paris, 1964, p. 53.
26. See Eduardo Galeano, *Days and Nights of Love and War,* translated by Judith Brister, foreword by Sandra Cisneros, Monthly Review Press, 2000. As quoted in *Searching for Justice: Counteracting Hate, Torture and Crimes Against Humanity,* one-day forum in advance of the UN International Day in Support of Victims of Torture, at Concordia University, Montreal, Canada, Saturday, June 19, 2004, preface.

3

Legal Instruments Against Torture

I. International Instruments

CONCERN FOR human rights and dignity is not a new phenomenon in human history. There are abundant references to minimum standards of treatment for defeated enemies in various religious, philosophical, and literary texts.[1] However, it took hundreds of years for common law to outlaw torture as "an institutionalized part" of the legal process: "Religion and law generated a complex moral paradox. Namely, torture was often deemed to be indispensable for the discovery of truth."[2]

Innumerable examples of torture occupy human history. In ancient Athens and under the Roman republic, torture was systematically used for the examination of slaves. Free citizens were also not immune from torture under special circumstances. Torture was in widespread use by the Inquisition and was a universal means of extracting confessions during witchcraft trials. It was not until 1816 that it was abandoned by a papal bull.

Attempts to outlaw torture began with the establishment of civil societies and the development of the concept of natural law. The creation of the League of Nations in the aftermath of World War I ushered in a new era for the adoption and ratification of human rights instruments outlawing the practice of torture. Unfortunately, the League had a short lifespan and it was only with the establishment of the United Nations Organizations in 1945 that we witnessed the evolution of the modern human rights instruments that led to the absolute prohibition of torture.[3]

The first document that laid a solid foundation for upcoming legal instruments against torture was the UN Charter of 1945. With its emphasis on the obligation of the members of the family of nations to avert aggression and work towards the peace and security of nations, the Charter prepared the grounds for the adoption of the *UN Declaration of Human Rights*, which focused on individual rights *vis-à-vis* the state's power (December 10, 1948). Article 5 of this Declaration specifies that "No one shall be subjected to torture or to cruel, inhuman or degrading treatment or punishment."

This was followed by the four *Geneva Conventions* of 1949 that acted as the main source of *International Humanitarian Law* (IHL), also called the laws of war. The *Geneva Conventions* outlawed physical or mental coercion against prisoners of war and detained civilians, deeming it a war crime. Women are protected against rape and any form of indecent assault. Detainees in an armed conflict or military occupation are also protected by common Article 3 to all four *Geneva Conventions* against murder, mutilation, cruel treatment and torture, humiliation and degrading treatment.

An important addition to the *Geneva Conventions* is Protocol 1, relating to the *Protection of Victims of International Armed Conflicts*, which entered into force on December 7, 1979. Article 75 of this customary international law[4] has prohibited the following acts "at any time and in any place whatsoever, whether committed by civilian or by military" personnel: violence to life, murder, torture of all kinds (whether physical or mental), corporal punishment, mutilation, humiliating or degrading treatment, hostage-taking, collective punishments, etc. Article 99 of the *Geneva Convention Relative to the Treatment of Prisoners of War* (adopted on August 12, 1949, and entered into force on October 21, 1950) is also vocal against torture: "No moral or physical coercion may be exerted on a prisoner of war in order to induce him to admit himself guilty of the act of which he is accused."

The first attempt to address the issue of torture in its totality was the UN General Assembly's adoption of the *Declaration on the Protection of All Persons from Being Subjected to Torture and Other Cruel, Inhuman or Degrading Treatment or Punishment* (December 9, 1975). This was not, however, a powerful instrument, because unlike UN covenants or conventions, it had no binding authority over nations. A major breakthrough occurred on March 23, 1976: The *International Covenant on Civil and Political Rights* and its first *Optional Protocol* entered into force. Article 7 of this binding document repeated the provision of the *UN Declaration of Human Rights* with an addendum: "In particular, no one shall be subjected without his free consent to medical or scientific experimentation."

The above Covenant and its first optional protocol paved the way for the establishment of the UN Human Rights Committee. Individuals were allowed to access the committee in cases of violation of their rights under the Covenant. Another major achievement was the adoption of the *Principles of Medical Ethics* by the General Assembly of the UN on December 18, 1982. This instrument prevents medical personnel from being involved in torture.

It was not until December 10, 1984 that the UN General Assembly adopted the comprehensive *Convention Against Torture and Other Cruel, Inhuman or Degrading Treatment or Punishment* (usually referred to as CAT). This Convention was enacted on June 26, 1987, and is the most important document to date that deals with the crime of torture and its prevention among the family of nations. In December 1997, the UN General Assembly declared June 26 (the day CAT entered into force) as the *International Day in Solidarity with Survivors of Torture*. Human rights organizations have been celebrating this day since then.

The adoption of the *Convention on the Rights of the Child* (CRC) on November 20, 1989, and its enforcement on September 2, 1990, was a major development in addressing the crime of torture against children. Article 37 of the CRC has protected children against torture.

Following are some non-binding UN instruments that are directly or indirectly connected with the struggle against torture. Several countries have incorporated parts of these instruments into their domestic legislation:

- *Declaration on the Elimination of Violence against Women* (December 20, 1993)
- *Declaration on the Protection of Women and Children in Emergency and Armed Conflicts* (December 14, 1974)
- *United Nations Rules for Protection of Juveniles Deprived of their Liberty* (December 14, 1990)
- *Body Principles for the Protection of All Persons under Any Form of Detention or Imprisonment* (December 9, 1988)
- *Basic Principles for the Treatment of Prisoners* (December 14, 1990)
- *Standard Minimum Rules for the Treatment of Prisoners* (July 31, 1957)
- *Code of Conduct for Law Enforcement Officials* (December 17, 1979)
- *Basic Principles for the Use of Force and Firearms by Law Enforcement Officials* (adopted by UN Congress in Cuba, August 27 to September 7, 1990)
- *Guidelines on the Role of Prosecutors* (adopted by UN Congress in Cuba August 27 to September 7, 1990)
- *Declaration on the Protection of All Persons from Enforced Disappearance* (December 18, 1992)

A major human rights achievement of the 20th century was the circulation of the *Rome Statute* of the International Criminal Court (ICC) on July 17, 1998. This instrument considers the widespread or systematic use of torture to be a war crime and a crime against humanity.[5] As will be shown in the chapter on impunity, the establishment of the ICC on July 1, 2002 ushered in a new era of the termination of impunity for torturers, war criminals and for those who have committed crimes against humanity.

CAT: Advantages and Limitations

CAT IS A useful instrument in codifying universally applicable standards against torture. It is implemented through the UN Committee Against Torture (Article 17 of CAT), which consists of ten independent experts designated by the UN Secretary General. The Committee's mandate is to monitor the practice of torture and ensure that the Convention is observed by the states' parties. To this aim, there is a Special Rapporteur designated by the UN Commission on Human Rights (UNCHR), whose mission is to monitor torture in all countries (whether a UN member or not) and to respond immediately. Anybody can communicate with the Special Rapporteur about the use of torture in any part of the world at any time.

The following articles from CAT are instrumental in any advocacy against the international evil of torture:

> Article 2 reiterates states' obligations in the prevention of torture. It leaves no doubt whatsoever about the absolute prohibition of torture: "No exceptional circumstances whatsoever, whether a state of war or a threat of war, internal political instability or any other public emergency, may be invoked as a justification of torture. An order from a superior officer or a public authority may not be invoked as a justification of torture."
>
> Article 3 stipulates that "No state party shall return or extradite a person to another state where there are substantial grounds for believing that he would be in danger of being subject to torture." This article is one of the most important tools of advocacy in favour of torture survivors. It is an absolute, which cannot be balanced with such considerations as danger to the security of the public or risks to national security.

Article 4 is about criminalization of torture: "Each State Party shall ensure that all acts of torture are offences under its criminal law."

Article 6 speaks to the prosecution of perpetrators of torture beyond any national boundary. Torturers should be apprehended and brought before the law in whatever country they escape to. This article considers torture to be a crime of international law and does not allow impunity for its perpetrators.

Article 10 emphasizes that education regarding the prohibition against torture must be included in the training programs of law enforcement personnel (civil or military), medical personnel, public officials and other persons who may be involved in the custody, interrogation or treatment of any individual subjected to any form of arrest, detention or imprisonment.

Article 11 delineates rules of interrogation, detention standards, and the treatment of prisoners. This is important because jails and detention centres are usually a hotbed for the perpetration of torture and other cruel, inhuman and degrading treatment or punishment.

Article 13 recognizes the rights of individuals to complain to authorities about torture in their countries. This article is a tool for holding those in positions of authority in jails or detention centres accountable to the laws of the nation.

Article 14 is about the responsibility of states to guarantee the rights of torture victims to redress, compensation and rehabilitation. This is an important tool in two respects. Firstly, it strengthens the mandate of the UN Voluntary Fund for Victims of Torture that was established by the UN General Assembly on December 16, 1981. The Fund receives "voluntary contributions from governments, non-governmental organizations and individuals for distribution to non-governmental organizations providing humanitarian assistance to victims of torture and members of their family."[6] Secondly, the article has prepared the background for the emergence of a private law dimension that greatly empowers private enforcement against public actors who are implicated in the practice of torture. This development signifies the extension of sanctions against torture from the public to the private sphere.

Article 15 is about the legal invalidity of statements obtained under torture. This is a useful tool enabling human rights institutions to call upon states to reform their judicial systems in ways that would negate the need for torture to obtain confessions or information from the accused.

Article 16 calls upon state parties to "prevent … other acts of cruel, inhuman or degrading treatment or punishment which do not amount to torture … ." This is an important tool to encourage the states to practice the humane treatment of visible minorities, people with different sexual orientations and non-citizens. It could also fill in the gaps of CAT to include lawfully sanctioned and religiously consecrated tortures such as stoning, suttee, and female genital mutilation as acts of cruel, inhuman or degrading treatment. It is unfortunate that such acts are not defined in international law.

Article 20 gives the UN Committee Against Torture a mandate to receive reliable information about the systematic practice of torture in the territory of state parties. It could bring the states to account and make possible investigations into the practice of torture.

Article 22 gives individuals of any country the right to submit communications (a euphemism for complaint) to the UN Committee Against Torture. This is a very important preventative measure which could ensure each state party meets its obligations. For the Committee to act upon such a communication, the state party should have recognized the competence of the Committee, and the individual should have exhausted all local proceedings. Out of 139 countries that had acceded or ratified the Convention by November 24, 2004, 41 of them had recognized the competence of the Committee.

CAT has made torture both a domestic and an international crime. It has also brought it to the institutions of private law. Torture is now a civil offence prosecutable through the institutions of civil society.

Despite the above advantages, there is a major contradiction in the implementation of the *Convention Against Torture*: while it is left to the state party to implement the Convention, torture is normally practiced with the sanction of the government and by those at the apex of political power. This fact is responsible for the impunity of torturers and the ineffectiveness of the international legal instruments.

Optional Protocol to the Convention Against Torture

HUMAN RIGHTS TREATIES are sometimes followed by *Optional Protocols* that can act as complementary procedures to the treaty or address a major area of it. *Optional Protocols* are treaties in their own right, and are open to signature, accession or ratification by states that are party to the main treaty.

The UN Commission on Human Rights established an open-ended working group in 1991 to draft an *Optional Protocol to the Convention Against Torture*. The intention was to establish a global system of inspection, which could allow the UN Committee Against Torture to make regular visits to places of detention. The Committee, on the basis of the draft protocol, could establish a sub-committee with the mandate to travel to any country at any time to monitor the implementation of the *Convention Against Torture*.

Unfortunately, some governments, not willing to have their detention systems subject to international inspection, did not show much interest in supporting the *Protocol*.[7] It took eleven years for the working group to come up with its final draft – a compromised document far removed from the effectiveness of its initial draft. It was not until December 18, 2002, in the fifty-seventh session of the General Assembly of the United Nations, that the *Protocol* was adopted. It was made available for signature and ratification on February 4, 2003. As of November 29, 2004, 29 countries had signed the *Protocol* but only 6 had actually ratified it. When it enters into force, the *Protocol* will create a sub-committee and allow in-country inspections of places of detention to be undertaken in collaboration with national institutions.

Cruel, Inhuman or Degrading Treatment or Punishment

THE DEFINITION OF the practice is the subject of legal debate. There are usually two criteria to establish whether a treatment or punishment is cruel, inhuman or degrading: 1) the act should be unusual to the extent that it shocks the conscience of humanity; 2) it is so excessive that it outrages standards of decency. In other words, there is the problem of disproportionality if the punishment does not fit the crime.

The above criteria do not make it clear whether treatments such as insults, verbal abuse, deprivation, humiliation, demoralization, and keeping individuals in a condition of uncertainty should be classified under this category. It is a widespread belief that the death penalty should be considered cruel and unusual punishment. With the intensification of the ill-treatment of visible minorities and non-citizens following the terrorist attacks of September 11, 2001, there is an urgent need for the UN system to come up with an appropriate definition of the acts that constitute "other cruel, inhuman or degrading treatment or punishment."

An Orphaned Instrument

DOCTORS, NURSES AND health personnel have always been vulnerable to forceful involvement in torture. They have been tortured and persecuted for their adherence to their ethics in the treatment of those who are considered *persona non grata* by military or tyrannical regimes. In its 1975 *Declaration of Tokyo,* the World Medical Association (WMA) provided medical doctors with guidelines on torture "in relation to detention and imprisonment." "The utmost respect," the preamble says, "for human life is to be maintained even under threat, and no use made of any medical knowledge contrary to the laws of humanity."[8] The WMA went a step forward with its resolution of 1981, announcing "it is unethical for physicians to participate in capital punishment."[9]

The above developments, along with the WMA's concerns for human rights,[10] paved the way for the adoption of the *Principles of Medical Ethics* on December 18, 1982 by the UN General Assembly. This document consists of six principles.[11] In the preamble, the General Assembly warns that "not infrequently members of the medical profession or other health personnel are engaged in activities which are difficult to reconcile with medical ethics."[12]

Principle 1 of the above instrument has made it the duty of medical personnel, particularly physicians, not to discriminate against those who are "imprisoned or detained." It is a "gross contravention of medical ethics" for them "to engage, actively or passively, in acts which constitute participation in, complicity in, incitement to or attempts to commit torture or other cruel, inhuman or degrading treatment or punishment" (Principle 2). They must not apply "their knowledge and skills in order to assist in the interrogation of prisoners" or to certify their fitness for punishment (Principle 4). They should not participate in "restraining a prisoner" unless it is necessary on medical grounds (Principle 5).

The widespread use of torture and other inhuman and unusual treatment as an after-effect of the terrorist incidents of September 11, 2001 has made the *UN Principles of Medical Ethics* more relevant. What follows is an excerpt from an article by American author and psychiatrist Dr. Robert J. Lifton:

> "There is increasing evidence that US doctors, nurses and medics have been complicit in torture and other illegal procedures in Iraq, Afghanistan and Guantánamo Bay. Such medical complicity suggests still another disturbing dimension of this broadening scandal. We know that medical personnel have failed to report to higher authorities wounds that were clearly caused by torture and that they have neglected to take steps to interrupt this torture. In addition, they have turned over prisoners' medical records to interrogators who could use them to exploit the prisoners' weaknesses or vulnerabilities. We have not yet learned the extent of medical involvement in delaying and possibly falsifying the death certificates of prisoners who have been killed by torturers."[13]

While condemning the practice of torture in jails, the Executive Director of the Physicians for Human Rights has referred to the lack of effective guidelines for medical professionals dealing with prisoners. He has reiterated that efforts must include "a robust examination of guidance provided to health professionals who work in settings where interrogations occur, since it appears that guidance for medical personnel is almost entirely lacking."[14]

It is an urgent necessity today for the international community to scrutinize the present legal instruments on the question of ethics on behalf of medical professionals on the one hand and their protection against forceful involvement in torture on the other. The present instrument is non-binding and impotent. There is no effective international body to monitor the implementation of the *UN Principles of Medical Ethics*. There is an immediate need for the implementation of a binding treaty among nations and an effective monitoring body to this effect.

II. Regional Instruments

DESPITE THEIR LIMITED scopes, regional human rights instruments are often broad and effective in dealing with the scourge of torture in a particular region. In the Americas, for example, efforts towards the protection of human rights predate the *UN Declaration of Human Rights*. The inter-American human rights system was born with the adoption of the *American Declaration of Rights and Duties of Man* by the 9th Conference of the American States, in Bogotá, Colombia, in April 1948. The Inter-American Commission on Human Rights (IACHR) was created in 1959 and held its first session in 1960. By 1961, the IACHR had started monitoring human rights conditions in member states through its on-site visits. In 1965, the IACHR was mandated to receive individual complaints on human rights violations including torture.

Another development is the adoption of the *American Convention on Human Rights* in 1969 and its enforcement in 1978. According to Article 5 of this document, "No one shall be subjected to torture or to cruel, inhuman or degrading treatment or punishment." A Commission of Human Rights and a Court of Human Rights were established in Costa Rica with a mandate of monitoring the implementation of the Convention and guaranteeing the fundamental rights of each and every person. Individuals can complain to the Commission regarding violations of the Convention (Article 44) provided that the particular state has accepted the competence of the Commission to receive complaints (Article 45). This Convention is a treaty among members of the Organization of American States, with 30 states from Latin America, the Caribbean and North America.

The instrument that specifically deals with torture in America is the *Inter-American Convention to Prevent and Punish Torture*. It was adopted in 1985 and entered into force in 1987. This Convention is also a treaty among members of the OAS. Article 2 of this Convention has a broad definition of torture. It includes "physical or mental pain or suffering" inflicted on a person "for purposes of criminal investigation" or "any other purpose." Torture is understood "to be the use of methods" to destroy "the personality of the victim ... even if they do not cause physical pain or mental anguish." Article 6 has made torture a criminal offence that should be prevented and punished by all member states. Articles 12 and 14 introduce universal jurisdiction for the prosecution of torturers.

There are well-established instruments and institutions in Europe for the protection of people against torture.[15] The *European Convention on Human Rights* (ECHR) was adopted in 1950 by the Council of Europe (the oldest inter-governmental organization, presently with 41 nations). The ECHR created two judicial bodies: the Court of Human Rights and Commission of Human Rights, based in Strasbourg. Article 3 of the ECHR provides that "No one shall be subjected to torture or to inhuman or degrading treatment or punishment." Under similar conditions to those mentioned above, individuals can complain against torture and other human rights violations.

Europe went a step further and accepted the *European Convention for the Prevention of Torture and Inhuman or Degrading Treatment or Punishment* (adopted on November 26, 1987 by the Council of Europe in Strasbourg and entered into force on February 1, 1989). This is the first instrument to emphasize the need for official visits to jails and detention centres under the control of member states.

In an attempt to take practical steps towards the prevention of torture, the European Convention created the European Committee for the Prevention of Torture and Inhuman or Degrading Treatment or Punishment (ECPT). The ECPT is composed of independent and impartial members and is occasionally assisted by experts. The Committee conducts periodic and *ad hoc* visits to places "where persons are deprived of their liberty by a public authority."

Africa is far ahead of Europe and America in terms of taking a multidimensional and comprehensive approach to the protection of the fundamental rights of humankind. The *African [Banjul] Charter on Human and Peoples' Rights* (known as the *African Charter*) was adopted on June 27, 1981 by the Organization of African Unity. This instrument, which entered into force on October 21, 1986, deals with a wide range of economic, social, cultural and peoples' (or community) rights. Article 5 provides that "All forms of exploitation and degrading treatment or punishment shall be prohibited."

The African Charter provided for the establishment of the African Commission on Human and Peoples' Rights. The Commission was officially inaugurated on November 2, 1987, in Addis Ababa, Ethiopia. It was mandated to ensure the promotion and protection of human and peoples' rights throughout the African Continent. Individuals, groups or NGOs can complain to the Commission about violations against the Convention (Article 55).

III. Non-governmental Instruments

THERE ARE NON-GOVERNMENTAL agencies with well-established rules and procedures that contribute continually towards the prevention, eradication and exposure of the crime of torture as well as to the rehabilitation of torture survivors. The following are some prominent agencies with an international mandate:

ICRC

THE INTERNATIONAL COMMITTEE of the Red Cross is one of the oldest NGOs working for the protection of victims of war and torture. It was founded in 1863 in Geneva, Switzerland, as an impartial and private humanitarian body. The ICRC works on the basis of neutrality between the parties in conflict. In cases of international conflicts among parties to the Geneva Conventions, the ICRC is permitted to visit all places where prisoners of war or civilians are held. In cases of non-international armed conflicts, the organization offers its services to the conflicting parties and – with their consent – can have access to places of detention. In situations of civil war or unrest, it extends humanitarian assistance, including visiting security detainees. Visits by the ICRC have, in many cases, improved the physical and psychological conditions of detainees and have prevented their torture and ill-treatment. The ICRC delegates try their best to meet the challenge of talking freely to detainees without witnesses. Individual follow-ups of the detainees' whereabouts are also part of ICRC visiting procedures.

Amnesty International

WITH ITS LONG-STANDING campaigns against abuses of human rights, Amnesty International is a global movement concerned with the protection and promotion of the human rights standards recognized by the international community. Founded in 1961 in London, England, Amnesty International has grown to become one of the world's most prominent non-governmental organizations with 1.8 million members in over 150 countries. Maintaining its independence, Amnesty International does not accept funding from governments nor does it support any particular political ideology or system, economic interest or religion.

Amnesty International campaigns on behalf of political prisoners and others who have been detained for political or religious beliefs or because of their ethnicity, gender, national origin or other status. It opposes the torture and killing of prisoners, the use of hostage-taking by opposition groups, and the death penalty. Amnesty International has worked to protect the human rights of refugees in cases of forcible return to a country where they may be subject to torture or execution. Amnesty International has also sent delegates to visit detention camps and areas. Based on comprehensive research efforts, Amnesty International regularly documents and publicizes specific cases of torture and other human rights abuses around the world.

Human Rights Watch

AS AN INDEPENDENT non-governmental organization based in New York City, Human Rights Watch monitors human rights developments all over the world. It began in 1978 as a small agency called Helsinki Watch with the initial mandate of monitoring the USSR's compliance with the Helsinki Accords. The organization evolved into its present structure in 1988, following the alliance with other watch organizations that covered human rights monitoring in other parts of the world. The mandate of this organization is similar to that of Amnesty International. It is also supported by private contributions and does not accept government funds, directly or indirectly.

IRCT

THE INTERNATIONAL REHABILITATION Council for Torture Victims (IRCT) is a global, independent health centre that contributes to the rehabilitation of torture survivors as well as to the exposure, eradication and prevention of this global evil. It was founded by Dr. Inge Genefke in Copenhagen, Denmark in 1982 "as an independent institution with its own premises." Today, the IRCT supports and collaborates with a global network of more than 200 rehabilitation centres across the world.[16]

Concluding Remarks

AS WAS SHOWN in this chapter, there is no lack of international, regional and domestic legal instruments and institutions against torture and other cruel, inhuman or degrading treatments or punishments. There is no doubt that without these instruments and institutions, torture would be much more prevalent in today's world. It is, however, unfortunate that torture is still widespread around the globe. This speaks to the need for more public education and advocacy against torture and harder work towards the protection of human rights and dignity. Power has always been a big hindrance. The absolute power of the sovereign states must be controlled by the national and international solidarity of grass-roots people and organizations.

Notes

1. The great Roman orator, man of letters and legal expert Cicero (106-43 BC) totally condemned the use of torture. There is a marvelous piece by the Iranian poet of the 14th Century AD, Sa'di Shirazi, in his masterpiece *Boostan* (*Orchard*), about a farmer who was bitten by a wild beast. He was taken home while screaming in pain. His little daughter asked him why he did not bite the beast in retaliation. The farmer smiled amidst his agonizing torment: "I didn't do it, darling daughter, because I'm not a beast." The great poet concludes that one can punish wicked people but must not treat them like a beast.
2. Winston P. Nagan and Lucie Atkin, "The International Law of Torture: From Universal Proscription to Effective Application and Enforcement," *Harvard Human Rights Journal*, Vol. 14, Spring 2001, p. 92.
3. There are plenty of sources about legal instruments against torture. For a detailed account interested readers can refer to the following:
   a) Durcan Forrest, *A Glimpse of Hell*, Amnesty International, UK, 1996, pp. 1-20; b) Amnesty International, *Combating Torture: a manual for action*, London, 2003; c) International Rehabilitation Council for Torture Victims (IRCT), *International Instruments and Mechanisms for the Fight against Torture - 1. Legal Instruments on Torture* at www.irct.org.
4. Customary international law refers to the group of international legal instruments that are binding on all states on a peremptory norm – laws that preempt all other customary laws. All states are bound to respect provisions of customary international instruments whether or not they have acceded to them.

5. See, for example, Article 7(f) and Article 8(2-a-ii).
6. Office of the High Commissioner for Human Rights, *Documents on United Nations Voluntary Fund for Victims of Torture, Part I, Mandate.*
7. During my trip in 1999 to Geneva, I spent a week attending the Working Group meeting of the *Optional Protocol*. The chair of the Working Group was Elizabeth Odio Benito, a well-known judge and expert on international law from Costa Rica. In the course of the delegates' discussions, I realized that opinions were divided. On the one hand, the conservative side (including US, Egypt, Iran, China, Cuba and Saudi Arabia) expressed reservations regarding the implementation of the *Optional Protocol*. They argued that unrestricted access would undermine national sovereignty and the individual's right to privacy. The progressive camp (including European countries, Australia and Canada), on the other hand, believed that there was no need for such reservations and that unrestricted access was essential to the effectiveness of the *Optional Protocol*. "If states," they argued, "can place limits on which sites can be inspected, then such restrictions hinder the comprehensive investigation of torture and may well provide states with the opportunity to avoid such scrutiny and hide the practice of torture." For more details see Ezat Mossallanejed, "Canada and the Global Prevention of Torture," *The First Light, Quarterly Journal of the CCVT,* Toronto, Spring 2000.
8. See *Declaration of Tokyo: Guidelines for medical doctors concerning torture or other cruel, inhuman or degrading treatment or punishment in relation to detention and imprisonment,* Adopted by the 29th World Medical Assembly, Tokyo, October 1975.
9. Resolution on "Physician Participation in Capital Punishment" adopted by the 34th World Medical Assembly, Lisbon, Portugal, September 28 to October 2, 1981.
10. It did not take long for the World Medical Association to develop its official position on the advancement of the "cause of human rights for all people." It called upon its member associations "to provide clear ethical advice to doctors working in the prison system" and "to support individual physicians who call attention to human rights violations in their own countries." See *World Medical Association Resolution on Human Rights,* adopted by the 42nd World Medical Assembly, 1990 and amended by the 45th Assembly, Hungary, October 1993, and by the 46th Assembly, Sweden, September 1994, and by the 47th Assembly, September 1995.
11. For the full text, see "Principles of Medical Ethics Relevant to the Role of Health Personnel," particularly "Physicians, in the Protection of Prisoners and Detainees against Torture and Other Cruel, Inhuman or Degrading Treatment or Punishment" adopted by General Assembly resolution

37/194 of December 18, 1982, UN Information Office, Ref: A/Res/37/194. See IRCT, *International Declarations and Conventions*, updated in December 1996, p. 16.
12. Quoted from the Office of the UN High Commissioner for Human Rights, *Combating Torture, Fact Sheet*, No. 4 (Rev. 1), New York Office, May 2002, p. 7.
13. Robert J. Lifton, "Doctors and Torture," *New England Journal of Medicine*, Volume 351, No. 5, July 29, 2004, pp. 415-416.
14. As quoted by Ken Agar-Newman in *American Journal of Nurses*, Vol. 105, No. 4, April 2005, pp. 15-17. Also see Statement of Leonard Rubenstein, Executive Director, Physicians for Human Rights, in American Civil Liberties Union, *International Human Rights*, July 2, 2004.
15. For more details see OSCE/ODIHR, *Preventing Torture: A Handbook for OSCE Field Staff*, First Edition, Warsaw 1999.
16. For more information see www.irct.org.

4

A Glimpse into the Global Picture of Torture Against Children

They kneel down,
The king and the beggar,
The saint and the sinner,
The wise and the fool, and cry:
Victory to Man, the new-born, the ever-living![1]

– Rabindranath Tagore

Introduction

THE GREAT INDIAN poet and Nobel Prize Laureate, Rabindranath Tagore, was of the opinion that when a child is born, it brings with it the message that God is not yet disappointed with humankind. He was thrilled anytime he learned that a woman had given birth to a child. He believed in the idea of a world committed to its moral responsibilities towards children: "On the seashore of endless worlds is the great meeting of children."[2] It is unfortunate that in the first decade of the 21st century, 64 years after the death of the great poet, one billion children around the globe are robbed of their childhood.

According to Kofi Annan, Secretary General of the United Nations, "childhood is starkly and brutally different from the ideal we all aspired to. Poverty denies their dignity, endangers their lives and limits their potential. Conflict and violence rob them of a secure family life and betray their trust and their hope. HIV/AIDS kills their parents, their teachers, their doctors and their nurses and also kills them."[3] However, Mr. Annan neglects to mention state-sanctioned tortures against children.

According to United Nations' estimates, 40,000 children die every day as a result of war and deprivation. Almost 11 million children under the age of 5 die every year from preventable causes. One hundred and twenty million school-age children have no access to school. About 150 million children suffer from malnutrition. There are 246 million child labourers working under abusive conditions. Sexual abuse, prostitution, slavery, and trafficking of children are widespread all over the globe.[4]

Over one billion children live in poverty. Of that number, more than 100 million are estimated to be abandoned in the streets of the world's largest cities. There are millions of refugees, internally displaced and stateless children. Since 1990, armed conflicts have killed 3.5 million people, over 45 percent of them children. The number of child soldiers is over 300,000. By the end of 2002, more than 20 million people had died of AIDS and another 24 million were infected with HIV. Over 5 million more are being infected annually. About half are young people between the ages of 15 and 24.[5] In 2003 alone, some 2.9 million people died of AIDS, mostly in underdeveloped regions of the world. HIV/AIDS has resulted in an ever-increasing rate of child mortality and millions of orphaned children.[6]

There are child marriages, forced marriages, and exchanges of women and girls in blood feuds between tribes and families. In more than 75 percent of the countries of the world, childhood is combined with tremendous suffering.

On November 20, 1989, after ten years of negotiations, the United Nations General Assembly unanimously adopted the *Convention on the Rights of the Child* (CRC), creating a comprehensive treaty for the protection of children. This "Magna Carta for Children" has become an indisputable component of customary international law. All countries, except Somalia and the United States of America, have ratified it. Although this is a significant step in the efforts to protect the rights of children, we must at the same time feel terribly upset that, sixteen years after the adoption of the CRC, the family of nations has failed to stop torture against children.

This chapter is a modest attempt to illustrate briefly only one area of the global suffering of children: torture and trauma as a result of war and gross human rights violations.

Types of Torture Against Children

DURING THE PERIOD of a year (March 2003 to April 2004), the Canadian Centre for Victims of Torture (CCVT) accepted 222 new children (out of the total number of 798 new clients) who had suffered directly or indirectly from physical or psychological tortures.[7] They came to Canada along with one or both of their parents and, in some cases, alone as separated children from 39 countries of the world. 118 of these children were girls. The countries that the children came from primarily were Afghanistan: 27, Iran: 26, Somalia: 23, Kosovo: 22, Albania: 18, Democratic Republic of Congo: 14, Angola: 10, Sudan: 8, Sri Lanka: 7, Turkey: 6, Colombia and Argentina: 5 each. The CCVT sister agency, the World Organization Against Torture (OMCT), has documented and acted upon 3,600 cases of torture and violence against children in 63 countries within a period of 6 years prior to August 2002.[8] The experience of CCVT and OMCT is the microcosm of a global tragedy: the crime of perpetration of torture against helpless and vulnerable children.

Children are subjected to torture and unusual treatment everywhere: at home, in the streets, in playgrounds, in orphanages, at work, in reformatory centres, in police custody and in war-ravaged areas. In Brazil, Guatemala, Colombia and many other countries street kids are not referred to as "children." They are called "vermin" and are regularly tortured and murdered by police. Torture against children has become common within the family, the community and government agencies.[9] According to Amnesty International, children are subjected to torture in all regions of the world. Children "suffer in silence, their stories never told, their torments never called into account."[10]

What is disturbing is the total impunity of those who commit torture against children. In some countries, beating children is considered a preventive punishment. Due to their age, fear and vulnerability, children are not in a position to raise their voice against their torturers. In many countries there is almost no protection from the government. The absence of any monitoring mechanism is also disturbing. If a family or an agency takes the risk of complaining against a particular officer, the complaint will be investigated, if at all, by the perpetrator's colleagues or even the suspect. It may lead to further violence against the plaintiff.[11]

Children remain absolutely helpless against torture in jails and detention centres. They have no one to speak to about their torture and ill-treatment except the guards or wardens who are involved in their systematic torture.

Children can be direct or indirect victims of torture and other cruel, inhuman or degrading treatment or punishment. At the most tender age they may face torture as a result of someone else's political activities. In many cases, torturers use children as tools to extract information or confessions from their parents or close relatives or to humiliate or degrade their families or communities. A client of mine told me that while in detention, his torturers tortured, raped and killed his nine- and ten-year-old sons before his eyes.

Children may experience torture directly as a result of their own political activism (attending a meeting or demonstration, distributing pamphlets, reading prohibited literature, asking an "irrelevant" question in school, etc.). During my imprisonment under the Shah of Iran (1973 to 1977), we had children between the ages of 14 and 17 years among us who had been tortured and imprisoned due to their own activities. They pretended that they enjoyed time with us, but this was not the case. In those days, all discussions were about politics and revolution, things that had nothing to do with the special needs of children. They loved to play, exercise and listen to stories but for all intents and purposes they did not feel at home. I remember a child of 16 was smoking a cigarette while everyone advised him not to do so. "You cannot advise me," he said. "I am not a child; I am a political prisoner."

Children may be detained and tortured due to their alleged criminality, gender and sexual orientation or simply for being street kids or living in slum areas and shanty towns. Children who suffer from abject poverty or those who belong to religious or ethnic minorities can be tortured as a result of the government's discriminatory policies or as a means of intimidating the whole community.

Children of political prisoners, even if they enjoy good care by the other parent or grandparents, are indirect victims of torture. The forceful and abrupt separation from a source of love and tender care is hard for small children to accept. They may feel sadness, anger, loneliness, and be fearful that they may never see that loved one again. To this one can add the child's feeling of abandonment and constant anxiety that the caregiver too may soon disappear. Sometimes, they feel guilty for the troubles their dear ones have gone through. Some develop the sense of being rejected, being no longer loved. Children with imprisoned parents or siblings may express their feelings by not playing, not eating, not sleeping, and by crying most of the time or by avoiding people and beautiful places.

Visiting imprisoned parents, specifically those who are in jail for political reasons, is both a source of joy and harassment for children. Imagine a labyrinth of brick or stone blocks guarded by rough people in uniforms, then a long corridor with a narrow hall with two rows of iron bars covered with screens and guards that are walking inside and listening to conversations between prisoners and their visitors. Along with scores of other visitors, the child visits her/his parent, whose face has turned pale and who is dressed in a prison uniform, on the other side of a barrier. They have to shout in order to hear each other's voices. If they are lucky enough to visit through a glass wall, they have to speak to each other on a telephone for a short period of time. A glass wall separates them by a few centimetres, but they may as well be hundreds of kilometres apart.

During jail visits, the families of political prisoners, including children, face humiliation, insults and more often than not physical abuse by guards and prison authorities. The impact on children, especially if the treatment continues for a long time, could be terrible. They may feel pity for their dear ones in jail, whom they feel are subjected to worse treatment. They may get frustrated with themselves and the whole world that cannot make any difference. Let me share another personal recollection. During a New Year's visit, prison authorities permitted me to see my two little nieces (my brother's and sister's children). They brought them to the jail's office. I embraced them and asked if they liked my beautiful palace. "You cannot fool us, uncle," they said. "You have no palace; this is your jail." The guards immediately intervened and took them away. They still remember the bitterness of that short visit.

In some countries, children are left with no choice but to lose their homes following the arrest and imprisonment of their parents. This may happen for various reasons, including harassment by the neighbourhood, government persecution, and finances. Children have to move from one place to another with the consequence of losing friends, teachers and everything that they love. It is, therefore, not surprising that they develop abnormal or even anti-social behaviour. They may not see their beloved parent or parents for years without knowing or understanding why.

Death Penalty

THERE ARE SEVEN countries in the world that have maintained the death penalty against children despite Article 6(5) of the *International Covenant on Civil and Political Rights* (ICCPR) and Article 37 of the *UN Convention on the Rights of the Child* that prohibit passing a death sentence on anyone aged less than eighteen at the time of the crime. The use of capital punishment against children is legal in the United States of America, Democratic Republic of Congo (DRC), Pakistan, Yemen, Saudi Arabia, Nigeria, and Iran.

Although the US government does not apply the death penalty to children under the age of 16, it has not been abolished for older children (16 to 18) in 24 states.[12] The Iranian clerical government has executed children under the age of 12, for their political and "anti-Islamic" activities. During the occupation of Kurdistan by the Islamic army, the notorious Iranian hanging judge, Ayatollah Khalkhali, executed the 12-year-old Kurdish boy, Azargoshasb Darabi, who had been arrested in a demonstration and who spat on his beard. The author's third cousin, Farzaneh Saboori Jahromi, was executed at the age of 12 for distributing anti-government pamphlets in the early 1980s.

The most recent attempt at child execution in Iran is the tragic case of Jila Izidi, a 13-year-old girl from the city of Marivan (Kurdistan). Jila was raped and impregnated by her brother, Bakhtiar, who was also 13, and a clerical judge sentenced her to death by stoning. The sentence was commuted under intense international pressure, but both children have been jailed for the rest of their lives.[13]

Alone in Jail

THOUSANDS OF CHILDREN in all corners of the globe are at risk of torture and ill-treatment in jails. States normally hide child imprisonment and use euphemistic terms like "reformatory centres" for places of child detention. According to a Quaker report, children in prison "are 'invisible' to the justice system and forgotten by social services."[14] Therefore, it is not easy to get accurate numbers of imprisoned children.

States use imprisonment as a short cut to resolve children's problems. In many cases, they confine children behind bars for minor offences such as theft or misbehaviour. They can be detained for their poverty, prostitution, homelessness, homosexuality, belonging to a minority group, or violation of immigration rules. Police in Central and Eastern Europe, for example, detain Roma children on sheer suspicion or as a "preventive measure." Children can be detained under the pretext of "safe custody."

Children may end up in jail due to their own or their family's political activities. In the Palestinian Occupied Territory and Gaza, for example, since the outbreak of the Intifada on September 28, 2000, about 3,000 children have been arrested.[15] According to Sufian Abu Zaida, the Palestinian Minister of Detainees, there are currently 360 children detained in Israeli jails and military camps, at least half of them between the ages of 12 and 15.[16] These children are subjected to all sorts of cruel, inhuman or degrading treatment including beating, intimidation, sexual harassment and sleep deprivation.[17]

According to Amnesty International, police and military forces use abhorrent methods of violence against imprisoned children in almost all countries. The US military, for instance, did not bother to find any alternative but to detain the 16-year-old Canadian-born Muslim child, Omar Khadr, initially in Bagram (Afghanistan) and later in Guantánamo Bay for almost 3 years. Under the accusation of killing an American soldier in Afghanistan, he was designated an enemy combatant and was maltreated in jail.[18]

There is barely any age limit for the imprisonment of children. In many countries, the minimum age for criminal responsibility is 7. In some "reformatory" centres in Sudan and Bangladesh, children between the ages of 7 and 18 are detained for long periods of time, as a preventive measure.

In many countries of the world, children are kept in overcrowded jails with adults and face sexual abuse. In Malawi, for instance, children are incarcerated in mixed jails. Adult prisoners, with the help of prison guards, recruit boys into their well-established prostitution rings. Police smuggle the boys into adult blocks for a bribe of 30 US cents. HIV/AIDS is prevalent in all prisons.[19]

Millions of children suffer every day due to their mothers' imprisonment. Although women constitute only 5 percent of the world's prison population, the rate of women's imprisonment is growing fast.[20] In the US, for example, there are approximately 2 million children with an incarcerated parent – 3 percent of all the children in the country.[21] Since 1990, the number of incarcerated women has increased by over 110 percent. This is mainly due to poverty, deprivation, discrimination and criminalization. It is unfortunate that the judicial system has disproportionately affected people of colour. Black and Hispanic children in the US are at greater risk of losing a parent to imprisonment.[22]

Studies show that the majority of imprisoned women, at the global level, are mothers. In Brazil's largest women's prison, Sao Paulo, for instance, 87 percent of women prisoners are mothers. In the US, 80 percent of female prisoners are mothers and three-quarters of them have children under the age of 18. In the UK, 66 percent of women prisoners are mothers, 55 percent of them with at least one child under 16.[23]

The Indian writer and journalist Anindita Ramaswamy has shown that the imprisonment of mothers leaves deep scars on them and their children: "Ask a man what he fears most in prison and he'll say loss of freedom. Ask a woman the same question and she'll be worried about her children."[24]

In many countries, mothers are usually the sole caregivers for children. If they end up in jail, their children are abandoned to a traumatic and miserable life. Most of them join street kids. Even if the child of an imprisoned mother is cared for by other family members, the abrupt and prolonged separation of mother and child has dire consequences for the child and may destroy the child's sense of security and ability to form bonds.

In a nutshell, children's imprisonment or their enforced separation from a parent is nothing but the death of innocence, the death of tenderness, the death of compassion, and the death of a better future for all.

In Jail with Mothers

THERE ARE THOUSANDS of children around the globe who have committed no offence whatsoever and are forced to stay in jail, sometimes in mixed prisons, due to their mothers' imprisonment.[25] They share cells or beds (if available) with their mothers. Prison guards do not count them as prisoners and never include them in their statistics.

Traumatized mothers have to take care of their children in the appalling conditions of jail: in overcrowded cells and lacking food, clean water and basic hygiene. In most jails, there are no toys and no playgrounds for children. In conditions of prolonged imprisonment, separation may come one day as the child gets older. It is painful for both the mother and the child.

Prison has become "home" for hundreds of children in India. They live an awkward life with their mothers in almost all jails – from Asia's largest prison, the high-security Tihar Prison in New Delhi, to women's jails in

Karnataka, Maharashtra, Rajasthan, Mehgalaya, Tamil Nadu, Vellore, Madurai, the Central Jail in West Bengal, Nari Bandi Niketan in Lucknow, and deplorable ones in Bihar and Madhya Pradesh.[26] Prison is the only world that these children know.[27]

Hundreds of jail-born children in Pakistan are living in horrible conditions in different jails along with their imprisoned mothers, as there is hardly any proper institution for their care. In Adiala prison alone, more than 167 women are held along with 67 children of different age groups. Most of these women are sentenced in connection with narcotics and *Zinna* – adultery.[28]

More than 1,000 children, under 18, are languishing in 65 jails all over Bangladesh.[29] Bangladeshi police keep some mothers and children in jail for "safety" purposes. These include victims of rape, domestic violence, trafficking, and prostitution. Girls who have married against their parents' will as well as lost and mentally disabled children are also kept under "safe custody." According to the Bangladesh National Women Lawyers' Association (BNWLA) these victims are virtually treated as convicts or under-trial prisoners. Mothers may live among male prisoners and innocent children may share cells with dangerous criminals who frequently, along with guards, subject them to physical and sexual abuse that has resulted in deaths. It has happened that after serving their sentence, the mother and child have not been able to return home, because they supposedly put the entire family to shame.[30]

The situation is no better in other parts of Asia. In the Philippines, for instance, there is a reported case of secret jail cells hidden in the back room of the Olongapo Center (a public shelter) where mothers and children as young as 8 are regularly imprisoned, beaten and deprived of food.[31]

In Myanmar, scores of young children are detained along with their mothers. Section 53 of the *Child Law* permits children to stay with their mothers until the age of six. In practice, however, children have to stay with their mothers much longer. The memory of a case that attracted the attention of the media some 17 years ago is still fresh in our minds: a Karen girl who had been born in jail was released in September 1988 when the government emptied all of Myanmar's prisons to make space for political prisoners. Her mother had died years before, and, at the time of her release, the girl was twenty-four years old.[32]

There are reports about children in prison in Africa as well. In Madagascar, for instance, children live in prisons with their mothers in wards not always kept separate from the general prison population. There are records of female inmates sold into prostitution by prison guards. Mothers and children suffer from starvation, infection, malaria, and tuberculosis.[33]

In Sudan, Omduman's Women's Prison accommodates dozens of women with their accompanying children. 90 percent of them are imprisoned for petty offences like brewing alcohol. Their abject poverty had driven them to brew alcohol to feed their starving children. There are frequent water cuts and a scarcity of food. Visits are not always allowed and cruel and degrading treatment is common. According to a report in the year 2000, there were 159 mothers with 181 accompanying children in this jail.[34]

In Rumbek (Southern Sudan), mothers have to languish in jail with their babies as a result of convictions for adultery. Under the customary law operating in the "chief's courts," the usual fine for the conviction is 7 cows (the equivalent of US $50). But, the poor women do not have the means to pay the fine.[35] They have to sleep on the bare floor along with their babies and face degrading treatment and horrible conditions in jail. In southern Sudan, a woman is the property of her father, brothers or husband. Girls are seen as sources of wealth and they may be sold at a very early age to an old man. Some girls commit adultery in a desperate attempt to get rid of their old husbands.

Children of prison lose their childhood and get used to the language of adults. Here are the words of five-year-old Arti, imprisoned with her mother (convicted in a cheating case) in Jaipur, India: "I know this is a jail. My mother did something bad, so I have to live here with her. I know what bail is. If my mother gets that then we can go back to our village."[36]

It should be borne in mind that keeping children in jail with their mothers is not a problem in just the countries of the South. It exists in countries of the North, including Canada, Australia and the United States of America. Apart from their own citizens, advanced industrial nations detain children of asylum seekers along with their parents more frequently. In the United Kingdom, for example, up to 2,000 children a year are detained, for the duration of one to nine months, along with their families, as a means of immigration deterrence and control. During a one month period in March and April 2004, a total of 323 children were taken into detention, half of whom were under the age of five.[37]

It is unfortunate that very few governments have implemented non-custodial sentencing options for mothers – an option that recognizes the crime but permits the offender to remain in the community and reform herself.

War-Affected Children

MODERN WARS ARE characteristically wars against civilians, particularly children. During the 60 years since World War II, the world has witnessed more than 150 major conflicts, of which 130 have occurred in countries of the South where people suffer from abject poverty, tyranny and ethnic conflicts.[38] Civilian casualties, which accounted for only 10 percent of all casualties during World War I, have since increased to 90 percent today, and 80 percent of these are women and children. The nature of civil war dictates that fighting takes place where people live, rather than on a battleground. In the period following the end of the Cold War in 1990, ethnic hatred has targeted all members of hostile groups, specifically their children.

It was in 1996 that Graça Machel proposed the immunity of children within armed conflicts: "Let us claim children as 'zones of peace.' In this way humankind will finally declare that childhood is inviolate and that all children must be spared the pernicious effects of armed conflicts."[39] Nine years have passed and the plight of war-affected children has become intolerable.

War may lead to the total destruction of infrastructure with the result of further underdevelopment and ever-increasing impoverishment. The ugly monster of war has forced thousands of young girls to accept the risk of HIV/AIDS and get involved in "survival sex" in exchange for money or food.

In every corner of the world, war is taking its toll on children and robbing them of their childhood. In some conflict zones, the fighting is older than the children are. There are children of war who have never experienced any other life. In some areas of heavy bombardment, when the bombs begin to drop, children run to shelters in pairs: one or two with their father and others with their mother. They are never all together: if a bomb hits, the whole family will be wiped out.

Here are the words of 14-year-old Linda, a child uprooted by armed conflict in Angola:

> "All of us suffer here all the time. We're all dirty. We have to save our money just to buy water from tanker trucks. The amount we can afford isn't enough for anything. Our clothes are filthy rags. I don't sleep well. We have to lay out pieces of paper on the ground and lie on them. I used to study in my hometown but I don't go to school here because I have to look after my brothers and sisters while my parents go to look for work. I'd like to live like normal people. I'd like to have a house and clothes like them, and to be able to study the same things that they

study. I'd like to go home but I don't think it's safe to go back yet; I think we will have to stay here a long time. I want there to be peace."[40]

In Iraq, before the coalition occupation, children under the age of 5 were dying at more than twice the rate they were 10 years before.[41] War, occupation and terrorist attacks have exacerbated the plight of children beyond imagination. Children are the main victims of war and occupation in Iraq. The clashes between Iraqis and coalition forces in Fallujah and Basra, for instance, resulted in the brutal killing of over 100 children – some of them on their way to school.[42] Mafia type gangs have also spared no time in kidnapping Iraqi children for ransom and subjecting them to all sorts of tortures and degrading treatment and punishments.[43]

Both Palestinian and Israeli children suffer as a result of the present conflict between Israelis and Palestinians. They are killed or wounded during actions of the Israeli army and security forces and terrorist attacks of Hamas and Hezbollah against Israeli citizens. Palestinian children have particularly suffered as a result of Israeli collective punishment of the Palestinian population including house demolitions. The latter have left thousands of Palestinian children permanently homeless. They have been deprived of living a normal life due to closures, roadblocks and curfews.

In their homes, in the street, in UN-run schools, Palestinian youth are not safe from Israeli bullets: "We're always listening for the helicopters, listening for the tanks, listening for the bombs."[44]

Israel has designated the Palestinian towns of Rafah and Khan Yunis (Gaza Strip), and Nablus and Jenin (in the West Bank) as war zones. This has given *carte blanche* to the Israeli army to shoot into residential areas and bulldoze Palestinian houses regularly. According to the Palestinian Centre for Human Rights, in four years of Intifada, the army has killed 136 children in Rafah and Khan Yunis, a quarter of all the Palestinian children who have died during the uprising, because of its "indiscriminate shooting, excessive force, a shoot-to-kill policy and the deliberate targeting of children."[45]

According to Amnesty International, throughout the year 2004, thousands of women and girls were raped and abducted by Janjawid, nomadic militia supported by the government of Sudan. The notorious Janjawid resorted to mass rapes, including gang rape of school children. They burned villages and massacred civilians while supported by the bombardments of Sudanese warplanes. The main victims of all these atrocities were children.[46]

The tragedy of Darfur, Sudan, is symptomatic of the world's failure to protect children against the evil of war. As of October 2004, over 1.2 million children had become displaced as a result of war.

Even after the conflict is over, children may be exposed to the explosive remnants of war that kill and maim thousands each year. Nearly two thirds of the 65 countries that suffered new mine casualities between 2002 and 2003 had not experienced active conflict during that period. A study by Human Rights Watch found that the use of cluster munitions by coalition forces in populated areas of Iraq was one of the major causes of civilian casualties in 2003.

More than 200 million landmines are stockpiled in the arsenals of 87 countries. Landmines cost as little as US $3 to produce. Clearing one landmine can cost up to US $1,000. Despite the existence of a Mine Ban Treaty, landmines kill or maim around 20,000 people annually.[47] Over 80 percent of landmine victims are civilians – one third of them are children and 90 percent of them have no access to medical care.[48]

Disruption of children's education and destruction of schools is another sinister by-product of war. This is being done despite the categorical provision of the *Rome Statute for ICC* that has, among other things, classified deliberate attacks on children and schools under war crimes. The tragic memory of the massacre of Russian children in their school is still fresh in our minds. In September 2004, the hostage-taking tragedy at a school in Beslan (a city in southern Russia) by a Chechen armed group and the counter-attack of the Russian security forces resulted in the massacre of more than 350 people, 150 of them small children. This tragic event shows the outrageous disdain for the most basic principle of human decency by the government and rebel forces.

The situation is not much better in other areas of conflict. In Aceh, Indonesia, for instance, 460 schools were burned to the ground during May 2003 as a result of fighting between government forces and rebels.[49] In Nepal, schools are regularly used as centres for propaganda and recruitment by the opposition and the government. Attacks on and abductions of teachers and students are frequent. In Afghanistan, non-state parties burn girls' schools and distribute night letters threatening girls who attend the school. In the Occupied Palestinian Territory, 1,300 schools have been disrupted as a result of curfews, sieges and closures. In the Bougainville region of Papua New Guinea, nine "no-go" zones are controlled by secessionist rebels. Children have no access to school in these areas.[50]

Children's education in Iraq is under constant threat from ongoing bombings, bloody demonstrations, kidnapping and other types of violence resulting from the occupation and war.[51] This was taken from the testimony of a sixth-grade Iraqi girl, Rana Rashid: "Our movement is extremely restricted. When we walk on the street we are vigilant and apprehensive, and we are suspicious of any person who looks in our direction."[52] According to UNICEF, "for children, going to school has become a daily calculated risk."[53]

In a nutshell, children are innocent victims of all wars. Even if children are not killed or injured, they can be orphaned, abducted, raped and left in psychological distress from direct exposure to violence, dislocation, poverty or the loss of loved ones. Those who survive often find themselves enveloped in a battle for survival of a different kind – against disease, inadequate shelter, a lack of basic services and poor nutrition.

Child Soldiers

A GREAT HUMAN tragedy is the recruitment of children by armed groups and government forces to fight in wars. They use children because they can easily brainwash them to obey orders and engage in fearless killings. The phenomenon of child soldiers is an ever-increasing problem.[54] There are currently 36 countries where it is reported that children under 18 are participating in armed conflicts.[55]

The exact number of child soldiers is unknown, but it is likely to run into more than 300,000 despite the *Optional Protocol to the Convention on the Rights of the Child* and the *Rome Statute* for the International Criminal Court, which have prohibited the participation of children in armed conflict.

Africa and Asia have the highest numbers of child soldiers. During 2003, there was a surge in the recruitment of children in Côte d'Ivoire, the Democratic Republic of the Congo (DRC) and Liberia. In the DRC, in particular, there have been widespread reports of atrocities, rapes and beatings involving children. In Somalia, children are recruited by all belligerent forces.[56] Thousands of children in northern Uganda have been abducted by the rebel group, Lord's Resistance Army, and forced into combat and servitude. Thousands more flee their homes and villages each night to seek refuge in towns where they can avoid attack or abduction. In Myanmar, there are still large numbers of children in armed forces, while the number of children used by armed groups and urban militias in Colombia has increased to around 14,000 in recent years.

A GLIMPSE INTO THE GLOBAL PICTURE OF TORTURE AGAINST CHILDREN

During the Iran-Iraq war (1980-1988), the Iranian clerical government recruited children as *Basijis* (mobilized militia), from the age of 10, to fight in war fronts. They "had about a fortnight's training before they were sent to fight. Death was probable and the belief that martyrdom would secure a passage to heaven was absolute."[57] In the course of war, scores of *Basiji* (mobilized) children were sent to the minefields *en masse* as human tools for clearing landmines.

In Cambodia, girls as young as eight years old are recruited as child soldiers. They play a role similar to boy soldiers; handling weapons, acting as spies, participating in battles, etc. More often than not, they are wounded or killed. Male commanders use them as objects for sex. Girls as young as 12 must use contraception and are required to go through the painful and dangerous process of abortion if they become pregnant.[58]

The 18-year conflict, with the participation of the government of Sudan, Uganda and rebel groups, in the north of Uganda and south of Sudan has turned the region into a zone of terror. The Lord's Resistance Army (LRA) has systematically attacked civilians in poor villages and kidnapped vulnerable children to join its ranks. Approximately 12,000 children have been abducted since the escalation of the conflict in June 2002. The LRA has used all its villainous techniques to brainwash these children and reduce them to professional killers. Some of them have been forced to murder their parents and other children. The LRA has created such fear across Uganda that thousands of children leave their homes each night, fearing forced abduction. These little "night commuters" spend the night in relatively safe shelters (ruined buildings, empty churches, bus stations, hospital compounds, etc.) and return home in the morning.[59]

On October 10, 1996, the LRA rebels raided the famous Ugandan boarding school, Saint Mary's, and abducted 139 girls. They released most of the girls, but they kept 30 captives, tortured them and turned them into child soldiers. Most of them were used as sex objects by the LRA commanders. This left a deep scar in the hearts of Saint Mary's teachers, staff and students. Every evening they prayed for the release of the abducted children and each year, on October 10th, they organize a remembrance ceremony.

Last year, ten of the girls managed to escape. One of them was Charlotte Awino, the daughter of Angelina Atyam, the great activist for the release of abducted girls and the founding member of the Concerned Parents of Uganda. I met Angelina during the International Conference on War-affected Children of September 2000, in Winnipeg, and was impressed by her passion for the fundamental rights of all children. I shed tears of joy when I saw on television Angelina's reunion with her daughter, Charlotte, after eight years. She was a 14-year-old child at the time of the abduction and a 22-year-old mother when she escaped. She made her way back home with her son whom she conceived after being raped by a warlord. Angelina remained steadfast and urged the release of the remaining abducted children. It is believed that some of the Saint Mary's girls were killed during their captivity.[60]

Children are conscripted, kidnapped or pressured into joining armed groups. Warlords have converted thousands of innocent children into participants of armed conflicts by providing them with lightweight weapons making it possible for children, even those under 10 years of age, to become effective killers.

Children are also forced into sexual slavery and to become labourers, cooks or servants, messengers or spies. Girls are particularly liable to be sexually exploited, whether by one commander or a whole troop. They may also join boys on the front line. Girls were part of government, militia, paramilitary and/or armed opposition forces in 55 countries between 1990 and 2003 and were actively involved in armed conflict in 38 of those countries.[61]

The abduction of girls is a worldwide phenomenon. In the past 10 years, girls have been kidnapped and forced into wartime services in at least 20 countries, including Angola, Burundi, Liberia, Mozambique, Rwanda, Sierra Leone and Uganda in sub-Saharan Africa; Colombia, El Salvador, Guatemala and Peru in Latin America; Cambodia, Myanmar, the Philippines, Sri Lanka and Timor-Leste in Asia; and the former Federal Republic of Yugoslavia and Turkey in Europe.[62]

Girls are sometimes given into armed service by their parents as a form of "tax payment," as happens in Colombia or Cambodia, for different reasons. After the rape of his 13-year-old daughter, a Kosovar Albanian refugee gave her to the Kosovo Liberation Army with the following justification: "She can do to the Serbs what they have done to us. She will probably be killed, but that would be for the best. She would have no future anyway after what they did to her."[63]

Some girls may also choose to become part of an armed group, since taking up arms can be safer than waiting to be raped, injured or killed. Girls' overall lower social status makes them more vulnerable to assault than boys, and rape is a common occurrence, often resulting in sexually transmitted infections. In Sierra Leone, health workers estimate that 70 to 90 percent of rape survivors tested positive for sexually transmitted diseases.[64]

Moreover, young women who were girls when they were abducted or forcibly recruited and return with "war babies" may be stigmatized and rejected by their families and communities because of the shame attached to rape and to giving birth to babies fathered by the girls' captors.

A positive trend is the program of demobilization, disarmament and reintegration of child soldiers in different countries including Sierra Leone, Afghanistan, Cambodia, and Sri Lanka. The World Bank also launched a joint effort in December, 2001 in support of regional Multi-Country Demobilization and Reintegration Program for the greater Great Lakes Region: Angola, Burundi, the Central African Republic, the Congo, the Democratic Republic of the Congo, Rwanda and Uganda. Under these programs demobilized children are transferred to temporary rehabilitation centres to receive comprehensive services.[65] They may also join educational and recreational programs and receive help in tracing their families and reuniting with them. However, it is unfortunate that war reproduces the traumatic conditions and makes most of the demobilization programs ineffective.

Despite recent efforts, the problem of child soldiers has remained unresolved. A multi-faceted initiative at all levels is needed to address the root cause of this evil and alleviate the problem of child soldiers. According to Archbishop Desmond Tutu: "We must not close our eyes to the fact that child soldiers are both victims and perpetrators. They sometimes carry out the most barbaric acts of violence. But no matter what the child is guilty of, the main responsibility lies with us, the adults. There is simply no excuse, no acceptable argument for arming children."[66]

Uprooted Children

DURING THE 1990S, millions of children were forced by conflict, environmental degradation or human rights violations to escape their homes. The period of exile runs into generations without any chance for children to have a taste of home.

Out of the 40 million uprooted people around the globe, about one third are refugees and the rest are people who are internally displaced mainly due to civil strife. More than 80 percent of these are women and children. They are left with minimal international relief because their national governments often consider this as "interference."[67]

The following is the list of the 16 top countries with a population of half a million or more internally displaced people (2004 or latest available estimates):

Sudan	4,000,000
Dem. Rep. of Congo	3,400,000
Colombia	3,100,000
Uganda	1,600,000
Turkey	1,000,000
Algeria	1,000,000
Myanmar	600,000 to 1,000,000
Iraq	900,000
Côte d'Ivoire	500,000 to 800,000
India	650,000
Azerbaijan	570,000
Indonesia	535,000
Bangladesh	150,000 to 520,000
Liberia	500,000
Sri Lanka	430,000 to 500,000
Syria	200,000 to 500,000

Source: Global IDP Project, Norwegian Refugee Council, as cited in UNICEF, *The State of World's Children 2005*, pp. 64-65.

Bereaved and traumatized, with most family members dead, there is little joy ahead for uprooted children. Most of them are incapable of imagining a life other than the one they live in violent and oppressive camps. Their basic needs are not even remotely satisfied and they lack the most fundamental standards required for the sound and healthy development of a child. War and violence have even penetrated the games children play. At worst, they play with explosives disguised as toys and at best with barbed wires. The violence and inhumanity children and their families have gone through are frequently reproduced in their games. This is, obviously, dangerous for the healthy upbringing of a child.

The plight of uprooted children is a microcosm of the global predicament in which women have been reduced to an inferior status. Refugee girls are suffering more. They have to take care of their baby sisters and brothers in the absence or death of their mothers. Children having to assume the responsibility of parents (sometimes at the age of six) are a normal phenomenon in camps. Given the difficult conditions of survival at camps, parenthood imposes a heavy responsibility on refugee children at an age when they themselves need parental care and affection.

More than 4 percent of uprooted children are "unaccompanied minors" (separated children) – children with no parents, relatives or friends. They are abandoned in refugee camps all over the world. When a parent dies in a camp, the child is left with no love, care or protection. In August 1996, along with a group of refugee rights workers affiliated with the Jesuit Refugee Service, I visited a camp on the border of Rwanda and Burundi. Refugees were not allowed to leave the camp and it took us a long time to get permission to visit. The camp was unbelievably overcrowded. A small, plastic UNHCR tent accommodated up to 14 women and children. We were followed by more than 400 children who left a storm of dust behind. Each of us was surrounded by 7 or 8 little girls and boys, some half-naked. They held our hands and wanted us to give them a pat on their heads or backs. They had lost their loved ones and more than anything else they looked for love.

Each year, an unprecedented number of children risk their lives to cross their national borders into a relatively safe place in a neighbouring country. These separated children are escaping both their governments and opposition forces that draft teenagers for military service. They are subjected to all sorts of financial, sexual and other types of exploitation by smugglers and officials on the other side of the border. Most of them end up in detention centres and, as is the case with separated children from Latin America reaching Mexico or the US, they may ultimately be forcibly returned to their native countries to face torture and death.

Uprooted children at camps live a helpless and vulnerable life. Most of them have never been registered. Many suffer from identity crises, which leave scars throughout their lives. They are subject to all sorts of abuse – rape, child prostitution, addiction, drug trafficking, robbery, etc. – by organized gangs of criminals or even those workers who are supposed to protect them.

Rape is commonplace in almost all camps. Young girls have to bear the extra burden of taking care of babies born to them as a result of rape. Eleven years after the crime of genocide, the protection of separated children and children born due to rape has not yet been resolved in Rwanda. In many areas, uprooted children suffer from chronic malnourishment and lethal epidemic diseases. Those who live in camps close to borders are subjected to cross-border armed raids that have frequently resulted in their murder, mutilation and abduction.

The harshness of life makes uprooted children feel, think, and act like mature persons at a very young age. It is not, therefore, surprising to hear the following words from a little boy in an overcrowded refugee camp in Thailand: "Sometimes I want to cry. But I don't want the other children to see it. So I cry when it rains."[68]

International Instruments

THE UN CONVENTION *on the Rights of the Child* (CRC) is the topmost instrument binding on almost all nations. According to Article 37 of CRC, no child shall be subjected to torture or other cruel, inhuman or degrading treatment or punishment. Article 38 stipulates that children must not be deprived of liberty "unlawfully or arbitrarily." Article 39 is about rehabilitation of children who are victims of "any form of neglect, exploitation, or abuse; torture or any other form of cruel, inhuman or degrading treatment or punishment; or armed conflicts." Article 40 provides various guarantees for children who are charged with infringing "the penal law." Detention shall only be a last resort and for the shortest possible time. A child deprived of liberty shall be treated with humanity and respect, taking into account the child's age; the child shall be detained separately from adults. A child deprived of liberty shall have the right to legal assistance and to challenge the legality of his or her detention.

There are many other international legal instruments for the protection of children against torture. The following are some examples:

- *The UN Second Optional Protocol to the International Covenant on Civil and Political Rights* (ICCPR)
- *The UN Standard Minimum Rules for the Administration of Juvenile Justice* (*The Beijing Rules*, 1985)
- *The UN Guidelines for the Prevention of Juvenile Delinquency* (*The Riyadh Guidelines*, 1990)
- *The UN Rules for the Protection of Juveniles Deprived of Their Liberty* (also known as JDL, 1990)
- *The UN Standard Minimum Rules on Non-Custodial Measures* (*The Tokyo Rules*, 1990)
- *The UN Optional Protocol to the Convention on the Rights of the Child*

on the involvement of children in armed conflict (adopted by the UN General Assembly on May 25, 2000 and entered into force on February 12, 2002)

- *The UN Optional Protocol to the Convention on the Rights of the Child* on the sale of children, child prostitution and child pornography (adopted by the UN General Assembly on May 25, 2000 and entered into force on January 18, 2002)

Convention number 182 of the International Labor Organization concerning the Prohibition and Immediate Action for the Elimination of the Worst Forms of Child Labor was adopted in June 1999 and entered into force in November 2000. This instrument declares that forced or compulsory recruitment of children for use in armed conflict is among "the worst forms of child labor."

The *Rome Statute* establishing the International Criminal Court defines conscription of "children under the age of 15 years" as war crimes.

The monitoring body for the implementation of the rights of the child is the UN Committee on the Rights of the Child (CRC). This an international body of 18 independent experts with a mandate of monitoring States Parties' compliance with and implementation of the *Convention on the Rights of the Child* and its two optional protocols. It is a body of independent experts that receives regular reports from the State Parties to the Convention and its two optional protocols on the way they implement the above instruments. The Committee studies each report and makes necessary recommendations to the State Party. It is unfortunate that the Committee cannot consider individual complaints on the violations of the fundamental rights of the children by State Parties.[69]

Are We Not Torturers?

TORTURE AGAINST children is, unfortunately, a common and hidden phenomenon everywhere. It is accepted in many countries on the basis of socio-cultural necessities, and perpetrators enjoy absolute impunity. Sometimes the general public, even good-hearted individuals, contribute towards torture and abuse of children unwillingly and unintentionally. Let me share a personal recollection.

While I was doing my Ph.D. in the city of Poona, India, my professor, K.

K. Das Gupta, gave me a beautiful watch as a gift. One Saturday morning, I heard a knock on my door. Two boys, about 11 years old, entered my room in the university hostel. I had just placed the watch on a table in preparation for taking a shower. The boys greeted me and handed me a piece of paper. They were asking for money as handicapped children who were deaf and mute. I refused to give them money as I didn't have any. They tried in vain to convince me through gestures that they were in desperate need. Altogether it did not take more than a few minutes for them to leave my room. I looked back at the table to check the time. The watch was missing.

The news spread rapidly through the campus. Everybody was sympathetic to me, especially a compassionate and charitable woman who was called "auntie" by everybody on campus. Another sympathetic person was the night guard, whom we all called Kaka Chokidar (Uncle Watchman) because he was protective towards everybody. People told me that the boys had possibly been a part of an organized criminal gang who were involved in robbery and even murder, in the manner Charles Dickens had illustrated in *Oliver Twist*. I came to know that professional criminals kidnap children from remote cities or neighbouring countries. They sometimes mutilate these children to make them objects of pity and then send them off to beg.

That same evening, I went to many friends and classmates and warned them against the boys' tricks. The next day, while studying in the library, somebody informed me that the children had been taken to the hostel by a friend of mine to whom I had told the story. I rushed to the hostel. The children were detained in the party room upstairs. They were surrounded by everybody in the hostel. When the boys saw me they became frightened. Everybody tried to persuade them to give my watch back. They refused and pretended that they were deaf-mutes and that they did not understand us. The kind and compassionate night guard slapped and kicked them. Our kind auntie lit a newspaper and held the fire close to their faces to make them confess. They remained steadfast.

I got a warning from the manager of the hostel that we could not keep the boys in custody anymore. I asked my professor for advice. He told me to give the boys a kick and let them go. I did not follow his advice because I was afraid that the children were part of a criminal gang and I had the responsibility to help in the detection of the gang behind the theft. I took the children to a school in the neighbourhood that was specifically for deaf-mute children. The principal examined the children and informed us that they were neither deaf nor mute.

As the boys were hungry, I took them to a restaurant and ordered food for them, but they ate very little. I told them that I was going to take them to the police station. At this point, they both ran away. I ran after them and took them to the police station. The police officer started shouting and threatening them and told them that they would be beaten to death if they didn't give the watch back. Their reaction was the same. The boys did not utter a word. I felt pity for them and withdrew my complaint. I then pleaded with the police officer to let them go. The officer assured me that he would keep them in detention for an hour and would then release them. He then asked me to leave. I left the police station.

To this day, I have not forgiven myself for the way I treated those children. Given the atrocities perpetrated by police in many countries, including India, there is no guarantee that the police did not further abuse the children.

Impact of Torture and War

CHILDHOOD PLAYS A crucial role in building the personality of each and every individual. Horrible experiences such as torture and war leave negative impacts on the social and emotional development of children. Devastating psychological effects may appear later in their adult lives. Younger children suffer more due to their vulnerability. Children's trauma resulting from torture and war may later develop into a collective trauma at the social level.

War-affected children are particularly at risk. By being direct witnesses to the massacre of their families and the destruction of their community, they may constantly blame themselves for not doing enough to protect their loved ones. This feeling of absolute helplessness and guilt of conscience may remain with them throughout their lives.

It is a well-known fact that children have a powerful sense of imitation. In conflict zones, they are at risk of imitating violence committed by belligerent forces. They see a gun as a source of power and therefore the solution to all problems. They internalize the indoctrination that killing is a short cut to overcome all difficulties. This is a great danger to the future peace within communities when children of war grow into a generation of adults. They may approach war or violence as the universal solution to all problems.

Children and adolescents, especially girls, who live in conflict zones are usually taken for granted. Here are some findings of the research done by the Palestinian scholar, Dr. Randa Farah, in a Palestinian refugee camp:

> "The youth feel they are suffocated socially since as they say no one is out there to listen or care about their opinion. They are often neglected. Programs for youth are very few and girls or young women suffer the most. While boys are allowed to play in the streets, girls end up most of the time at home, caring for younger siblings or the elderly in the family and doing domestic chores. One ten-year-old said she had only left the camp once in her life."[70]

Children who are affected by war and torture rarely trust others and are not normally capable of establishing close relationships at the social and individual levels. The trauma may remain with them for many years after its initial experience. They lose the joy of childhood and behave like gloomy old persons with a strong sense of cynicism. The following is taken from the statement of an adolescent girl from Bosnia:

> "The war takes everything away – everything – you don't have any more of that happy face. There are no more jokes that are funny. If someone says a joke, you just sit there. It is not funny anymore – you understand it in a different way. The war takes simply everything that you have. You don't have yourself again. You're a totally different person like you're born again with a different personality in some different world that is now so ugly. And you see all those bad sides; there is no more good side to anything. There is no point; there is simply no point of living anymore. I don't trust anybody now ... When somebody simply kills somebody that you love the most ... you don't believe anybody."[71]

Let me share my experience of helping a teenager who was suffering from the after-effects of torture and war. Between the ages of 5 and 7 she had to live in a war-ravaged area and witness torture and atrocities of the armed conflict. She was 6 when a soldier abused her sexually. I saw her for the first time at CCVT when she was 17. She was suffering from constant fear, insomnia, hypervigilance, violent behaviour, hypersensitivity, amnesia and severe anxiety. She was restless and uneasy all the time. She was terribly afraid of the dark; she was fearful of staying alone in any place. I referred her to one of our experienced psychiatrists and provided her with the holistic services of the CCVT. She continued using our services for a few weeks when she developed a sense of withdrawal and stopped seeking help from any source. Sometime later, I learned from the police that she had been arrested for assaulting a close friend.

Another client of the CCVT was tortured and experienced sexual abuse at the tender age of 5 due to his father's political activities. The torturers murdered his father in jail and he had to escape to Canada with his mother and siblings. They are all clients of the CCVT. He unfortunately developed violent behavior, initially on the domestic front and later at the social level. He is now 15 and is facing five charges – assault, drug trafficking, theft, etc.

A study of 1,000 Palestinian children between the ages of 12 and 16, selected from public, private, and UN-run schools in East Jerusalem and the West Bank revealed that 54.7 percent of children had experienced at least one lifetime trauma. Post-Traumatic Stress Disorder (PTSD) was diagnosed in 34.1 percent of the children.[72]

The trauma of war and perpetual violence may reproduce itself on a daily basis and spare not a single child. The following is an excerpt from the observation of Mr. Mohammed abu Yusuf, a counsellor at the Palestinian Raghda Alassar's school:

> "We work in a lot of schools to treat the children. In the one next to Kfar Darom [a Jewish settlement in Gaza], all the children are suffering from post-traumatic stress disorder. Most of them were crying and shaking when they were speaking about their experiences. There is a lot of bedwetting."[73]

War affects the system of values and beliefs and destroys the normal relationship between parents and children. According to Mulugeta Abai, the Executive Director of the CCVT, "parents who carry an unresolved burden of fear, guilt, depression and anger cannot easily establish balanced or adequate relationships with their children."[74]

Under the condition of war, parents fail to provide normal protection for their children. The failures of a Palestinian father, Jamal Al Dura, to protect his 12-year-old son, Mohammed, from the gunfire of the Israeli soldiers have scarred the consciousness of Palestinian children. This Gaza boy was killed in the arms of his father on the second day of the Intifada (September 30, 2000) despite his father's desperate attempt to protect him from gunfire.

Such events leave a deep impact on the mentality of war-affected children, who stop seeing their parents as sources of protection and support. The outcome is the collapse of respect for parental authority. According to a Palestinian social worker:

"The respect for authority is shattered because children see their fathers beaten in front of them. The authority of the father, who used to just have to utter one word for the child to obey, is shattered. The father is helpless to protect the child and the children think they are alone."[75]

Another impact of war on children is their tendency towards expecting an early death. They may welcome the prospect of becoming a "martyr." According to a Palestinian service provider:

"The martyr is in paradise, he has glory here and in the afterlife where it is so much better than life in Rafah. The children see many people killed, so they come to expect to be killed. This is horrible, that children should accept the possibility of death."[76]

Constant fear and anxiety are the rule of life in war-ravaged areas. Parents and children are reciprocally concerned about each other's security and well being. Here is the story of a little child in Gaza:

"Suzanne, a 5-year-old girl from Gaza, suddenly asks her mother, 'Where did my father go?' although she knows that he was only in the other room. She quickly runs to him and shouts: 'Father, I heard a sound like an airplane. Did the airplane attack us? Hurry! Close the window and curtain!' Even after the sounds of missiles have stopped, she does not let her parents out of her sight."[77]

Feelings of uncertainty and anxiety, as seen in the case of Suzanne, may not leave war-affected children for the rest of their lives. What follows is an excerpt from the testimony of Visna, a war-affected child from Cambodia:

"The nights are the worst. Sometimes I am too afraid to sleep, for when I sleep, I dream I am dead. In my dream, a soldier in uniform comes to find me. He is angry with me and I am arrested and taken away. The soldier questions me for a long time. I say I don't know what I have done. No one listens to me. I see someone take a gun and then they shoot me – not just once but three times."[78]

Visna was 16 when he was interviewed in the town of Battambang (Cambodia). He is 19 now. The hope for a durable peace in Cambodia is the only guarantee for hundreds of child soldiers there to promote their coping capacity and recover from the after-effects of war and torture.

Conclusion

WE HAVE SO far illustrated the gloomy picture of torture against children. It is unfortunate that the world has so far been shortsighted in not giving priority to its children. This unjustifiable negligence will lead to the irreparable destruction of the future of humanity on earth.

There will be no solution for the plight of children until and unless the world overcomes its present fatal apathy. We are facing a merciless Frankensteinian global system that is not accountable to anybody and sets its own rules. There is an undeniable link between the growing desperate plight of children and the policies of the transnational and international financial corporations. The tragedy of child soldiers and war-affected children is also connected with the war-mongering policies of superpowers and arms-producing companies. According to Amnesty International:

> "The majority of current armed conflicts could not be sustained without the supply of small arms and light weapons and associated ammunition ... The failure to control the international arms trade has also enabled guerrilla groups to obtain large supplies of arms."[79]

The world should be proactive and allocate adequate resources to address the causes of torture and violence against the most vulnerable members of its population. There is also a need for an end to the culture of impunity. The International Criminal Court as well as other international and regional tribunals should be provided with human and financial resources to bring perpetrators of crimes against children to justice.

Existing institutions such as the UN Committee on the Rights of the Child and the office of UN Special Rapporteur on Violence against Children should be strengthened. It is time to enable children and adolescents to advocate for themselves and the rights of other children around the globe. Children have both the capability and competency to participate actively in identification, exposure, eradication and prevention of torture and other forms of violence against themselves. Even under the terrible conditions of war and generalized violence, they have demonstrated creative initiatives to join community activities and improve their lives.

Finally, it should be borne in mind that change comes from grassroots initiatives. According to Amnesty International, "Global activism is a dynamic and growing force. It is also the best hope for achieving freedom and justice for all humanity."[80]

Notes

1. See "The Child" in Vinayak Krishna Gokak, ed., *The Golden Treasury of Indo-Anglian Poetry 1828-1965* (New Delhi, Sahitya Akademi, 1970), pp. 57-58.
2. From the poem "On the Seashore" in the above collection.
3. UNICEF, *The State of World's Children 2005: Childhood under Threat*, The United Nations Children's Fund, New York, 2004, p. vii.
4. UNICEF, *Building a World Fit for Children: The United Nations General Assembly Special Session on Children*, UNICEF, 2002, p. 5.
5. UNICEF, UNAIDS, *What Parliamentarians can do about HIV/AIDS; Action for Children and Young People*, The United Nations Children's Fund, New York, 2003, p. 1.
6. Footnote No. 3, pp. 9-10.
7. Canadian Centre for Victims of Torture, *Annual Report: 2003-2004*, Toronto, 2004, p. 24.
8. From the OMCT Press Release entitled "Children, Torture and other Forms of Violence: Facing the Facts, Forging the Future," August 29, 2002.
9. In a short story written more than 40 years ago, the Iranian writer, dramatist and psychiatrist Dr. Gholamhossein Saedi has exposed paternal torture in the tyrannical and traditional society of Iran. He has illustrated the tragedy of a father's torture and ill-treatment of his little son and the latter's unfortunate resistance. See G. Saedi, "The Game is Over," translated from Persian by Robert A. Campbell in Leo Hamilian and John D. Yohannan (The City College of New York), N*ew Writings from the Middle East*, New American Library, New York, pp. 352-374. In June, 2005, a young female client of the CCVT received Protected Status in Canada. Her refugee claim was against her father who had tortured her for disobedience and violation of traditions since the age of 4.
10. Amnesty International, *Hidden Scandal, Secret Shame: Torture and Ill-Treatment of Children*, London 2000, p. 25. This book of 100 pages provides a detailed account of torture and ill-treatment against children in almost all areas.
11. Ibid.
12. From the statement of the President of the American Ethical Union and the President of the National Leaders Council of the American Ethical Union entitled "Death Penalty: Against the Execution of Children" (December 12, 2002). See http://roots.ethicalmanifold.net/archives/000085.html.
13. From the Press Release of Nahid Riazi, Co-ordinator and Spokesperson for Campaign to save Zhila and Bakhtiyar, October 14, 2004.

14. Marlene Alejos, *Babies and Small Children Residing in Prison*, Quaker United Nations Office, Geneva and New York, March, 2005, p. 30.
15. Samoud Newsfeed, 03/15/2005, http://sumoud.tao.ca/?q=node/view/204.
16. Saed Bannoura, "360 Child Detainees in Israeli Prisons," IMEMC & Agencies, March 24, 2005.
17. From *Jerusalemite Daily News*, March 8, 2005. See http://www.jerusalemites.org/news/english/march2005/8.htm.
18. See Colin Perkel, "Canada Complicit in Detention of Khadr," *The Toronto Star*, February 9, 2005.
19. Amnesty International, Library Online Documentation Archive, AI Index: ACT 76/007/2000, September 29, 2000.
20. International Centre for Prison Studies, *A Human Rights Approach to Prison Management*, 2002, p. 133.
21. *Criminal Justice Magazine*, American Bar Association, Spring 2001, Volume 16, Issue 1.
22. Makebra M. Anderson, "Criminal Justice System Neglects Children of Imprisoned Mothers," *The Wilmington Journal*, March 14, 2005.
23. As cited in *Women in Prison*, a written statement of the Friends World Committee for Consultation (Quakers) to the 66th Session of the UN Commission on Human Rights.
24. See Anindita Ramaswamy, "Losing More than Freedom," *The Hindu Magazine*, Sunday, April 20, 2003.
25. For more information, see Rachel Taylor, *Women in Prison and Children of Imprisoned Mothers: A Preliminary Research Paper*, Quaker United Nations Office, Geneva, July, 2004.
26. See *The Hindu Magazine*, Online edition of India's National Newspaper, Sunday, April 20, 2003.
27. While getting released from Bhagalpur jail after 7 years, the nine-year-old Sunita Kumari, who had not seen a pig in her lifetime, jumped with excitement the moment she saw a drove of pigs outside jail. "Such big rats!" she exclaimed in amazement. See *Deccan Herald*, May 4, 2005.
28. From an article entitled "Jail-born children living miserable life," in *Pakistan Observer*, Islamabad, January 10, 2005.
29. "Religious Perspective on Human Rights," *E-Newsletter*, Vol. 4, No. 38, September 23, 2002.
30. From UN Economic and Social Council, Distribution, GENERAL, E/CN.4/2003/NGO/98, March 10, 2003.
31. From a piece called "Call to help women and children in secret cells," June 24, 2003, from *Child Rescue Page* (http://www.preda.org).
32. See Jo Boyden, *Myanmar: Children in Especially Difficult Circumstances* (Rangoon: UNICEF, February, 1992).

33. From "Crime and Society: a comparative criminology tour of the world" at http://wwwrohan.sdsu.edu/faculty/rwinslow/africa/madagascar.html.
34. See Leonardo Franco, Special Rapporteur, "Situation of Human Rights in Sudan," United Nations General Assembly, 55th Session, October, 2000, *Vigil Sudan,* English Edition, 4th Quarter 2000.
35. From "SUDAN: Women and children in prison," in *IRIN News,* UN Office for Coordination of Humanitarian Affairs, Sunday, May 15, 2005.
36. From *The Hindu,* Online edition of India's National Newspaper, Sunday, April 6, 2003.
37. *Save the Children, Detention of children seeking asylum is unnecessary and harmful,* a 96-page research paper released on February 28, 2005.
38. United Nations Children's Fund, *UNICEF Actions on Behalf of Children Affected by Armed Conflict,* UNICEF, August, 2000, p. 2.
39. Graça Machel Report, *Impact of Armed Conflict on Children,* 1996, para. 318.
40. As quoted in Save the Children Fund, *War Brought Us Here: Protecting Children Displaced within Their Own Countries by Conflict,* 2000, p. 23.
41. Footnote No. 38, p. 51.
42. Footnote No. 3, p. 60.
43. Amnesty International Report 2005, *The state of the world's human rights,* p. 7.
44. From the testimony of Khitam abu Shawarib, the only social worker in Rafah refugee camp, on the southern tip of the Gaza Strip. See Dorothy Naor, "The Death and Disorientation of the Children of Gaza," *The Guardian,* Saturday, September 18, 2004.
45. Ibid.
46. Footnote No. 43, p. 2.
47. The *Convention on the Prohibition of the Use, Stockpiling, Production and Transfer of Anti-Personnel Mines and on their Destruction* (the "Mine Ban Treaty") entered into force in March, 1999. By September, 2004, 143 countries had acceded to the treaty. See p. 54.
48. International Campaign to Ban Landmines. *Landmine Monitor Report 1999* and *Landmine Monitor Report 2002,* and the Landmine Service Network, as cited in UNICEF 2005, p. 46.
49. Footnote No. 3, p. 41.
50. Ibid., p. 59.
51. Ibid., p. 60.
52. Ibid., p. 61.
53. Ibid.
54. United Nations, *Children and Armed Conflict, Report of the Secretary General,* A/58/546/-S/2003/1053, UN, New York, November 10, 2003, p. 6.

55. Laura A. Barnitz, *Child Soldiers: Youth Who Participate in Armed Conflict,* Booklet No. 1 in a Series on International Youth Issues, Youth Advocate Program International, 1999, p. 2.
56. Footnote No. 3, p. 53.
57. Haleh Afshar, "Women and War: some trajectories towards a feminist peace," *Development, Women and War,* p. 52. A PDF version of this brilliant article is available at www.oxfam.org.uk/what_we_do/resources/downloads/dww_afshar.pdf.
58. UNICEF, *Guide to the Optional Protocol on the Involvement of Children in Armed Conflict,* UNICEF, New York, December 2003, Box 2, p. 11.
59. Footnote No. 3, p. 48.
60. Ibid., p. 49.
61. Ibid., p. 42.
62. Ibid.
63. Ibid.
64. Ibid., p. 43.
65. Footnote No. 58, p. 45.
66. As quoted on the back page of the source given in footnote No. 55.
67. For more information see Roberta Cohen, "The Guiding Principles on International Displacement: An Innovation in International Standard Setting," *Global Governance,* No. 10, 2004, pp. 459-480.
68. As quoted in the article "Uprooted Children: A Glimpse into a Global Disaster," *The First Light,* Winter 2000.
69. For more information see the Office of the UN High Commissioner for Human Rights, Committee on the Rights of the Child http://www.ohchr.org/english/bodies/crc.
70. Randa Farah, Ph.D., *Children and Adolescents in Palestinian Households: Living with the Effects of Prolonged Conflict and Forced Migration,* paper presented at International Conference on War-Affected Children, Winnipeg, Canada, September 11-17, 2000. Dr. Farah was at the time a team leader in Jordan working with The Refugee Studies Centre, Oxford University, UK. I sincerely thank Dr. Farah for providing me with a copy of her unpublished paper.
71. Canadian Centre for Victims of Torture, *Coming to Terms with Torture and Organized Violence,* p. 53.
72. Vivian Khamis, *Post-Traumatic Stress Disorder Among School Age Palestinian Children,* Department of Special Education, United Arab Emirates University, Faculty of Education, United Arab Emirates, July 1, 2002.
73. Chris McGreal, "The death and disorientation of the children of Gaza," *The Guardian,* London, Friday, September 17, 2004.

74. Mulugeta Abai, "Torture and Its Effects on Families," *The First Light,* Toronto, Spring /Summer 2005, p. 18.
75. As quoted from Mrs. Abu Shawarib in footnote No. 73.
76. Ibid.
77. As quoted in Samir Qouta, Raija-Leena Punamäki, Eyad El Sarraj, "Mother-Child Expression of Psychological Distress in War Trauma," *Clinical Child Psychology and Psychiatry,* Sage Publications, London, Thousand Oak, and New Delhi, Vol. 10(2), 2005, p. 136.
78. UNICEF, *Adult Wars, Child Soldiers: Voices of children involved in armed conflict in East Asia and Pacific Region,* UNICEF, 2002, p. 6.
79. Footnote No. 43, p. 4.
80. Ibid., p. 11.

5

Children of Prison

Monireh Baradaran

IN MARCH 2001, I attended Ms. Baradaran's presentation at the University of Toronto. I was so impressed by her experience with children in Iranian political prisons that I stayed to the end and asked for a copy of her presentation. With the generous help of my colleagues Peri Matthew and Paulina Wyrzykowski, I translated the text from the original Farsi into English. I mailed the text to the author and received her kind permission to include it in this book.

Monireh Baradaran spent nine years (October 1981 until October 1990) in Iranian political prisons and experienced different techniques of torture. She was born in Iran in 1955 and graduated in sociology from the University of Tehran. She is also a social sciences graduate from the University of Hanover, Germany. She has been living in Germany as a political refugee since 1991.

Monireh Baradaran has shared the story of her torture and resistance in her book *Haghighat-e Sadeh (The Plain Truth)*, which has been translated into German and Dutch. Her other book, *Ravanshenassi-e Shekanjeh (The Psychology of Torture)*, was published in 2001. Monireh is also a literary critic and writes in exile for various Iranian journals. She is a member of the Association of Iranian Writers in Exile and provides Iranian and non-Iranian communities with her sagacious lectures on the issues of prison and torture. In 1999, she received a prestigious international award named after a 1936 Nobel Prize Laureate, the German anti-fascist publisher and journalist, Karl von Ossinezsky.

I WANT TO TALK to you about children. One of the conspicuous features of prison in the Islamic Republic of Iran is the existence of a relatively large number of children in the female wards, particularly in the 1360s (1981–1991). During that time, children were forced to stay alongside their mothers and go through the various ordeals of jail life from interrogation to punishment, in addition to enduring the sad tedium of days on the ward.

The first child I saw in prison was Ali, who was a one-year-old boy. Ali and his mother were hostages. Security had gone to arrest Ali's father and as they couldn't find him, they brought his wife and son to jail instead and kept them as hostages. Ali was forced to spend long, monotonous days among hundreds of women and girls who called themselves his "aunties." He was witness to their anxieties and extremely violent outbursts of emotion. He had to tolerate loud and overcrowded conditions. He did not even have a simple toy to enjoy in a moment of peace and quiet. Therefore it was not altogether surprising that little Ali was always nervous and nagging. In those days, in the autumn of 1981, he was the only child in our ward. I don't know whether later, when the number of children was increased, Ali was still in prison or not. I lost track of him in the transfer schedule of the jail.

I spent the summer of 1984 in a ward where 10 to 15 children were being kept alongside the adult women. The eldest was a six-year-old girl, quiet and solemn. She was involved in the daily chores of the cell and her name was on the list of prisoners responsible for chores in the ward as well. In contrast to the other minors, she was old enough to understand the limitations of prison life because she had experienced life on the outside. She was not, however, old enough to understand why she should be imprisoned. I think for this reason, prison was more painful for her than for the other children.

All the children played strangely. Sometimes they would stand behind one another in a row, and chant slogans: "God is great; Khomeini is the leader." Sometimes they blindfolded another child and dragged the boy or girl behind them. Little boys liked to play the role of male guards and of the *pasdars* (guards and sentries). Once, one of these little ones shouted from the entrance of the ward: "Sisters, cover yourselves with the *hejab*. The technician brothers are coming." ("Technician brothers" was a term used for prisoners who fixed plumbing on the wards.) All the inmates stopped their work and searched hurriedly for their veils. We had been tricked because, in fact, there were no "technician brothers" coming; it was little Yavar holding a jug and followed by many children pretending to be "technician brothers."

F. Azad writes in her memoirs that one of the children's tragic games consisted of bandaging each other's legs. They would put ointment on one another's feet and wrap bandages around them. They nursed each other and in that way would amuse themselves for an hour. They had learned this from their elders.

Children's games are partially a reflection of their observations and experiences. For most of them their only experience of life was prison. The only car most of them had ever seen was the minibus, which used to take them from the ward to the visitor's hall. Usually this ride was more exciting for them than the visits themselves.

F. Azad writes about a woman who had to keep her daughter, Sahar, with her inside the jail for a year and a half, and describes the girl's internal world in her memoirs:

> Sahar did not go out of the ward even for visits. Her mother had no visiting rights for years. All Sahar's learning was limited to her observations in the ward. She would very quickly learn the names of the prisoners. She knew all the new inmates, and it was she who introduced them to me. Normal things in the world of children, like animals, parks, ice cream, sandwiches, etc., she knew only through television. As a result, funny accidents took place. Once in our room there was an empty cheese bucket with a picture of a sheep that had not been erased from the surface. Prisoners used it as a stool and called it "the calf." There was a bigger bucket that had the same use and we called it "the cow." One day, while watching a television program for children, Sahar saw a cow. As usual, she asked, "What is this?" She was told that it was a cow. Sahar laughed and said, "No." She went and brought the bucket and said, "This is a cow." Everybody laughed. But Sahar insisted on her interpretation for a long time after. [F. Azad, *Prison Memoirs*, page 69]

The rules on "cleanliness" and "uncleanliness" were extended to children. Drawing demarcation lines between human beings because of their ideals or religions is one of the most inhumane and painful aspects of the "ideological" jails. The Baha'is, people who followed the Baha'i faith, the leftist groups, or whoever did not pray, were called infidels and treated as untouchable. The "repentants" (those prisoners who had been brainwashed in the course of their torture and imprisonment into acting as spies and informers against other prisoners) and the fanatical Muslim prisoners did their utmost to avoid the "untouchables" in order to protect their "cleanliness." The repentants had learned a system of belief from the authorities, which they in turn codified into prison rules and regulations. The outcome was a system of apartheid on the basis of religion.

RUMINA AND RUFIA were two sisters, two and four years old, in jail with their mother. They had been arrested because they belonged to the Baha'i faith. According to repentants and Muslim fundamentalists, these two children were considered untouchable like their mother. They were kept in the "untouchable" cell that was designated for the leftist prisoners. They had no right to step into the "Muslim" cell. It was interesting that at the same time a two-year-old child called Mehdi was imprisoned in the adjacent cell. Mehdi had no playmate. Yet I never saw Mehdi approach the girls even for a moment. Mehdi's parents were killed during an armed confrontation with *pasdars*. Mehdi had been saved and brought to the prison. The story given out was that because Mehdi did not have a family, he should be taken care of in the prison. Responsibility for this was given to three repentant sisters.[1] These three sisters had named him and cared for him with all their love. Mehdi was an extremely intelligent boy but there was something in his behavior and in his way of talking that did not fit at all with his age, and that disturbed anyone who spoke with him. Faranek, from our cell, who was doubly untouchable as both a leftist and a Zoroastrian, loved Mehdi very much. But Mehdi knew his boundaries and was aware that that he did not have permission to approach Faranek. Mehdi knew all of us by the name of our cell, "room six," which to him meant the room of people who did not pray. The family of the three repentant sisters had announced that they were quite willing to adopt Mehdi, but the jail authorities had given him to the family of a martyr instead. The day when Mehdi left forever was a day of lamentation for the three sisters. Yet, they tried not to show their feelings and they pretended to agree with the jail authorities that Mehdi would be happier with his new family and that they had made the decision with his best interests in mind.

IN ANOTHER WARD, the mother of Saeed did not pray. According to the rules of the Islamic jail she belonged to the group of "untouchables," and again her baby was included in this category. Saeed was born in jail and when he learned to crawl, his only opportunity for moving and exploring the world was a place the size of a blanket. He was not permitted to go beyond that blanket lest he make others unclean. When Saeed's mother was forced to go out of the room, she had to fasten his leg to the bars of a radiator in an attempt to keep him from moving beyond his permitted boundary.

CHESHME WAS BORN in jail to a mother who was steadfast in her ideals. In ward number three of Evin prison she was among the few prisoners who did not pray. The guards and repentants were highly hostile towards her and had boycotted her and her daughter. Even her friends had succumbed to this inhumane boycott. Although she commanded the respect of others, the atmosphere of intimidation was such that this respect could not be expressed and remained secret. Cheshme's mother felt these limitations and preferred to do her work alone so as not to put others under pressure. She used to get up earlier than the others to wash Cheshme's clothes and diapers while the bathroom was empty. During the daytime the bathroom was always crowded. We used the bathroom for washing dishes and clothes as well and Cheshme's mother had to be vigilant that drops of water from her hands and clothes would not fall on any Muslim.

Cheshme had green eyes as clear as a mountain spring. She created a feeling in everybody of wanting to embrace and kiss her. However, on her apron was stitched: "Do not kiss me!" Little Cheshme, almost one year old, was always nervous and bitter. Perhaps she was able to see and feel the realities of her environment. Perhaps she was able to observe her mother's anxiety and sorrow, and fear the day when she would be separated from her forever. Cheshme's mother was given a sentence of execution but it had been postponed because of Cheshme. Cheshme's father had been executed before she was born.

Later they transferred all of us to another prison and Cheshme's mother remained there alone. Her days must have been difficult among repentants who had animosity for her in their hearts.

THERE WAS ANOTHER mother in the same ward with a similar story. She was, according to prison terminology, "on death row." This was because she had refused to be interviewed on television as a repentant and had refused to pray. She had given birth to her daughter in jail and had named her Sona, which means white swan. She was always alone and except for one or two inmates, had no friends or acquaintances. One day they called her for interrogation. She came back nervous and broken; they had told her that her husband had been executed. The news spread in the ward immediately, and all glances went to her. Nobody saw her weeping. Lamentation for the death of an "infidel" was considered a crime. Perhaps the mother of Sona, in her own loneliness and in private, had shed tears – but that was only possible by going under a blanket or inside a toilet stall for a few minutes.

IN WARD THREE, where I spent a short time, Sima was the littlest child in our cell. She was three years old and spoke very sweetly. She was in love with our stories and poems, and had a strange power of imagination. In my experience, children of prison usually show much imagination and a rich vocabulary. Sima's father and aunt had been executed, and when she was bored of everything she used to cry incessantly. It was only reciting a story that could somehow relieve her boredom and even that would not always work.

THE CHILDREN IN prison were frequently agitated and nervous. Their games usually led to quarrels and avoidance of each other. Navid, a four-year-old boy, was always the cause of complaints because he was agitated, rebellious, and used to bite children who were younger than him. His mother, who was ashamed of his behaviour, would explain that her son was not so aggressive outside of prison.

Three-year-old Rowshan had spent more than two years of his life in jail. During those years the number of imprisoned children had been reduced and most of the time he was the only child remaining in our ward. His behavior and the way he spoke did not fit his age. His games had little similarity with children's games. Even when they brought little Yashar and Rosa to our ward, Rowshan did not have much inclination to play with them. During his last year in prison he was openly tired of all of us. He used to wake up in the morning angry and bitter. On his way to the washroom he used to cover his eyes with his hands in an attempt not to see us, and when one of us would run enthusiastically to him and say hello, he used to say: "No hello," with boredom. His patient mother would tell us that her son was tired and that we shouldn't disturb him. It is possible that if happy and sociable Yashar, who always smiled generously at everybody, spent more years in prison, he would have ended up avoiding us as well.

These children had seen and felt realities that could not be explained by logic alone. They used to directly or indirectly participate in their mother's interrogations. They had heard the screams, insults and threats of interrogators and the cries and howls of torture victims, and they had seen their bandaged, injured feet and legs.

THEY HAD SEPARATED Roozbeh from his mother for the period of her initial interrogation, which was interspersed with prolonged torture. The mother had no news from her son for a few days and nights. She thought that they had taken her son away from her forever. Later, they took two-year-old Roozbeh with his mother to the corridor known as Ward 2000, where they had to live together with one blanket between them. He was forced to learn to spend day after day on the same blanket, with only the traffic of the prisoners' comings and goings for entertainment. Roozbeh was also an assistant and guide to his mother, since she could not walk on her injured feet and had to use her hands to move around. Roozbeh helped his mother to go to the washroom and acted as her eyes, since she was blindfolded at all times. Roozbeh used to explain the events of that small world and the story of his acquaintance with other prisoners to his mother in his sweet, childish language.

THE NUMBER OF children who were imprisoned in solitary cells was more than those who were in public wards. The newly arrested prisoners had to spend a long time in cells. They kept them all alone, or sometimes when there were many prisoners they kept a few people together in a very small space with no window. Prisoners under interrogation (which sometimes continued for up to a year) had no contact with their families. This naturally included newly arrested mothers. They had no option but to keep their children with them for months in a cell the length of which you could walk in six steps. Mothers and "aunts" were forced to entertain little ones by games they invented especially for that small world. We recited stories and made up all sorts of games with hands or mouths.

I remember ten-month-old Siavash, who used to be our cellmate along with his mother for some time. It was bad luck that he learned to walk prematurely when he was nine months old and still in the cell. To entertain him we recited all of the children's poems that we could remember. Sometimes we even became poets ourselves and made up lines to entertain him. We also imitated the sounds of different animals for him, or pretended to be an animal and give him a ride. But all of this was not enough for Siavash. He used to stand and stare out of the slot low in the door, which was intended for passing the food tray to the prisoners. For his sake, the guards left it open during those days to allow a bit of fresh air into the cell. The boy used to put his mouth in front of the slot and repeat the word "come," which he had recently learned. By using this word he was asking for help. When he heard the sound of steps he would start moving his hands and legs. One of the many guards had developed a kind of affection for him. He used to take Siavash with him out of the cell whenever he got an opportunity. But where? We didn't know. His mother was anxious but she yielded and let her son go. When he returned, Siavash was not willing to leave the guard's arms. The mother had no option but to pull him away by force and this scene was the most painful of all.

There were a small number of other guards who at least behaved humanely towards children. In a book called *The Tiny Window of My Cell*, we read about Fakhri. He was a guard in a jail named "Ward Number 2000" (the former Joint Committee).[2] Fakhri was concerned about children. He used to take children who were imprisoned in locked and semi-dark cells out for fresh air and buy them toys from time to time.

DESPITE ALL OF the difficulties, children inside the prison were a gift to all of us. The beauty and tenderness of their world was capable of taking us out of our monotonous and coarse existence and even sometimes of giving us back a passion for life. The little Siavash whom I mentioned before gave me back the will to live at a time when it had lulled in my heart and I was driven to the point of suicide. He came to me when despair drenched the four walls of my cell. I had taken the right to happiness from my fellow cellmates with my own despair. Then ten-month-old Siavash imposed his own rules on us. This little dictator told us that we should all pay attention to him. He made us laugh because he wanted our laughter. He also created work for us. His mother used to be taken for interrogation every day and I had to replace her, giving him his milk on time and washing his diapers. When it was time for bed, he used to fall asleep in my lap listening to lullabies I sang, and so I knew I was still useful in life. I had no time to think about the trials of my continued interrogation and the dangers of the retrial which lay ahead.

Playing with children and reciting stories to them was perhaps more delightful to us than to the children themselves. By inventing a game, providing toys, and stitching clothes for them we developed our own interests and artistic talents. I remember *Farvardin* (the first month of spring in the Iranian calendar beginning on March 20th and ending on April 22nd) of the year 1362 (1983) and the passion and enthusiasm with which we prepared a birthday party for Eliar and Sara. Both children were born in *Farvardin*, 1361 (March 1982), in Ghezel Hessar prison. Their father had been executed, and now they were being held in a punishment ward, where they would celebrate their first birthday. Everybody was thinking of preparing something. Some of us decided to stitch traditional, indigenous clothes for them: Azerbaijani for Eliar and Baluchi for Sara. Everyone helped us find the cloth and string. It was unbelievable how so much coloured cloth and yarn and string could be hidden in *boghcheh-ha* (the large cloths in which we wrapped up and stored our clothing). Handicraft work was prohibited and during the inspections that used to take place by repentants, everything, except prisoners' clothes, was confiscated. But the prisoners, especially those who were in that ward because of their steadfastness in keeping to their ideals, knew how to hide precious things in prison. They had learned to hide them in places that would never occur to the minds of the repentants, despite their knowledge of each and every prisoner's trick.

It was therefore natural that sewing clothes should happen out of sight of the repentant guards. In the meantime, we wanted to surprise the mothers of Sara and Eliar, and therefore we had to hide our work from them as well. All this used to add to our excitement. The birthday was on the 15th of *Farvardin* (April 5th). On that day the ward had a different, quiet atmosphere. Some had prepared cakes by using bread and mixing it with sugar and butter, a little piece of which we could still find in our breakfast in those days. Others had made toy dogs and cats by stitching towels together. Both mothers shed tears of joy at the sight of such a celebration. The only people who did not participate in this delightful party were the children themselves. They could not stand that much noise and our excitement. They felt uncomfortable in the clothes that we had made for them and they wanted to get rid of the ostentatious finery and hats as soon as possible.

Years later little Rosa had the same problem with us. She didn't want to be our doll. Our eagerness, our enthusiasm about the natural manifestation of life, sometimes prevented us from paying attention to the needs and aspirations of our little princess. We used to sew and weave unique and strange clothes for her out of the most beautiful cloth that we could find in our ward and from the yarn taken from our torn sweaters. We were so happy to see her wearing those dresses and would get so much pleasure out of seeing her in the clothes that we had made for her. But she chafed under our attention and did not want to be our doll. The first word she learned was "No."

WHAT IS THE DEMARCATION line between childhood and adulthood, in Iranian jails in particular, and in Iranian society in general? In the year 1360 (1981), there was a twelve-year-old girl in our ward. She was held as a hostage for her brother and was lucky to have her mother with her in jail. Apart from her, there were quite a few thirteen- and fourteen-year-old girls in those years. In the absence of their mothers, we witnessed them going through puberty.

At the time of her arrest Maryam was thirteen and had not yet completed her junior high school. She was severely tortured and in the process her kidneys were injured. Other injuries caused by whipping had left permanent scars on her young legs. Sometimes even woollen socks were not able to relieve her pain. She was sentenced to eight years in prison and would be released at the age of twenty-one.

One of the other adolescent girls in our cell, when she heard her name being called by loudspeaker for interrogation, threw herself in the arms of a middle-aged woman and started pleading with her and weeping. With a still childlike voice and childish gestures she insisted that she did not want to go. The day before, she had spent all day undergoing interrogation. She had been tortured and had heard the screaming and howling of others who had been flogged. She had also seen wounded bodies. Despite being called a few times by loudspeaker she would not go, until at last a guard came and took her by force.

In the decade of the 1360s (the 1980s), when we were taken to Hosseinieh (a place of worship and lamentation named after the third Imam of the Shi'ite Muslims), from the top of the curtain that separated us from male prisoners we could see adolescent boys. In their faces and behavior you could still observe a remnant of childhood. Some of them gathered around Lajvardi (the chief interrogator and head manager of the prison who was later assassinated by the militant Mujaheddin). The face of this man, who pretended that his tyranny stemmed out of his concern for these adolescents, engendered in me feelings of hatred.

Let's go back to the previous question. What is really the borderline between childhood and adulthood? Is a twelve-year-old girl a child or an adult who has legal responsibility? According to international norms, people are usually considered adults at the age of eighteen. The civil law of the Islamic Republic of Iran, however, defines the age of adulthood according to Islamic jurisprudence. According to Note No. 1 of Article 1210 of the Civil Law that was passed by the Islamic Consultative Assembly, in 1361 (1982), the age of religious maturity or adulthood for boys is fifteen lunar years (just under 15 years old), and for girls, nine lunar years (just under 9 years old). Accordingly, when a girl reaches the age of nine full lunar years she has legal responsibility, because Article 49 of the Criminal Act demarcates the borderline between childhood and adulthood. According to these laws, it is possible to subject this group to "divine punishment" (torture), to sentence them to prison, and even to execute them.

ANOTHER GROUP OF children in prison were the children of female guards who used to come to work with their mothers. They had been taught that we were dangerous outsiders, different from other human beings, and that they had to keep their distance from us. We could understand the prejudices that their impressionable minds had been indoctrinated with through their looks, behavior and the way they avoided us. Melika was a four- or five-year-old girl who used to come to us every other day with her mother, who was a guard in the ward. She was beautiful, precocious and extremely intelligent. Her honey-colored eyes and stubborn look created a kind of fascination in us to touch and exchange a few words with her. But it was useless. They had even taught her to order prisoners to do or not do certain things, such as: "Lower your blindfold, don't look at me!"

In the year 1368 (1989), when I was in a solitary cell called a sanatorium, Melika let slip to me the news that another woman had hanged herself in her cell. A few days later, I read the news on the wall of the bathroom. Melika was of an age where she could understand the relationships and events within the jail. But with her limited experience, how was she capable of interpreting them for herself and creating meaning? This was a question with no answer.

In the year 1360 (1981), a small boy worked in a building designated for torture and interrogation. I heard that he was the son of Mohammad Kachooei, the manager of Evin jail, who had been shot by one of the guards during the mass execution of a group of prisoners in June of that year. I saw this boy helping his grandfather and other guards distribute food or give water to prisoners. I can imagine that they had told him we were the murderers of his father. I don't know how this boy could stomach the atmosphere which prevailed in Evin jail during the year 1361 (1982). With such rancour and violence, what type of future awaited him?

IT IS NOT POSSIBLE to speak about imprisoned children and forget their mothers. Imprisoned women and mothers constituted a significant portion of the political prisoner population, and was one of the characteristic features of prisons under the Islamic Republic. As a result of our gender, we women were always subjected to double humiliation and psychological persecution. These types of sexual pressures were more severe for mothers, both those whose children were brought up in jails and the ones who had children on the outside. In either case, the apprehension and responsibility for childcare fell on their shoulders.

One of the imprisoned mothers writes:

> The male prisoners did not understand this phenomenon. In male wards there were no children. The child problem was not their problem. Only in cases like naming a child who was born in jail did they intervene. Or else they made recommendations for bringing up the child that they conveyed through letters or during visits which sometimes took place. [*The Book of Prison*, Noghteh Publication, 1377]

No father had been forced to take his child with him to prison when they arrested him. No father had to add the apprehension of taking care of his child to the usual anxieties related to interrogation and living in jail. And even when it was decided that a child should be sent outside, frequently it was the family of the wife who used to take care of their grandchild. The contradiction in this issue is clear and self-evident; the anti-women laws of the Islamic Republic of Iran give legal custody of children to fathers, and in the case of the death or execution of the father, to the grandfather. It happened frequently that these children had no relationship whatsoever with their grandfathers and had not even met them. Nevertheless, when a decision had to be made about the fate of the child, the law, which did not recognize any rights for the mother, except the so-called "holy" duty of caring for the child and breastfeeding it up to the age of four, would interfere.

At the time of her arrest, Maryam had to bring her newborn baby with her to jail. They had executed her husband. After about one year, she sent the baby to her family and they accepted responsibility for taking care of the child up to the age of six, which was the time when Maryam was released from jail. Later on, Maryam found an opportunity to leave the country, but had to postpone this for years in order to get the consent of her father-in-law to take his grandchild out of the country. Let me add that, fortunately, among the families of political prisoners, these anti-women and anti-human laws did not usually lead to a crisis, because of the trust and understanding among families.

I frequently heard mothers confess that in the decisions they had to make in jail, they used to think more about the fate of their children than their own fate. And if there was an apparent conflict between the two, usually stemming from the mother's ideological commitments, the result was a guilty conscience. This feeling was accentuated by families who sometimes allied themselves with the prison authorities in accusing the mother of selfishness.

I was not a mother. I could not even imagine this double and extremely heavy responsibility and I confess that my understanding of their predicament is thus limited. I cannot know what they felt, just as I cannot truly know what a three-year-old girl felt when she used to fold her hands behind her back and slowly and thoughtfully pace in the cell, or in the yard when they sent us out for fresh air.

Translator's Notes

1. To "repent" means to acknowledge one's sins, but in the context of Iranian jails repentants had become dangerous torturers and sometimes executioners while they were serving their terms in prison. This was a unique phenomenon of the Iranian prison system under the new Islamic regime. Repentants lived alongside other prisoners, playing the roles of both victims and victimizers. With the intensification of torture and execution they became so powerful that even prison guards would obey their orders. Yet this did not ultimately spare them from the harsh conditions of jail life – several were even executed by the regime they supported wholeheartedly.

2.· A medieval jail run jointly by police, Intelligence and gendarmerie under the Shah of Iran notorious for torturing political opponents of the regime.

6

With My Child in Jail

The author of this chapter, Saeideh, is my client at the Canadian Centre for Victims of Torture. She was accepted as a refugee about two and a half years ago and is presently living in Canada as a permanent resident. It took her a long time to share the story of her torture and trauma in Iran with me, her CCVT counsellor. Building trust between client and counsellor is very difficult. Victims of torture, war, and gender related persecution are reluctant to tell their stories for many reasons including shame, fear, avoidance of retraumatization, etc. The author is now in a stronger psychological condition and is able share her story in the hope that what happened to her may never happen to anyone else in any corner of the globe. I have tried my best to translate as accurately as I could. My colleagues Zorana Alimpic and Indira Rodrigo have helped me throughout this endeavour.

I COME FROM AN extended family in the small city of Ardabil in the province of Azerbaijan, Iran. My family was very poor but culturally and politically rich. My father was an old man and extremely wise and knowledgeable. He was illiterate but well aware of what was happening in the world. From childhood I became socially aware, particularly about women's oppression, especially when I looked at the lives of my older sisters, who were suffering in unsuccessful marriages.

In the course of growing up, I developed an aspiration to work for the emancipation of humankind, specifically from poverty and patriarchal oppression. Soon I found myself in a circle of likeminded women. We used to visit different groups of women and young girls to discuss with them their lives and the state of their society.

Iranian society went through political turmoil and a full-fledged revolutionary movement in 1978. We intensified our activities in our city and soon we became a small, active group, well known to everybody. When the oppression came it not only affected me but it affected my entire family. Many of my family members escaped and lived underground while the rest were harassed on a continuous basis. I escaped to Tabriz, the capital of Azerbaijan.

During these years of living in the capital I developed a friendship with a gentleman who was politically active and well-respected in the community. Eventually we married. We loved each other and cherished the hope that by furthering our human rights activities we would establish a fruitful and affectionate family life. We lived together for only fifteen months and the fruit of this relationship was a baby boy. Everything seemed to be going well; we had a warm house, a handsome baby, and hope for a bright future.

Our house was invaded on a cold, dark winter night in late 1982. That night we had a guest; a village boy had come to the big city to complete administrative work for his impending military service. He was a friend and student of my husband – who used to go to the nearby villages and offer literacy courses to illiterate children of the poor, including that boy. The boy had no one in the big city and had come to stay with us for a day or two. Around 4:30 a.m. I awoke to the cry of my baby. He was hungry and I began breastfeeding him. Suddenly the silence was broken with the horrible sound of boots in the hall and on the roof. The door was kicked open by *pasdars* (guards). Everybody was asleep except for me and my baby. A *pasdar* took a veil from a hanger, threw it over me and ordered: "Wear this! Get up! Stand in front of the wall!"

They then awoke my husband by kicking him with their boots. Our guest, the village boy, was so tired that a guard asked, "Is he dead?" With this they proceeded to beat him until he awakened. They sent us to different corners of the room, and began conducting body searches. A group of *pasdars* searched our closets and the rest of the room. They found a piece of paper in the pocket of the semi-literate village boy; it was his homework. They beat him and told him that he had used secret scripts about his political activities. The boy didn't know anything and they continued to beat him for absolutely no reason. They called my husband by his organizational nickname. This was how we came to know that somebody had betrayed us.

All of the guards were armed. They blindfolded us and did not even permit me to change my baby's diaper. We were guided outside. I looked through the blindfold to see a blind alley, a cul-de-sac with many cars and several armed *pasdars*. I saw a person blindfolded getting out of a car. I recognized him by his stature; he was the person who had betrayed us and had guided the guards to our home. They forced us into a car. At this point my husband told me: "We have reached the end of the line. Forgive me if I ever did anything bad to you." I responded with affection, comforting him and saying that he had provided me a sweet and pleasant life and that there was no need for forgiveness. The *pasdars* separated us immediately and took him to another car. It was the last time that I would sit together with my husband.

We were separated in jail; they threw me in a small, dirty cell with no heating system. There was a blanket stained with blood, urine, and dried excrement. I even saw parts of a human body there. The walls of the cell were stained with blood and the handwriting of ex-prisoners. Some of them highlighted the need for courage, fortitude and resistance.

It was not long before they took me for interrogation. I had to take my child with me. They began by stating that if I did not provide them with the necessary information they would kill me. The interrogator began looking over the file he had received about me from my home town of Ardabil. I saw a paper about my elder brother. He was a teacher of philosophy in a high school. The paper was a petition signed by the school principal and many others proclaiming my brother to be an infidel. They had testified that my brother had called Imam Hossein (the third Imam of the Shia sect of Islam who is considered the martyr of all martyrs) a reactionary person. I knew that this could lead to my brother's execution and I was in a state of shock. At that moment someone called the interrogator on his walkie-talkie. The interrogator put down the file to move to the other side of the room in order to answer the person on the line. It was a rare opportunity. I grabbed the paper from the file and in a moment I chewed and swallowed it.

The interrogator resumed his work. The blindfold played a big role in his interrogation. He used to put it on and then take it off. Although my child was only four months old, whenever they put the blindfold over my eyes he started to cry. They would tie my hands and feet to the bar of a stretcher and beat the soles of my feet and sometimes my back. This was all done while my baby was left in the corner of the torture chamber on the bare, dirty floor. My son would cry as they tortured me. Initially I tried to tolerate the pain and not scream. I was tortured by two people who quickly became furious with my resistance. One of the torturers told his friend, "You aren't beating her hard enough; if you beat her harder you will have a greater reward from God Almighty."

I pleaded with them to take the baby outside of the room. They then started to insult me, beating me harder and threatening:

"The baby is not yours; it belongs to the Islamic Republic of Iran. If you don't give us information we will take the baby from you forever. These days are the best days of your life. We know what to do with you next."

When one of the torturers got tired he would hand his whip to the other man, who, before starting, would bless his friend: "May God reward you for your holy work."

After delivering blows to the soles of my feet they would stop and call in a female *pasdar* who would force me to walk. The males were not supposed to touch me. Before the torture began, a female *pasdar* used to strip me down leaving only my underwear, removing even my bra. Then she covered me with linen bed sheets and started flogging me. Sometimes when they flogged my back the linen would tear. I used to faint after severe torture; they would then bring me back to consciousness by pouring very hot or very cold water over my body. Then they let me go back to the cell. I could barely pick up my child, but they forced me to do so. With injuries to many parts of my body, I used to carry my baby in my arms to my cell. They degraded me by making comments about not adhering to the dress code of the Islamic Republic: "Be careful! Your veil has slipped from your head! You should be ashamed of yourself."

I was alone with my four-month-old baby and did not know what they were doing to my husband. They put me through all kinds of torture and degrading treatment and punishment in an attempt to extract information about my husband and his activities. My worst experience was the time when they tortured my husband in a neighbouring cell so that I could hear his screams. They mentioned my name and insulted me, threatening to rape and kill me if he didn't confess. They brought him to such a point that his screams sounded like those of a dying beast. I was ready to be tortured ten times more to stop my husband's torture by those butchers of humankind.

Three days after my arrest, they took me to be interrogated again. They demanded that I provide them with all the information I had. I withstood their threats and insisted that I had no information whatsoever. This made both of my interrogators furious. They tortured me to the point of death and then raped me, one after the other. Each offered my body to the other before their sordid action:

"You go first."

"No, brother, please. You go first."

I don't want to describe the details here, as it is too traumatic. Suffice it to say that I suffered from bleeding and menstruation problems for a long time afterwards.

I would like to mention here that the religious Puritanism of the interrogators was perversely hypocritical. It was un-Islamic for men to touch a woman. Female guards were not supposed to touch us as we were leftist, non-believers and therefore untouchable. It frequently happened that a male or female guard, with a stick in his or her hand, opened the cell door and asked me to put on the blindfold.

They asked us to hold one end of the stick and follow them while they held the other end. Their religious Puritanism did not allow them to hold the hand of prisoners whom they regarded as "belligerent to God and corrupted on earth." In their torture chamber, however, there was no sign of piety. Male guards, assisted by their female colleagues, had no shame and did not spare women political prisoners from sexual abuse, rape or even gang rape. They legitimized their hateful crimes by reciting verses from the Quran or other religious texts:

"You are non-believers; you cannot enjoy Islamic rules; we can do anything we like with infidels."

LIVING WITH THE baby in jail and resisting torture was not an easy task. I had no diapers, only two old ragged pieces of cloth. A stench permeated my cell. I could only go to the bathroom three times a day for the duration of twenty minutes. I had to very quickly wash the cloth I used as a diaper, the baby and myself in order to return to the cell on time. The baby had to wear his diapers, drenched with urine and stool, for hours. His skin was burning and covered with bruises. The wounds were bleeding. Anytime I knocked on the door, there was no answer. The guards hated to open our cell unless they were taking us to be tortured.

The food was poor, and very soon, as a result of torture and poor nutrition, my breast milk dried up. I begged the guards for milk or powdered milk. They answered me with insults and beatings. They told me that there was a ration of food for one prisoner and that the baby was not counted as a prisoner. As an "incommunicado" prisoner, I was not allowed to ask my family to bring us food. I could not bear my baby's starvation. I was left with no choice but to feed him with my own meager food. As it was too hard for the little baby, I chewed the food first, made it as soft as possible and put it into his mouth. But the food had no nutritional value. The baby was always hungry and so was I. This, along with the burning pain in his thighs and buttocks, made him restless. He cried all the time.

My darling child became so weak that I thought it would be difficult for him to survive. A male guard sympathized with me. There was a hole in the door with a flap that could only be opened from the outside. From time to time the guard used to open the flap and speak with me through the hole. "I am sorry that I cannot save you from this damned place, but at least I can bring milk and diapers for the baby." This was a glimpse of hope amidst the darkness. I thanked him and begged him to do it before it was too late. My hope turned to despair when he told me that he loved me and wanted sexual intercourse with me. Alas! He wanted to make a deal with me.

I rejected the deal and told him that an extra-marital relationship, specifically with a helpless captive mother, is considered an unforgivable sin according to his Islamic belief. I even threatened to bring the issue to the attention of his superiors. He backed off momentarily. However, he again tried to take advantage of me, when he saw my baby's deteriorating condition. Nothing is more painful for a mother than to see her child dying gradually before her eyes.

I was facing one of the most difficult dilemmas of my life. On the one hand, there was no doubt in my mind that I must not submit to his will. On the other hand, I found it selfish to reject the deal and to allow my child to die. I frequently challenged myself, "What's more important: your integrity or the life of your poor, innocent, starving child?" At last I decided to surrender, telling myself, "I have to save my child. They have already raped me. Let this be another torture on top of that."

I received small concessions. The guard brought me milk, diapers and cookies. However, he gradually discontinued his help on the pretext that it would enrage prison authorities. This intensified my hate tenfold. More than twenty-two years have passed since this incident in my life and I have not been able to forgive myself. I shared the story with my psychiatrist twenty years later and I am still under her care. She has assured me that I made the right decision. She might be correct, but I am not capable of overcoming my emotional obsession. I had a choice and could have rejected the dirty deal. The baby is now a young man. I have never told him the price I paid for his survival. What will his reaction be if he comes to know about it? Will he forgive me? These questions haunt my mind constantly.

Two months later, they transferred me to a new cell and I never saw the guard again. The cell had no window. I did not know whether it was day or night. I could only guess the time of day when they brought my food. We had not had a bath for a month and a half; both my child and I were stinking. One day a government delegation visited the jail. They entered my cell and asked I if had been tortured. "Don't you see my injured feet?" I asked. I also showed them the baby's infected thighs, buttocks and armpits. I told them about my back that was injured as a result of being tortured and added: "Obviously, I can't show you, because you would then subject me to the Law of *Taazir* (divine punishment) that would result in many more lashes." According to the Law of *Taazir,* a woman was strictly forbidden to show any part of her body to a man (except her husband).

When my child was about six months old I noticed some sores on his head; he had long hair and I hadn't noticed them earlier. When I looked carefully I found many infected sores and worms coming out of the wounds. This was because of the lack of sanitation and the fact that we had not been allowed to wash for more than two months.

Altogether, I saw my husband twice in jail. The first time was three months after our arrest. As part of an inter-prison visiting program, they allowed me to see my husband behind a glass barrier for a few minutes. The second meeting happened by sheer chance in the course of a transfer.

It did not take long until they detected all of our connections and arrested whoever was affiliated with us. In their terms I became "information depleted" and was no longer an interesting subject for interrogation. It was the right time for them to transfer me to the public jail and send me for trial.

They told me:

"We are now sending you to a new facility. It is upsetting that you didn't collaborate with us. You must reform yourself, if not for your own sake, at least for the sake of this baby. We hope that you will feel pity for your child and behave yourself."

THIS TIME, INSTEAD of a blindfold, they put a cap on my head and pushed it down to cover my eyes. My body was stinking to the point that I could not even tolerate myself.

They pushed us into a car. After some time I found myself in the corridor of the police court. I could hear the voices of many other prisoners. They started exchanging information. Someone, who had seen my child in the torture chamber, recognized him, and informed me that my husband was among the prisoners. After some time, I heard a quiet voice: "Don't talk;

don't trust anyone." I recognized my husband's voice. I felt great emotion. I was happy to know that he was still alive. I longed to see him and tell him that we too had survived all their tortures.

They took us to another room and permitted us to uncover our eyes. I pulled the cap away from my eyes and head and looked around. I recognized my husband. His face was pale and he looked fatigued. He smiled and told me to remain calm and relaxed. He was taking advantage of every moment to see our six-month-old son. During the time we were together, he kept staring at the baby. Unfortunately, living in the cells had created such a devastating impact on the child that he did not react well to anybody; he was afraid of the many seated men with beards and moustaches. The baby would not even look at his father. When I tried to persuade him to go to his father, he hid his face in my bosom. This meeting with my husband was too short. It was our second and last meeting since our arrest.

They separated us and transferred me, along with my baby, to a public ward that was run by the police. There, I encountered many prisoners, including a few from my own town. They welcomed us with joy. But when they stepped forward to embrace us, they immediately stepped back due to the rotten smell coming from our bodies. We had to wait to shower until the next day.

There were thirty small cubicles in the showering area, each with one shower inside. The cubicles were dark and without any ventilation. They pushed three or more prisoners inside each cubicle to shower together. Twenty minutes after closing the gate of the shower site, we were expected to have finished everything. Altogether we had ten minutes to bathe. The water was either freezing-cold or boiling-hot. Sometimes, we had to stop with soap still on our bodies.

One day they took me for fingerprinting. Upon seeing my name the officer got confused. He asked me, with astonishment, why I was being fingerprinted twice. I assured him that it was my first fingerprinting. He checked his list carefully and accepted my explanation. "That was somebody else with the same surname." He mentioned the first name spontaneously. It was shocking news for me. My younger brother was among the prisoners.

We had to adapt ourselves to the new environment. Life would have been more miserable without the generous assistance of other prisoners. They used to help me with everything related to the baby – especially his clothing. There were four rooms in our ward, each with a total area of 24 square metres. Rooms were overcrowded, each with 100 inmates. We could not sleep at the same time due to the lack of space. We had divided ourselves into three groups: sitting, standing and sleeping prisoners. In an attempt to get more space, we slept in reverse directions. To obtain extra space for babies, prisoners who were shorter slept in the same area. There were four other babies in jail with their mothers. No child could sleep with their mother due to the lack of space. The smell emanating from the babies' diapers was a source of annoyance for all prisoners. I wrapped my baby's dirty diapers inside my own dresses to save other inmates from the smell.

We had to sleep at 10:00 p.m. sharp. We were not allowed to feed the babies during sleeping hours. Babies were strictly forbidden from crying. If they did, the guards would punish their mothers severely. One night, the baby had diarrhea and I had to remain awake and change his diapers frequently. I used all possible precautions, but a guard noticed. She woke everyone up. I showed her the diapers and told her about the exceptional situation. She did not believe me and shouted: "You are lying to me. You are using this as an excuse to organize a nightly discussion circle. You are conspiring against Islam. Tomorrow I will tell the brothers (male guards) about your conspiracy." I could not control my anger. I showed her my baby's diapers and told her, "Then tell the brother guards that I used my baby's diapers as a tool of my conspiracy."

She ordered me to shut up and left. Next day they called me for interrogation and gave me 60 lashes for my remarks.

I had to take the baby when they interrogated me. He was afraid of people. Sometimes they called me before 9:00 a.m. and returned us to the cell in the evening, during which time we had no food or water and were not permitted to go to the washroom. Interrogators were annoyed by the presence of my baby. It happened many times that they threatened that if I brought the baby the next time, they would separate us forever. I could not comply with their orders because the child would not stay with anybody else.

With the passage of time, the baby became bigger. He soon started hating the blindfold. One day the torturers prolonged the interrogation to the extent that both of us fainted. They brought me back to consciousness and sent one of the jail-mates to carry the baby to the ward.

Food was poor in terms of both quality and quantity. Prisoners had no food during the course of their interrogation. It happened many times that the baby was hungry for many hours when I was going through the ordeal of interrogation.

The baby developed affection for my fellow prisoners. He enjoyed having many "aunties." He understood all three languages spoken in the ward: Azari, Farsi and Kurdish. His "aunties" had taught him. It was interesting that he spoke with each "auntie" in her native tongue. If a Kurdish girl, for instance, tried to speak Farsi with him, he would respond in Kurdish. No one could play a trick upon him.

He was ten months old when he got an infection that blocked his urinary tract. He stopped urinating. It took a painful effort to convince guards to take the child to the clinic in prison. The doctor, a political prisoner himself, prescribed an antibiotic ointment. He told me, in the presence of two guards, that the ointment should be applied deep inside the child's penis; otherwise, he would die. He gave me a thin barometer and advised me to smear it with the ointment and insert it inside. It was a painful practice. He would lose consciousness during the process and I used to cry, because I had no choice but to inflict pain on my child. All the other prisoners used to cry with me. The doctor told me that outside the jail doctors used anesthesia prior to implementing this treatment.

The child's health was deteriorating. He was crying all the time and making life miserable for everyone in the ward. This prompted all the jail-mates to write a joint petition to the jail authorities and request to have my child transferred to the hospital immediately. The authorities were reluctant to transfer him because I was in limbo and they usually did not transfer any inmates to outside hospitals before their conviction. I pleaded with them for three days; my child was slowly dying. They finally transferred us, escorted with two *pasdars* (paramilitary guards) and two policemen.

UPON ARRIVAL AT the hospital's premises, I remained handcuffed and the guards escorted me until we reached the special ward in the hospital. They did not want to enter the actual hospital unit because they were afraid of people's reactions that were generally against prison guards. They left and stayed on guard outside. It was in the hospital ward that the police officers finally took off my handcuffs. They had been ordered to take us to the hospital in such a way that no one would know that we had come from jail. They behaved as if we were friends. Despite these attempts, the doctors and nurses immediately sensed that they had brought us from a political prison.

It was unbelievable! I could feel kind and compassionate glances everywhere. There was a high level of cooperation and collaboration among medical personnel to save my child. I received friendly messages both directly and indirectly from all corners. One of the doctors began having a friendly chat with the police officers in an attempt to distract their attention. In the meantime another doctor took us inside a room and asked me about the conditions in jail. I informed him that I did not feel secure. He assured me that everybody in that ward was a friend.

They undressed my child and put new clothing on him. They then put the old clothing on top of the new in order to hide the new dress from the guards and police officers. They fed my baby with chocolate he had never tasted before. They filled his pockets with chocolates to take with him. They attempted to prolong the process of treatment to give me some time to rest. The medical staff told me that they would prepare any type of food I liked.

Their kindness was like refreshing water in a parched desert. These were people who did not know me. They were only driven by their altruism and good will. One of the nurses gave me one hundred toomans, which was a lot of money. Since she knew that they would search me in the jail she hid the money inside the baby's diapers.

It did not take long for almost everyone in the ward to come to know about the helpless political prisoner and her little baby. I felt empathy from the many nurses and medical personnel who came and visited us; they pretended that they were there to check the baby. They gave us whatever they could gather, including everything they had in their own pockets. The staff did everything for the baby.

In an attempt to give us another day of rest and comfort the doctor made up an excuse and told the guards and officers that he needed to take a blood sample from my child the following day before he had eaten his breakfast. He wrote a very persuasive letter to the authorities in jail and told them the child's health was in danger. After a few hours they took me back to my jail.

The next day there was general reluctance from the guards and the jail manager to let us out. I also came to know from their conversation that the doctors had made frequent calls warning them about the health risks facing the baby. Finally they let us go to the hospital.

When we reached the hospital I felt that I had been moved from hell to paradise. The abundance of food and drink gave me the feeling that we were invited to a banquet. They said, "This is all for you and your baby."

They had brought many pairs of shoes and socks. It was not possible to take all of them back to the prison. I had to dress him in many pairs of socks, one on top of the other. They asked officers to wait outside and they took us to a nursing room – a place where no patient was permitted to enter. There, the most pleasant and unexpected event was waiting for me: I found a woman who was standing with her back to us. "Who is she?" I asked myself. The lady turned around. I could not believe my eyes. She was my sister-in-law, my husband's sister. She embraced me and started kissing her nephew. As a nurse in the hospital, her colleagues had informed her of our coming and had taken the risk of arranging a private visit between us. She gave us money and gifts. This visit did not last for more than a few minutes due to the life threatening risk we were all taking.

They kept us there until late afternoon. Food and beverages were so attractive that everybody joined the banquet – even the police officers. The most delectable fruit on the table were grapes and watermelon. These were not allowed in jail due to the guards' suspicion that we might make wine from them.

The doctor asked me if I had experienced torture and unusual or degrading treatment. I politely apologized and told him that as a prisoner I was not able to speak on those issues. The doctor appreciated my honesty and told me: "But, I am sure something terrible has happened to you. Your baby is afraid of men including myself."

A nurse brought the test result. I saw the doctor's hands shaking. He remained silent for a moment and in his silence started wiping away his tears: "I have bad news for you. The level of sugar in your baby's blood is extremely low; he should drink lots of fruit juice and eat things that are rich in protein."

I told him that in jail there was no food quota for the baby. He wrote a letter to the doctor in jail and explained the life-threatening danger of low glucose in the baby's blood. It was with the help of that letter that the jail doctor was able to get fresh and canned fruits for the baby after that.

THE GUARDS HATED to see us happy in jail even for a moment. Spontaneous manifestations of happiness such as singing, dancing and even tapping rhythms on the wall were strictly prohibited. The guards considered the actions un-Islamic and punished "perpetrators" with lashes. One day, along with two inmates and my child, we decided to go to a room that was used both as a library and a place of worship. One of the girls started tapping on the door in a rhythmic manner. My baby started laughing and dancing with joy. A guard observed the scene and reported it. It did not take long before we were called by loudspeaker to report to the jail's office.

In our jail, guards used two different terms when they called a prisoner to report to the office: *Ezaam* (expedition) or *Edaam* (execution). Often, they purposefully pronounced "z" like "d" to create panic among the prisoners. Children hated these terms and anytime authorities called a prisoner to the office they stopped and pleaded with her not to go. They had instinctually come to know that those who go for *Edaam* (execution) would never return. The moment we heard the word "Edaam" from the loudspeaker, we were all electrified. A female guard was sent to take us to the office. On the way, my child started begging the guard to forgive us, repeatedly mentioning that it was his fault that he danced.

They hastened us to a room called "Chamber No. 15" where we found a man other than the interrogators who were known to us. He blamed us by saying:

"Shame on you! You performed a wedding ceremony in a holy place of worship. You have ridiculed the sacred traditions of Islam."

Both girls were terrified. In an attempt to boost their morale, I took a risk and responded angrily:

"I have made frequent verbal and written requests in vain for food and clothes for my baby. Ignoring these requests has nothing to do with your Islamic tradition, but you find knocking on the door against the sacred traditions of Islam."

I paused for a moment and continued:

"We have frequently asked authorities not to use the term *Ezaam*, that has the same sound as *Edaam* (execution), but no one has paid any attention. Don't you notice that this child is on the verge of having a stroke because he heard this word a few minutes earlier?"

My words softened the heart of the man who lowered his voice and said:

"Go back to your jail. Whatever mistakes you have committed so far I forgive you. Don't do it again."

CHILDREN OF PRISON used to show a great deal of empathy for tortured inmates, but in their own ways. There was a girl in our room whose intestines had been twisted under torture. With the intensification of her pain she used to have convulsions and lose consciousness. At these times, we wrapped her in a blanket. Four prisoners held four sides of the blanket, and we delivered her to the guards to send her to the hospital.

One day her condition deteriorated and we all insisted that she be taken immediately to the jail's hospital. Amidst general anxiety, my child stopped everybody and told us in his childish language:

"Don't take auntie to the hospital; I know what her problem is."

For a moment all the weeping inmates stopped and turned back to my child:

"Tell us the problem with auntie."

He raised both his hands and said with great self-confidence:

"She has urine and cannot urinate the way I couldn't urinate. Take her to the toilet."

For a few seconds our weeping turned to laughter. It was astonishing that such a small baby had his own diagnosis and acted like an experienced doctor.

IN AN ATTEMPT to pass the time and make the tedious life of the prison tolerable, prisoners used the most elementary materials to make interesting handicrafts. The handmade crafts were so valued in our prison cell that we took the utmost care to keep them away from the children. We felt lucky that after a long time we had acquired needle and thread. We had got thread by pulling it out of our towels. We got needles from our families. They hid them inside fruits that they sent to us in jail. During visiting hours they gave us hints about which fruits had needles inside.

We used colourful thread to make art and do embroidery. A talented Kurdish girl made such a beautiful piece of embroidery that it brought a sense of pride to all of us. Everybody praised her work. The children were enthusiastic to see her work but they were not allowed to touch it.

One day inmates were showing the Kurdish girl's embroidery to each other and exchanging words of praise. This made my child so enthusiastic and joyful that he went ahead with full confidence and in a plausible tone ordered in Kurdish: "Give way! Give way!" He took the embroidery and said, "I am tired of getting orders all the time not to touch. I want to touch. I want to see what it is."

We tried to explain to him that preventing him from touching her work was necessary to protect his hands from the needle. "If you teach me how to sew," he said, "I won't injure my hands."

There were so many mice in our jail that sometimes we found a dead mouse in our food. Catching mice had become one of our frequent entertainments. Except for a human being, the first inmate that my son saw in his prison life was a mouse. With much difficulty we tied a thread to the tail of the mouse. My child took the other end of the thread and played with the tiny animal.

My husband was extremely eager and anxious to see his son. I found out that he was constantly trying to visit the baby. I was not permitted to see my husband and the baby would not go with anyone else. I repeatedly asked the authorities why I should not be allowed to visit my legal and legitimate spouse. They used to reply all the time with a ready-made answer: "You are non-believers, therefore your marriage is illegitimate; not only your touch, but even your glance at each other is considered an unforgivable sin."

One day they allowed the baby to see his father, but they were suspicious of political prisoners taking him. They brought non-political prisoners to carry the baby to his father. The visit did not take more than half an hour. The child cried until he almost fainted. He did not like to be carried by a strange woman on the one hand and he was not used to seeing a man on the other. He was terribly afraid of seeing his father.

The father visited his child once more. As I was not allowed to see my husband I asked one of my closest friends to take him to his father. This time also he started crying and screaming. The visit was too short. A few days later the guards gave me a letter from my husband, in which he referred to the visit:

"It was an unpleasant visit; whenever he visits me, he starts crying. I can't stand my child weeping. Therefore, it is better for both of us not to visit each other anymore."

And that was the last visit.

FIFTEEN MONTHS AFTER the initial arrest they executed my husband without permitting me to see him before his death. He was twenty-eight years old. He was a human rights activist, a man of letters, a poet, a writer and a master of the arts. He had great passion for life and a hope for the ultimate salvation of humankind. I still have twelve letters he wrote to me in prison, each full of love, hope, and passion for life.

I came to know about my husband's execution two months after his death. When I met the Shariah judge (the judge of Islamic jurisprudence) who was the hanging judge as well, I asked him why they killed my husband. Neither one of us believed in violence; nor had we been involved in any kind of violent activities. He smiled and told me that he ordered the execution of my husband because he was intelligent, resisted all tortures, refused to give them any information and his spirit could not be broken.

Those of us who were imprisoned with our babies had an especially difficult life. My child had no idea of the outside world; his world was limited to a small cell and the most vivid events in his life were when I was brought back to the cell, my body covered in wounds. The child, however, loved listening to stories and I had plenty of time to narrate different tales to him. This was not without difficulty. He had no idea about many things in the story, such as animals and people. I had to explain these through drawings and pictures in the newspapers. The child used to ask intelligent questions.

After many months of languishing in jail, a small change brightened our monotonous life. We were transferred to a room from where it was possible to see a glimpse of the outside world. There was a window close to the ceiling far from the prisoners' access. We were lucky as the screen that covered the window had been torn apart. We could see the light and a tiny portion of the sky. Another fortunate incident happened: they brought us three-storied beds. My child used to climb the ladder to the bed on top that was close to the window. He was eager to look outside and discover things that he observed. He used to ask with astonishment:

"What is this in the sky?"

"It is a bird."

"Something is moving; what's that?"

"It is called a car."

"I am seeing a pile of something green. What's that?

"It's a tree."

The child was very happy during the visiting day of the week. That was a different day. People used to come and go and laugh. Children were not allowed to go for a visit. My child and I were "incommunicado" prisoners and therefore had no visitors. Still my child was overjoyed. Visitors brought lots of food and fruits and the prisoners left the best items for the children.

FINALLY THE DAY came when the prospect of our freedom could be seen on the horizon. When the child reached the age of four, I heard rumours about "amnesty." I had been sentenced to eight years of imprisonment, but they commuted it to four. Besides, the child had reached the age of four and according to the guards he was a mature person and was not allowed to see his mother's body. I could no longer take him with me for bathing. They told me:

"We are going to release you because of your child."

Everybody was happy about our imminent release and congratulated us on our upcoming freedom.

Although my child had no idea of freedom, he was happy as a result of the general happiness. He used to confuse the term "freedom" with "free" and declare repeatedly:

"I want to go for free; I love free."

It did not take long before the child found himself in a strange world. He was unbelievably panicky with men. At home, when he saw me sitting without a scarf, he used to come to me shaking with fear and warning me:

"Hide your hair, mom; cover it with a scarf; there is a man here."

I tried to calm him down:

"Don't be afraid son; he is my brother and that one is my father."

I could not, however, convince him and he responded with fear:

"No, mom, these men will beat your head."

He was panicky at the sound of the wind and music. He used to get angry upon hearing the sound of electric appliances and moving vehicles and I had to pay for that. After hearing such sounds, he used to come to me and bite me. I was covered with bruises from his bites.

He missed his "aunties" a lot. He had become so attached to them that it was difficult for him to live without them. Here was something surprising: he never made a remark about going back to prison and seeing them. He used to say all the time:

"Mom, we are very lonely; let's bring all my aunts here."

Then he would name them one by one.

Outside jail, the child behaved in an abnormal way. He was curious to know about many things and had lots of questions. I had to live in my late husband's house under the strict supervision of my father-in-law. This left a negative impact on his upbringing. He had become lonelier.

One day we went to the market place. I was holding his hand. I saw an apple in his other hand. I asked him where he got it. He pointed to a fruit shop's basket. When I told him not to do it again, he told me with surprise:

"Why not? They have put it there for us to take."

He had no idea about private property or about buying and selling. He took everything from anywhere and used it immediately. When he saw shoes he took them and immediately put them on and threw his old shoes away. If it was food, he ate it immediately. Although he was a grown-up child, we had to carry him in our arms or on our shoulders to prevent his pilfering.

I remained out of jail for one year. My father had put up his property and his life as a guarantee for my release. I had to report to the prison authorities every month. On one of these occasions, they re-arrested me because they didn't like the "fast-paced manner" with which I was climbing the stairs, and the apparent "aggressive" way in which I signed my name in the reporting book. They did not allow me to take my child with me; he was left with very little protection. When they released me after six months, I found my child in a desperate situation. He had been passed around, sometimes taken care of by my relatives, sometimes by neighbours, and at other times, had no protection at all. He was not initially ready to accept me as his mother because of the tremendous hardship he had gone through.

It took my child two years to adapt to the new environment outside jail. However, for many years when he saw a guard or someone in a paramilitary uniform, he avoided him and refused to speak with him.

Soon, much before I was expecting it, he asked me who his father was. We had made a family decision not to tell him. We had made a joint decision to present his grandfather as his dad, but he did not believe me:

"No, mom, I do not believe it. You are young and my father should be much younger than this gentleman."

He was not yet six.

One day, he came to me with a disturbing question. His cousin had told him that the guards had decapitated his father. I felt that I could no longer hide the story from him. I asked him to be patient. I thought for a couple of days and developed a method based on the stories told by Shahrzad in the book of the *Arabian Nights*. Every day, I narrated a part of the story, beginning with the formation of history, establishment of governments, and development of empires. Gradually I made him understand concepts like tyranny, injustice, freedom, and struggle. Then I told him about the Iranian society, the lack of freedom, and his father's campaigns as a freedom fighter. He learned about the fear his father had caused in the hearts of his oppressors and why they had killed him. The young fellow accepted the reality of his life quietly and rationally. He never showed any negative reaction. He did, however, remain silent. When I would ask him why, he would nod and say:

"Mom, I'm thinking of why this happened."

He was seven at the time.

He was a good and intelligent student but he preferred to be by himself and live in isolation. He did not like to socialize with other people or argue with them. He wanted to be with me all the time, but this did not happen and he grudgingly accepted that.

WHEN HE REACHED fourteen, he was no longer the same person. His silence turned to anger, as if a big bang had happened in his life. He was reluctant to tell me the reason. When I insisted repeatedly, he burst into tears and told me: "I'm very unhappy because my destiny was determined before my birth and I'm now facing a *fait accompli*. I have no freedom of action or thought."

With the passage of time my life, as a woman, became more and more difficult. I reached a point when I felt living outside of jail was not much better. I had been left with no job, no money, and no accommodation. A shadow was following me all the time. My father-in-law blamed me for everything and began harassing me. I was left with no choice but to accept a traditional arranged marriage in an attempt to protect my child and myself. A year later I became pregnant and delivered another baby boy.

Unfortunately, my second marriage turned out to be an abusive one; it was a kind of slavery. At home I was constantly abused and harassed by my husband and outside of my home I was harassed by security forces that were suspicious of me. Life was becoming harder and harder every day. I reached a point where internal and external forces of evil put my very survival at risk. I do not want to enter into this entirely different story here. My son was approaching his 18th birthday (the age of military service) and was not allowed to leave Iran before completing his compulsory service in the army. Life had taught him to withstand hardship and he had acquired a premature maturity. I was not worried about his safety because, unlike his father and myself, he was politically innocent, and therefore not at immediate risk.

When he came to know about my predicament, he insisted that I escape to a safe haven along with his vulnerable brother. He was so worried about our safety that he offered his support by saying that he would work hard to save money in order to save our lives. He comforted me by saying that he would join us when we were established in our new home. I was left with no other option but to leave him in Iran and come to Canada with my youngest son. I was so sad to have to leave my son and face an unknown destiny.

I have been in Canada for around four-and-a-half years. I am very thankful to all of the people in Canada who understood my torture and trauma and helped me with my refugee claim. That includes my lawyers, physicians, psychiatrists, nurses, befriender and counsellor from the Canadian Centre for Victims of Torture and many other people. I'm presently a permanent resident of Canada and cherish the hope that one day I will become a citizen of this great country. Unfortunately, I am still separated from my eldest son who is now twenty-two years old and has suffered such trauma in his childhood. He is presently doing his compulsory military service in Iran. He initially served in a border town and was soon transferred to a remote area.

He does not have a permanent address and our communication has become very difficult. He will soon complete his military service and hopes to join us.

I'm a single mother and a divorced woman. I cherish the hope that Immigration Canada will accelerate the process of the unification of my family. My youngest child also shares my aspiration and is looking forward to the day when he will be re-united with his older brother. I live in hope that I will see my beloved jail-mate again.

7

Surviving Torture Through Self-Rehabilitation and Love

MY ENTIRE LIFE is a story of trauma and exile on one hand, and love and happiness on the other. I have escaped tyranny and persecution three times in my life, and I am a victim and survivor of torture, having spent four years in jail in Iran because of my human rights activities. I came to Canada as a political refugee on February 12, 1985. Devastated by my past and living as a refugee in Canada, I experienced both tremendous hardship and unbelievable grass-roots generosity. I chose to work for and with refugees and traumatized people as a way of creating meaning in my life and recognizing that we exist only in relationships to others, and that this interdependency is at the heart of all human connections. I am pleased with my present job as a Counsellor and Policy Analyst with the Canadian Centre for Victims of Torture. Prior to that, I worked for seven years as a Refugee Policy Analyst and later as the Coordinator of the Jesuit Refugee Service of Canada. I found these jobs highly rewarding because of their direct impact on the lives of those most vulnerable people who had experiences similar to mine.

I was a human rights activist during the late 60s and early 70s under the Shah of Iran. I was involved in civil and human rights movements at the University of Tehran, and later some friends and I tried to organize small groups of students and intellectuals to fight against tyranny. There was a notorious secret police in those days called SAVAK. This unscrupulous intelligence service was omnipresent, monitoring each and every citizen. Very little dissent was tolerated, even from the moderate reformists. The Shah was considered the shadow of God and SAVAK committed crimes of torture and murder in his name.

Nevertheless, I found it possible to function as a human rights activist in this environment, provided I was circumspect in my activities and did not attract the attention of SAVAK, or so I thought. Then, one day, I too was arrested.

It was on a beautiful April day in 1973, when two well-dressed and quite nice-looking men entered my office, wearing civilian clothes. At that time, I was working as the Deputy General Manager of Organization, Education, and Methods in the Ministry of Water and Power. They asked if my name was Mr. Mossallanejed and I said yes. Then they ordered me to put both my hands on the top of my head, and began searching me. They were tense and panicky; I could hear the sound of their panting. I don't know why they were so nervous. Perhaps they were worried that I had a bomb strapped to me. Next, they searched my desk and took some documents, none of which happened to be of a political nature. Finally, I was handcuffed and blindfolded and taken away in a car. I did not know where they were taking me or where I was when they stopped. I was led into a building where the men left me alone for a few minutes. Eventually they returned and the interrogation began in earnest. They yelled obscenities at me for a while before taking off the blindfold, at which point I found myself in a dungeon.

They tied me to a metal bed, spread-eagled, and a large, burly man who looked like a gorilla began beating me with a wooden stick. I later found out that his name was Mr. Husseini. He struck me so hard that the stick broke in half after four blows. After a few more blows, the remaining stick broke into two pieces. He beat me another twenty times with the thickest part and then exchanged his stick for a thick, black electrical cable. Over the next several hours, I was beaten with a variety of instruments. Every once in a while new people would come into the room, always elegant and well-groomed, and I used to think they would surely put a stop to the beating. Instead they would laugh and take a turn. I was beaten on the soles of my feet and forced to run around the room and pushed from one man to another. In that way the interrogators sought to restore the circulation in my feet so that I would continue to feel pain when they hit me.

The object of this beating was to extract information about my friends and associates. I was supposed to give the names of guerrillas and their safe houses, despite the fact that I was not involved with any violent faction and had no idea about their whereabouts. After a while I began to scream. At one point, one of the interrogators held his hand over my mouth and held my nose so I was unable to breathe. He would only allow me to breathe if I gave him the information he wanted. I indicated that I would talk. Then I insisted that they untie me before I would say anything. Finally, I began to talk about myself – where I was born, how beautiful the city was, where I went to school – none of it having to do with politics and none of it the kind of information they wanted. They tied me back down and resumed beating me.

At some point, they took me back to my house and searched it in front of me. I remember one of the torturers, the Gorilla that had beaten me on the soles of the feet, whispering that I shouldn't be limping because it was shameful; my neighbors would feel that I was ridiculing them. Yet I couldn't walk normally because my feet were badly injured. They did not find anything in my house except a single pair of hiking boots, which they made a fuss over, insisting they must belong to a guerilla, and quite a few fresh dates, which they also said were there to feed my guerilla friends.

After I was taken back to jail, they blindfolded me again and ordered me to stand facing the wall in front of the torture chamber. I could hear the sound of lashes followed by torturers' shouting and insults mixed with the pleading, weeping, and screaming of the victims. I waited for half an hour or so – that seemed like an eternity to me – until my turn came again.

A boy I knew, a second year law student to whom I had given two pamphlets on human rights, was brought in and I was asked to identify him. It was then I learned that he had been arrested and had given my name along with some others to SAVAK, implicating me in guerilla activities. All the information he had given them was false; he must have simply told them anything he could think of in order to end his own torture. So all my pain was over a false confession extracted under torture. When I contradicted him and asked whether he was not ashamed of himself, they immediately took him away and intensified my torture. It was so difficult to stand the pain. With every blow I felt an intolerable pain running through my body. After some time the man who had arrested me (he was, in fact, the chief interrogator) entered, and said my interrogators had permission to torture me to death, and that they should not worry about the consequences.

The beating continued until I could not feel any more pain, only a vague tingling sensation each time I was hit. It was at that point that the Gorilla decided to stop, since there was no point in continuing. All the torturers went away and left me in an agonizing limbo in the middle of the night in the dark torture chamber. After some time two soldiers entered. They took me by the arms and helped me towards a large brightly-lit room. There are moments in life that one never forgets: when I glanced back I saw the trail of my footprints on the bright mosaic of the floor. They were made by blood dripping from my soles. In that room I found the Gorilla and three of my torturers, including the person who had arrested me. He told me:

"I am Dr. Hosseinzadeh. I am the inventor of torture. I will design a torture suited to your nature and character. We'll extract all the information you have."

In SAVAK, all torturers called themselves doctors. Later, I found out that his real name was Reza Attarpour, the most notorious torturer and the chief of all interrogators in Iran. He threatened me with burning and said that he would pump boiling water into my rectum. Thankfully, neither threat was carried out.

The moment when I saw my cell was one of the happiest in my life. It was a small room, but it had a mattress on the floor and four pillows, and I knew I would have at least a small reprieve from the torture. Yet, paradoxically, as soon as the door closed behind me, I felt everything that had happened wash over me and I became desperate. If I could have died then, I would have. Every single person I have spoken to who has been tortured has confirmed that there always comes a point when you wish to die.

In the morning, all four pillows on which I had rested my legs were stained with blood. (The cell had probably been occupied by four prisoners before me.) Since I was unable to walk, one of the guards carried me to the prison doctor. When the doctor unwrapped the bandages from my legs, I saw that strips of flesh were hanging off the bottoms of my feet. The doctor said to me:

"You must be an extremely dangerous man, one of the guerrilla leaders, to have been tortured so badly."

I told him I was merely a human rights activist and had been falsely accused. After that the doctor apologized for having to cause me more pain. He said that he had no anaesthetic, but in order to prevent gangrene he would have to trim the flesh off my legs and feet before dressing the wounds. It hurt, but not as much as the beatings had.

Both of my legs, especially the left one, were completely black right up to the knees. I passed blood instead of urine for 24 hours. For one week I could not walk at all. A guard had to carry me to the bathroom in his arms. For fifty days I walked with great difficulty. Over the next four years I spent time in many prisons and was beaten on numerous occasions, but I was never tortured as badly as that first time.

In time, I learned that they had arrested me because the boy who broke under torture told them I was a liaison between the Marxist guerillas and the fundamentalists, which would have made me extremely dangerous. SAVAK must have realized their mistake soon enough, certainly within a short time of the arrest. Yet I was kept in prison for another four years. At first because they feared that if I were released before my wounds had healed the story of the torture would get out, and later because they hoped I would eventually give them some excuse that would allow them to justify the initial arrest. For four years, I lived in constant fear that one of my former associates would be arrested and would give my name under torture, which would cause SAVAK to make new attempts at extracting information from me. I remain proud to this day that while I gave them bits and pieces of information about myself in order to get them to leave me alone, I never incriminated anyone and no person was arrested because of me.

They kept me in the limbo of torture and interrogation until they sent me to a military tribunal. Although I was a civilian and a civil rights activist, I was sentenced to three years imprisonment. Just before the end of my sentence, the Shah had established his one-party system and ordered SAVAK not to release any political prisoners. Thus, people like me, who had served their sentence, were transferred to a new prison and kept in indefinite limbo. Eventually, President Carter came to power in the United States and put pressure on the Shah of Iran to release certain political prisoners. I fell into this category and was allowed to go free.

My troubles did not end with my release. I felt as if I had been transferred from the small prison of a cell to the larger prison of a police state. I was terrified of being arrested again and felt as if a shadow followed me everywhere. Finding work was impossible, as any kind of job required security clearance, which was routinely denied to former political prisoners. For all of these reasons I decided to escape to India, where I registered for a Ph.D. program. It wasn't until after the Shah was overthrown that I returned to Iran.

THE SOCIETY I found when I went home was very different from the one I had left behind. There was much upheaval, and the religious fundamentalists had by that point gained a near monopoly on political power. They did not believe in the democratic process and I suddenly found myself persecuted by my former friends from prison who now occupied important positions in government. Often I had to change locations four or five times each day to evade capture and once spent a night hiding out on a battlefield, with bullets flying all around.

Life was impossible in such circumstances and I fled Iran again, this time seeking refuge in Turkey. If things were difficult back home, they were certainly not easy in Turkey either, particularly for an alien with no residence permit. This feeling of living under constant threat became part of my experience and followed me for many years to come. Soon I left Turkey and sought refuge in various European countries, eventually returning to India, where I continued my studies. The situation in India was far from stable, however. I discovered that the Iranian Hezbollah had organized in the country and were busy persecuting political refugees such as myself. Many of my friends were beaten and two were killed when they were attacked by an angry mob. While all this was going on, my son was killed in an accident. Still grieving and in shock, my wife and I decided to leave for Canada. We arrived in Montreal on February 12, 1985.

MY FIRST JOBS in Canada were all for minimum wage or less. I worked in a bakery from 9:00 p.m. until 10:00 a.m. with no break, for a wage of $3.25 per hour (the minimum wage at that time was $4.25 per hour). My next job was working on demolitions at a construction site for a year and a half. It was hard, physical labour for which unionized workers were paid at least $15.00 per hour. It could be done mechanically, but the cheapest way for the employer was to use a needy refugee like myself who would do it manually for $5.00 an hour. Very quickly, demolition became part of my psychology. I used to demolish buildings in my dreams and plan various demolitions in my mind. One day, a friend invited me for supper. When I entered his house, I noticed that it was built of stone and concrete. I reacted spontaneously:

"It will be an extremely hard job."

"Which job?" my host reacted with astonishment.

"Demolishing your house," I answered.

"You are my friend, why are you going to demolish my newly-built house?"

I realized my mistake and made a sincere effort to convince him of the psychological impact of my job.

In the following years, to 1990, I did whatever was necessary to support my family and myself. For a long time I worked as a mover, which later caused me severe back pain. I was a ditch digger. I worked in a sausage-making factory and even in a travelling circus. Along with a friend, I was responsible for loading and unloading circus equipment. We were not permitted to be clowns because that was considered a professional job. I resigned when the racist supervisor harassed and then fired my friend.

Wherever I applied for jobs, they considered me overqualified because of my Ph.D. degree. For at least five years in Montreal, I got used to being overqualified and unemployed.

THROUGHOUT MY LIFE, when I felt most hopeless and desperate, several things helped to sustain me and give me hope. It is those things I wish to share with you, my beloved readers, in the hope that they may help others, including CCVT clients, who have had similar experiences.

First among these is physical activity. In the four years I was in prison I discovered the value of regular exercise. It may sound trivial, but exercise is also a method of resistance, a way of regaining control over your life. If you are healthy, you are better able to withstand torture. Since the goal of torture is to destroy you as a person, by refusing to be broken you gain a victory over your oppressors. Even when I was so badly injured that I could barely move, I made a point of flexing those parts of my body, such as my arms and my neck, which had not been injured. This regime, which I established for myself while in prison, continued after my release, and to this day, hardly a day passes when I do not engage in some form of exercise.

The second coping mechanism that I found useful was that of task-setting. I discovered something important when I first began to exercise in jail. If I set a task for myself, it allowed me not to think about my surroundings and not to worry about the future. During the time it took me to exercise my arms, I was not unhappy, and this occasional escape allowed me to survive the rest of the time. To do nothing in prison, day after day for four years, is to go mad. My friends and I knew this, and so we would invent all sorts of distractions for ourselves. For instance, we would take out the less cooked inner part of our bread, mix it with our saliva by chewing, and knead the bread for hours until we got a dough similar to Playdoh. We would use the dust off the walls, flakes of medicine pills or cigarette ash to colour our creations, and we made everything from chess pieces to pipes out of the dough. I never had any inclination towards visual art before my imprisonment, yet in jail I became known among the guards as an artist, and it afforded me some measure of respect.

From my little figurines I learned the next lesson of survival: that no matter what happens, we must always look for alternatives. I was not an artist. But when it became necessary, I found myself capable of creating art in order to survive, and seeing the finished products in my hand gave me great joy. Such experiences help me to appreciate the Art Therapy Program of the Canadian Centre for Victims of Torture. Under this program, survivors of torture and trauma express their feelings by involving themselves in visual arts and receive counselling in the process.

I also learned that aesthetic appreciation is yet another way of discovering some goodness in our surroundings. Singing, for instance, was a common pastime and those with good voices were considered a blessing. We would all join in with them as they sang their songs of love or resistance. The second day after I had been tortured, as I lay in my cell I began singing songs about courage to give myself heart and the will to survive. I always used to tell myself that I must not give up, no matter what.

Whenever we were transferred to a new cell, everyone would exchange information: who you were, what had happened to you, who you knew. We never shared more than we had told the torturers, because we knew that there were informers in every cell, but nevertheless, it was a valuable source of information for us. It was a paradoxical situation living as we did in tiny, crowded cells under extremely harsh conditions. Our cellmates were our only source of support, yet we also knew that we could never fully trust anyone in case they turned out to be an informer. Immediately after the exchange of information an exchange of song would follow. I remember one particularly good singer who used to go to the bedside of a severely ill cellmate and sing the most beautiful songs. That inmate was a very young boy, perhaps eighteen, who had been arrested at random and severely tortured by burning before the interrogators realized he simply didn't know anything. He was ill for a long time, and also severely traumatized by his experience, and the singing was one of the few things that seemed to make him happy. Ever since then I have valued music as a way to overcome feelings of depression. I listen to cheerful music to make myself happy and sad music if I want to find some outlet for my feelings.

I myself have no talent for singing, and so in prison I learned to tell stories instead. I found that humour in particular was valued and that by laughing at things we could relieve our tensions. We could make ourselves feel better by making our oppressors appear ridiculous. For example, when I was transferred from my first cell, I told everyone in the new cell about being tortured. They all laughed at the stupidity of the interrogators and the Gorilla before telling me their stories. When I think back on it, it seems that my time in prison was full of this kind of contradiction; torture on the one hand, humour and satire on the other, mistrust and friendship at the same time. I remember one time when we were all led to the showers together, people began to sing and dance spontaneously, for no reason. On another occasion, we were all told that we would be executed in the morning in retaliation for the assassination of a government official by the guerillas. We thought we only had a single night left to live, and chose to spend it telling jokes and laughing about our predicament.

Satire was a form of humour particularly suited to our situation, since it is as much about pointing out the absurdity and injustice of a system as it is about laughter. In this way it became another form of resistance and it minimized the amount of power that our torturers and interrogators held over us. Again, the lessons I learned about humour in prison helped me survive later on in life. I published my first satire shortly after the death of my son, when I was suffering and in pain, because I felt I had to have some way of conveying the absurdity of human existence to others. Throughout life, I have continued to cultivate a sense of the absurd, which stems from the knowledge that in the end things have no meaning other than that which we ourselves create. Realizing this has made me able to appreciate the humour and irony in life and literature alike, and to live for the moment, enjoying small things as they come my way.

Humour, music, work and physical activity helped me survive in prison and afterwards. But, the most important thing that helped me to survive was love. Love for me is a general and profound feeling of passion and good will and devotion towards the universe. Love is the free manifestation of the depths of human – and also animal – nature. It may bring with it an intellectual ecstasy that can surpass personal suffering and bitter experiences. I agree with Hegel when he says, "The true essence of love lies in forgoing one's consciousness of self. Forgetting one's own self in another 'I' and yet, in this very disappearance and oblivion, winning one's self and taking possession of one's own self for the very first time."

Love lifts you to the top of the world. You are yourself and at the same time you are not yourself. You transcend your "self" and anxiously seek a unity with the subject of your love. Rumi (1207-1273 AD) depicted the healing impact of love in his masterpiece *Massnavi*:

> So shrinks from love the tender heart
> as from threat of being slain
> for, when true love awakens, dies
> the Self, that Despot, dark and vain
> then let him die in night's black hour
> and freely breathe in dawn again.

As a survivor of torture, if you feel that you have suffered for a cause you loved, you can deal with your trauma in the context of love and understanding. Love opens up a vast horizon before your eyes. Love provides you with a generous gift that can heal most wounds. Saint Paul is right when he declares that

> Love is always patient and kind: it is never jealous; love is never boastful or conceited; it is never rude or selfish; it does not take offence, and is not resentful. Love takes no pleasure in other people's sins but delights in the truth; it is always ready to excuse, to trust, to hope, and to endure whatever comes … There are three things that last: faith, hope and love; and the greatest of these is love.

Based on my experience in jail and exile and as a frontline worker helping refugees and survivors of torture, all the components of love mentioned by Saint Paul have healing impacts: hope, faith, forgiveness, patience, compassion, gentleness, devotion, trust, peace of mind, and stoicism.

You cannot have healing without hope. After twenty-eight years of hard work and frontline experiences, the Canadian Centre for Victims of Torture (CCVT) has made it an essential part of its mandate to provide its clients with "hope after horror."

I will never forget an engineer who became totally dysfunctional as a result of the tortures he had undergone. We made a desperate attempt to take him out of his self-imposed isolation. Our complete failure made some of our friends believe that the poor victim was suffering from paranoia and schizophrenia. A few weeks passed and a man from his town was brought in. He started caring for the so-called lunatic engineer. They spoke the same dialect and shared sweet memories about their town. The new inmate took it upon himself to wash the engineer's clothes and persuaded him to eat well. He provided him with love and hope. Within a period of two months, an unbelievable miracle happened. Our engineer was completely cured.

Loving others and being loved by them has frequently saved my life. When, for example, I lost my son in India, I received support from many Indian and Iranian friends who went far out of their way to show my wife and me their love and affection. Without that genuine love we would probably not have survived.

I am a living witness to the positive impact of the CCVT befriending program for survivors of torture, war, and organized violence. This program has proved to be effective in bringing meaning to the lives of both CCVT's clients and its volunteer "befrienders." One of our clients had gone through such a devastating trauma that the befriender was unable to teach him English. The befriender became so committed to his friend that he learned his friend's language and was able to communicate with him in his own mother tongue. The befriender is now an expert in that language and is enjoying the friendship of many people from his friend's ethnic community.

On another occasion, we matched a client suffering from PTSD with a befriender who was a poet. Our client is now in good condition and has just started composing poetry again in his own language.

We are by nature social beings; we do not exist in isolation. We cannot exist at all without the help and support of others, and the acknowledgement of this interdependency lies at the heart of love.

Prison taught me that survival means depending on the love of others and having them depend on yours in return. And this insight, born as a survival strategy, gradually became part of my character so that I was able to worry more about others and less about myself. Just as one can discover places, one can also discover people. There is beauty in human relationships.

I REMEMBER ONE day I received forty lashes on the soles of my feet. When I was brought back into the cell, many people rushed over to try and help, giving me strips of torn fabric for bandages and offering backrubs to ease the pain. It is such exchanges that give rise to enduring friendship, and such love that gives rise to the willingness to make personal sacrifices. It is because of this passion for others and the idea of reciprocity that I became involved in refugee protection long before coming to Canada. In India, I was the founder of the Union of Iranian Refugees and became active in the People's Science Movement there.

In my experience, sharing common goals and understanding can be extremely helpful in recovering from trauma. It is part of what I think of as cultivating a general passion for life. Sometimes it seems as if we are living in a heartless world and in a spiritless situation. It is important for survivors of torture and war to create an atmosphere of love, sympathy, and support among themselves. There is a saying in Farsi, that "one who is sorrow-hearted knows sorrow." If nobody understands us, we should try to understand one another. During the years of working with CCVT, I have frequently observed the effectiveness of our mutual support groups organized for our clients in their own native languages.

Another aspect of the same passion is recognizing the importance of a unity with nature. We are all part of nature; we cannot exist without it, and to disrespect nature is to disrespect ourselves. I frequently read and pause on the prophetic message of Chief Seattle to the US President:

> But if we sell you our land, you must remember that the air is precious to us, that the air shares its spirit with all the life it supports. The wind that gave our grandfathers his first breath also receives his last sigh. And the wind must also give our children the spirit of life. And if we sell you our land, you must keep it apart and sacred, as a place where even the white man can go to taste the wind that is sweetened by the meadow flowers.

Some may laugh to hear it, but nature is beautiful to me and spending time in it and developing an appreciation for aesthetic beauty, has helped me survive many hardships. I will never forget an early morning during the first week of my arrest. The shadow of death was hanging over my head. A soldier entered my cell. I could not move due to the severity of my wounds and the loss of blood as a result of torture. He carried me in his arms. In that atmosphere of panic the brave soldier revealed his compassion to me by his comforting words. To my surprise, I soon found myself in the jail's garden behind my cell. The prison doctor was waiting there to change the dressing on my wounds. I saw the sunrays coming to me generously through the thick branches of the trees. It was the most beautiful sunrise I have ever seen in my life.

When I first moved to Canada, I used to plant flowers on a bit of public land along the street in front of my apartment building. I didn't know anyone in the neighbourhood, but people used to stop and ask me if I was from the City. When I told them no, they asked me why I was planting things. I told them it was just because I liked to do it. Gradually, they began to come by offering me tea, giving me flowers, and talking to me about their dogs and their memories of home. Suddenly, I had friends.

Finally, there is the idea of "travel." By travel I do not mean getting on a plane and going to the other side of the world. Rather, I mean what in Arabic is described as *t'aamol*, the action of seeing something, pausing and considering it very carefully before taking action. For me, the purpose of education is to discover yourself and to explore things and phenomena in order to further your own knowledge. Since we are always changing, it is a continuing process; each day we discover a new person in ourselves. Travel, whether through space or in our thoughts, is an essential part of this educational and rehabilitative process.

After the death of my son in India, I began to attend the lectures of Krishna Murti with a doctor friend of mine. Murti talked about the need for education to be a completely voluntary process, without any element of coercion. He was completely non-judgmental, asking questions and allowing people to debate them freely, each individual contributing a different point of view. People of all sorts were welcome. Once, I saw a beggar dressed in rags, being addressed with great respect by my doctor friend. I asked my friend if he was simply making fun of the man. My friend said no, the beggar had been a very respected professor and the dean of homeopathic medicine at the university. Nobody knew quite what had happened, only that he had left his job and family one day, and had taken up begging. He wouldn't accept money, only some food, and because of his former status nobody questioned him about the reasons for this change in lifestyle. All this was very novel to me, and different from my previous educational experiences, which generally consisted of the presentation of a series of facts to be learned.

These sessions made me realize the extent to which truth is constructed. Opposites can sometimes be equally true and a single thought can be arrived at from many different directions. I began to think about my own suffering in this way, to understand what had happened to me from a global perspective. Philosophy allowed me to recognize that my trauma was not somehow separate and unique, but part of the ongoing struggle of humankind. It made me question human nature and human values, but it also made me notice all the things that were right and beautiful with the world. I came to recognize that everyone suffers, and that sadness is part of our human condition. At the very root of this suffering is the recognition of our own mortality. Yet we cannot surrender to sadness, but must try to be as happy as possible given the circumstances.

In this way, I came to see happiness as a virtue, but also to recognize that it was counterproductive to think only about myself and my own suffering. Rather, I felt I needed to use my own experiences to help others in order to address some of the root causes of the tragedy that had taken place in my life. I think that it may sometimes be easy to become trapped in one's own suffering, remembering things over and over and dissecting them to the point that even once the original suffering is forgotten, we create new sources of pain in our lives. Recognizing our underlying mortality, on the other hand, leads to a kind of acceptance both of sadness and of our own limitations. It is important to recognize that there are, inevitably, things we cannot change as individuals; that some events are beyond our control, and that even those things we can affect sometimes take a long time, years or even generations, to change. This understanding has helped me to see patience and tolerance as an effective way of coping with personal tragedies.

I do not belong to any organized religion, although I grew up among people whose religion was strong and well-organized. My faith stems from the belief, perhaps irrational, in the ultimate emancipation of humankind, in the idea that, for all the mistakes we make and all the atrocities now taking place, we are moving towards a future when people will no longer inflict suffering on one another. This faith, along with the drive to continually assimilate new experiences and to see exile not as a prison but as an opportunity to understand and appreciate different people and ways of life, gives me the will to survive and strive continually for my own happiness and that of others.

IN CONCLUSION, LET me reiterate that the after-effects of torture are not something that can go away. The scars, especially the psychological ones, remain for the rest of the victim's life. When I used to be under torture in jail, I often dreamed that I had returned to my childhood, working in our family garden. It was a beautiful garden of date palms and citrus fruit where my brother, father and I worked together. My mother and sisters used to bring food and sweets, and we had pleasant family parties. Then, years before my imprisonment, the trees died due to a very cold winter and the garden turned to a wasteland. It was surprising to me why it appeared in my dreams so frequently in jail. The worst part of this dream was when I woke up and saw myself imprisoned in the limbo of torture. My dreams still continue, albeit in a totally opposite way. Now after more than thirty years, at least twice a week, I see myself either in jail under tremendous torture or waiting on death row or among my family members in Iran (alive or deceased) while authorities are looking for me in order to arrest me. The best part of these nightmares is when I wake up and see myself in my safe home and comfortable bed. I heave a sigh of relief.

In attempting to cope with my trauma of torture and exile, I have tried my best to acquire internal richness and strength. I strongly feel that if we train ourselves to go beyond the self and see the source of love and life in nature, society and other individuals, no burden will be too heavy and no suffering intolerable.

8

Impunity

Introduction

THE TERM IMPUNITY is used when a person who has committed a criminal act is exempt from punishment or uses various methods to escape legal prosecution. There is a regrettable tendency in human history to leave perpetrators of massive, horrific crimes unpunished. Impunity is highly detrimental to the prevention and eradication of torture, war crimes and crimes against humanity.[1]

Impunity is entangled in a web of complex power relations that spans the world. Power, for instance, is the source of a major contradiction in the implementation of the *Convention Against Torture*: while it is left up to contracting states to implement the Convention, torture is normally practiced with the sanction of the government and by those at the apex of political power. Thus, the very same regime which perpetrates an abuse to begin with is entrusted with its prosecution and prevention. This fact is responsible for the impunity of torturers and the ineffectiveness of the international legal instruments for human rights. It is noteworthy that under the existing legal framework, individuals who have committed war crimes and crimes against humanity (including torture) cannot face legal prosecution before losing political power. There is, therefore, little accountability for scores of criminals so long as they remain part of the ruling cliques.

The Impact of Impunity

DURING THE TRANSITIONAL period between a horrific past and a more humane present, it is difficult for victims to move forward towards building a better future while agents of tyranny and darkness – torturers, rapists, and perpetrators of genocide and war crimes – walk freely without compunction. In 1996, I travelled to Rwanda and visited seven cities, speaking to people about what was needed to build a peaceful post-genocide society. What I encountered was a common belief in the need for reconciliation as a prerequisite for reconstruction. Reconciliation was, however, considered impossible without achieving some kind of justice for the victims of the 1994 genocide.

It is by addressing the problem of impunity against the agents of death under an *ancien régime* that a society under a new government can show its commitment to human rights.

Failure to prosecute torturers and war criminals may provide a green light for the public to go easy on crime in general. Impunity for perpetrators of unspeakable massive crimes may encourage ordinary criminals to continue with their actions on an unprecedented scale. In addition, the lack of justice as such, during the period of transition, may provoke hatred and encourage survivors to take justice into their own hands by resorting to various retaliatory measures. The result could be chaos.

Let me share some of my own experiences with the impact of impunity on the well-being of torture survivors. In early 1998, a lawyer referred a young girl to me, a survivor of torture and rape, from my country of origin, Iran. She refused to accept any help from me and instead asked my associate, a student of Social Work, to provide her with CCVT services. My student told me later that she refused my help because my dialect resembled that of her torturer and rapist in jail. I persuaded the student to extend her help to the vulnerable girl while I removed myself from the case. For a long time I used to leave the CCVT premises before the client's arrival.

Another client of mine had an urgent appointment with me. He badly needed a letter of support from CCVT. Before entering my office, he saw a man with a long beard waiting outside. No sooner had this client reached my office than he started shaking. He told me in a voice filled with desperation: "What is this bloody torturer doing at CCVT? He tortured me, my friends and siblings …"

I asked him to let me investigate. He was so agitated that he forgot about his urgent work and left the Centre hurriedly. I informed Mr. Mulugeta Abaï, the CCVT director, and we initiated an investigation. My client called four times within half an hour to find out about the man with the beard. I shared the result of our inquiry and assured him the man was a CCVT volunteer from another country in another continent who spoke a totally different language. The client accepted my explanation, but it took him one week to return.

At mid-day, in the summer of 2002, a man rushed into my office at the CCVT and immediately collapsed. He had been a client at the CCVT for more than a decade and my client for five years. To this day he continues to suffer from multiple after-effects of trauma as a result of the torture he experienced in his country of origin. When his torturers failed to extract information from him, they proceeded to torture both his parents (murdering one of them in the process) as he was forced to look on.

After collapsing on the floor in my office, the client began to shiver in the midst of the overwhelming mid-summer heat. I covered him with a blanket as everyone at CCVT hurried to help. The two physicians on staff, Dr. Teresa Dremetsikas and Dr. Mohammad Ahmad, attended to him but it took a full four hours for him to recover from his initial shock. When he was able to speak clearly he described the events that led to his collapse. It seemed that he had run into his torturer face-to-face in broad daylight. "I didn't know what to do," he said. "I took a cab and rushed to you." When mental health professionals assessed him a short while later, he was found to be at risk and was admitted to a psychiatric facility where he spent a week. It was not until some time later that I learned the identity of my client's "attacker." The person who had acted as a trigger for his retraumatization was in fact a passer-by who merely resembled the offender.

THE PSYCHOLOGICAL IMPACT of impunity runs through generations. The case of Mennonite persecution by both Catholics and Protestants during the 15th and 16th centuries is a fitting historical example. The Mennonites rejected all authority except that of the Bible and their own conscience, but adhered to the Christian doctrine of non-violence. For this belief they withstood brutality and torture. In my frequent encounter with Mennonite colleagues, I have found them to be forgiving, but not forgetful. I believe that the Mennonites deserve an apology for the atrocities they suffered as a means to the ultimate healing of their historical wounds.[2]

Between 1915 and 1922, approximately 1.5 million Armenians perished as a result of a well-planned genocide by the rulers of the Ottoman Empire. Mass deportation and the relentless slaughter of Armenian civilians resulted in one of history's greatest disasters, a holocaust by any definition. Entire families were murdered; women and girls were violated and raped, and children were sold into slavery or sent to their deaths, some perhaps even taking their own lives to escape suffering and starvation. Only a few years later, Hitler, in conceiving his plan of the Jewish genocide, uttered these words:

"Who after all speaks today of the annihilation of the Armenians?"[3]

To this day, Turkish authorities and heads of government have denied the Armenian request for an acknowledgement of the genocide and a public apology for the crimes committed against them. Individual Armenians still carry a collective burden as a result of the complete impunity of their persecutors. The House of Commons in Canada adopted a private motion on April 21, 2004 stating that the "House acknowledges the Armenian genocide of 1915 and condemns this act as a crime against humanity." The government of Turkey condemned this motion as "narrow-minded."[4]

The barbaric genocide of approximately six million European Jews for merely being Jewish has traumatized the entire Jewish population of the world so that even today they have not emerged from the initial acute trauma. Germany's belated acknowledgement of the atrocities of the Holocaust and the endeavours of the German people to compensate for the past have gradually resulted in a positive impact on survivors. Successive German governments have tried to ease the historic tension between the two peoples through reparations, frequent public apologies, financial compensation, and memorials to the survivors.

Why Impunity?

THE LACK OF transparent domestic legal provisions criminalizing torture, and the absence of political will in implementing existing laws, have always paved the road for impunity for those who perpetrate this heinous crime. There are few states in the world with statutes that provide for the exercise of universal jurisdiction over torture as specified in Article 5-8 of the *UN Convention Against Torture*. Even these countries are reluctant to enact their legislation and initiate actual prosecution.

The fear and silence of torture survivors and the absence of mechanisms to conduct full and effective investigations into complaints and reports of torture are other obstacles in addressing the problem of impunity. Under tyrannical regimes complaints are turned against victims and there is normally no protection for witnesses and others involved in the proceedings, including lawyers, prosecutors and judges.

Governments that emerge during transitional periods are normally unwilling or unable to address the problem of impunity for the following reasons:

1. amnesty laws and pardons

2. corruption or weakness of the judicial system

3. a two-tier judicial system in which perpetrators are tried in secret by special military tribunals.

Military courts are infamous for their inaction, long delays, indecision, and lukewarm responses in limiting punishment to mere reprimands. For instance, a military tribunal in Chile gave Pedro Fernandez Dittus, head of a military patrol, a 600-day suspended sentence. He had been charged with setting two Chileans on fire in Santiago and leaving them on the road.[5]

The prevalence of a culture of impunity in many countries creates insurmountable barriers on the long road towards removing impunity. There is a structural problem as well. Addressing the problem of impunity becomes an almost impossible task after the collapse of fascist and semi-fascist regimes during which the outgoing government had reduced millions of people to the role of collaborators. It is not uncommon for individuals to participate in crimes as a means to ensure their own survival. The novelist Maggie Helwig has illustrated this situation as follows:

> "In situations of massive crimes against humanity, there is invariably widespread involvement and responsibility throughout entire populations. No court could ever prosecute all those who committed crimes in the former Yugoslavia or Rwanda ... we have not found a way to deal with this problem, and as a result hatred continues to fester in many postwar situations."[6]

A Glimpse into the History of Anti-impunity Campaigns

1. The UN Charter

THE GLOBAL CAMPAIGN against impunity goes back to the philosophy of the establishment of the United Nations. Chapter 7 of the *UN Charter* (entered into force on October 24, 1945) introduced the principle of "collective security" of the family of nations and the possible use of force in case of "threats to the peace, breaches of the peace, and acts of aggression." This powerful anti-impunity provision was directed against states and of course had nothing to do with individual perpetrators. It did, however, act as a basis for further developments.

2. The Nuremberg Trial

The first attempt at addressing the question of impunity at a global level was initiated immediately after World War II. The Nuremberg International Military Tribunal should be considered a landmark in the fight to end impunity. It is symbolic that it took place in Nuremberg, a city that was once characterized by Hitler as being of pure German character and was witness to many Nazi rallies and congresses. It was in Nuremberg that the notorious anti-Semitic *Nuremberg Law* was declared in 1935.

On October 18, 1945, the first session of an international military tribunal for the prosecution of 24 Nazi leaders was held in Berlin. They were responsible for the horrible torture, death, and extermination of millions of innocent people and the destruction of a civilization built over the course of centuries. All subsequent sessions of this historic tribunal (216 trial days), beginning on November 20, 1945, were held in Nuremberg. The Nuremberg tribunal was composed of four judges and four chief prosecutors from the US, the UK, the USSR and France. This tribunal *par excellence* relied on the then inadequate international agreements as the legal basis for its prosecutions.

After more than 10 months, the Nuremberg International Military Tribunal rendered its decision on October 1, 1946.[7] During the course of the trial, the tribunal rejected the notion that states rather than individuals could be prosecuted for war crimes. The tribunal maintained that state-sanctioned crimes are implemented by individuals. The tribunal also rejected the *ex post facto* argument and held that crimes committed by the defendants had been considered crimes of international law before the outbreak of the war.

Despite its limited scope as the tribunal of triumphant Allied powers, the Nuremberg military tribunal revolutionized international law and set a solid foundation for subsequent international legal instruments against impunity, including the *Genocide Convention* of 1948, the *International Humanitarian Law* (four *Geneva Conventions* of 1949), the *Convention Against Torture* (1984), and the *Rome Statute for ICC* (July 1998). It was during the Nuremberg trials that new concepts were introduced for the first time in human history. Among these were the concepts of crimes of aggression and crimes against humanity. These include murder, enslavement, extermination, deportations, and other massive crimes against civilians before or during the war, as well as persecution or torture against conquered racial and religious minorities.[8]

3. Russell's Tribunal

A MAJOR CHALLENGE in the area of international justice is to prosecute the torturers and war criminals who are at the apex of power and against whom there is no superior force which can be invoked. The British humanist, philosopher and mathematician Bertrand Russell proposed an innovative answer to this question with the establishment of the International War Crimes Tribunal in 1966 to assess the nature of the US military involvement in Vietnam. With no formal legal recourse at his disposal, Russell carried out "extensive study and planning." He wrote to an international panel of distinguished intellectuals, including French philosopher Jean-Paul Sartre, the British political scholar Isaac Deutscher, and the Yugoslav writer Vladimir Dedijer. He then invited all the members to London, England in November 1966. The Tribunal had no clear historical precedent. Russell relied on the "integrity of the members" as the best guarantee for the impartiality of the tribunal:

> "I believed that the integrity of the members of the Tribunal, the fact that they represented no state power and the complete openness of the hearings would ensure the objectivity of the proceedings. We also decided to accept possible evidence from any source, so I wrote to President Johnson inviting him to attend the Tribunal."[9]

They organized a symbolic international tribunal with the mandate of assessing the US culpability in five areas by adopting the standards applied in the Nuremberg Trial:
1. the crime of aggression, involving violation of international treaties
2. the use of experimental weapons, such as gas and chemicals
3. the bombing of hospitals, schools, and other civilian areas
4. the torture and mutilation of prisoners
5. the pursuit of genocidal policies

The tribunal examined written documents and heard from Vietnamese witnesses as well as professional investigating teams who travelled to the region to collect information. The proceedings of twelve weeks of public hearings were published in a report entitled *Crimes of Silence*.

Despite having no legal authority, the tribunal awakened the world to its moral responsibility to break the conspiracy of silence and address the problem of global impunity. A document outlining the "Aims and

Objectives of the Tribunal" states:

> "Even though we have not been entrusted with this task by any organized authority, we have taken the responsibility in the interest of humanity and the preservation of civilization. We act on our own accord, in complete independence from any government and any official or semi-official organization, in the firm belief that we express a deep anxiety and remorse felt by many of our fellow humans in many countries. We trust that our action will help to arouse the conscience of the world." [10]

Arousing the conscience of the world has indeed been the greatest legacy of the International War Crimes Tribunal. While the Tribunal took on a formal organizational structure and continued for a time to hear evidence with regard to other international conflicts, it failed to achieve prominent status. Nevertheless, the idea of a people's court to pass judgment on crimes systematically denied by those in power has continued to serve as an effective tool for granting voice to survivors and raising the awareness of the international public. Among its many important initiatives, the Women's International War Crimes Tribunal broke the silence surrounding the wartime sexual slavery of Asian "comfort women" and in 2000 found Emperor Hirohito of Japan guilty of crimes against humanity.

4. Convention Against Torture

THE ADOPTION OF the *UN Convention Against Torture* (CAT) on December 10, 1984 and its entry into force on June 26, 1987 was a breakthrough in the global campaign against torture and impunity. It provided a global system through which the contracting states were bound together to prosecute torturers present in any territory under their jurisdiction. Provisions on universal jurisdiction, similar to those in the CAT, also exist in regional conventions such as the *Inter-American Convention to Prevent and Punish Torture* (adopted on December 9, 1985), and the *European Convention on Human Rights*.

5. International Tribunals

THROUGHOUT THE 1990S, the world witnessed the horrendous genocides in Rwanda and the former Yugoslavia. These tragic events laid the foundation for the establishment of the International Criminal Tribunal for the former Yugoslavia (ICTY) and the International Criminal Tribunal for Rwanda (ICTR) in addition to paving the way for the upcoming *Rome Statute for the International Criminal Court* (ICC).

While impunity is a global problem, impunity for perpetrators of gender-related tortures is more widespread. Sexual crimes against women like gang rapes, forced prostitution, and sexual enslavement have always occurred in the course of genocides, wars, and even in times of peace. Yet until recently little international attention was paid to this abhorrent human tragedy. Rape was considered a component of every war and not a form of international crime. For a long time, national systems and international tribunals failed to investigate or prosecute crimes of sexual or gender torture.

One cannot underestimate the tremendous difficulties involved in the investigation and prosecution of gender-related international crimes. Survivors of sexual tortures suffer from ostracism and stigmatization and are usually reluctant to share their horrible experiences – especially with male investigators. It is also difficult to find witnesses to crimes of this type. Investigations need to be carried out with the utmost care and vigilance. There is always a risk of retraumatization for victims during the process of the investigation and the need for debriefing services may arise at any time during this process.

Despite initial reservations, the ICTR recognized sexual violence (rape, sexual enslavement, forced prostitution, etc.) as a form of genocide and torture.

The ICTY, sitting in The Hague, and the ICTR, in Arusha, have endeavoured to overcome the above difficulties and bring perpetrators of rape and other sexual crimes to justice. They had convicted 28 Yugoslav and 6 Rwandan defendants by June 30, 2002, among them the former Prime Minister of Rwanda.

6. Towards the Establishment of the International Criminal Court

THE IDEA OF an International Criminal Court (ICC) was developed within the UN system following the bitter experiences of genocide in the former

Yugoslavia and in Rwanda. A coalition of supportive states, called the "Like-Minded Group," was formed to push for a Diplomatic Conference to finalize and adopt the ICC Statute in 1998. Philippe Kirsch from Canada chaired this group in its attempt to promote an independent and effective ICC.

The Like-Minded Group reached the conclusion that an effective international court must have:

1. Jurisdiction over crimes of an international nature including those committed during internal armed conflicts
2. A positive relationship with the UN Security Council, while allowing its independence and impartiality to be maintained
3. A distinguished Prosecutor with complete independence, capable of going beyond state complaints and referrals from the UN Security Council and initiating new prosecutions
4. The recognition of the experiences of women and children in armed conflict

The efforts of the Like-Minded Group resulted in the establishment of a Diplomatic Conference in Rome between June 15 and July 17, 1998. The Canadian delegation played a facilitating role throughout the negotiations and tried to bridge the gap between different countries in areas such as the jurisdiction of the Court, the definition of crimes, etc. At last, a global proposal was prepared. As Chair of the Conference, Philippe Kirsch played a crucial role in developing the final draft. The package was adopted on July 17, 1998, by a vote of 120 states in favour, 7 against, and 21 abstentions.

Following the adoption of the *Rome Statute for ICC*, a Preparatory Commission (PrepCom) was created, with Philippe Kirsch as its Chair, to negotiate specific supplementary documents, such as the *Rules of Procedure and Evidence of the Court*, the *Elements of Crimes*, the *Financial Rules and Regulations*, the *Relationship Agreement between the Court and the UN*, and the *Agreement on the Privileges and Immunities of the Court*.

Following the election of 18 competent and distinguished judges, including Navanethem Pillay from South Africa and Elizabeth Odio Benito from Costa Rica, the International Criminal Court began its work. Phillippe Kirsh was elected as the President.

The Rome Statute and the ICC

THE *Rome Statute for ICC* established the International Criminal Court as a permanent institution with jurisdiction over "persons for the most serious crimes of international concern" which "shall be complementary to national criminal jurisdictions" (Article 1). The court has jurisdiction with respect to: a) the crime of genocide b) crimes against humanity c) war crimes d) the crime of aggression (Article 5).

The *Rome Statute* is mandated to deal with "the crime of aggression" (Article 5-d). The Statute, however, has not provided any definition for the crime of aggression and has subjected the exercise of its jurisdiction over this type of crime to future definition. The definition of the crime of genocide in the *Rome Statute* is similar to the definition given in Article 2 of the 1948 *Convention on the Prevention and Punishment of the Crime of Genocide*. Genocide is defined as "acts committed with intent to destroy, in whole or in part, a national, ethnic, racial or religious group" (Article 6).

The concept of "crime against humanity" that was introduced by the Nuremberg Tribunal is well defined in Article 7 of the *Rome Statute*:

> "the following acts constitute crimes against humanity when committed as part of a widespread or systematic attack directed against any civilian population, with knowledge of the attack: (a) Murder (b) Extermination (c) Enslavement (d) Deportation or forcible transfer of population (e) Imprisonment or other severe deprivation of physical liberty in violation of fundamental rules of international law (f) Torture (g) Rape, sexual slavery, enforced prostitution, forced pregnancy, enforced sterilization, or any other form of sexual violence of comparable gravity (h) Persecution against any identifiable group or collectivity on political, racial, national, ethnic, cultural, religious, gender grounds ... (i) Enforced disappearance of persons (j) The crime of apartheid (k) Other inhumane acts of a similar character ..."

The definition of war crimes in the *Rome Statute* is based on the provisions of the *International Humanitarian Law* (the four *Geneva Conventions* of 1949). They consist of the serious violation of the above Conventions through such acts as willful killing, torture, extensive destruction and appropriation of property, compelling a prisoner of war to serve in the forces of a hostile power, etc.[11]

The *Rome Statute for the International Criminal Court* is based upon the principle of "complementarity." The ICC intervenes only when national courts are unwilling or unable to prosecute. Its jurisdiction is not retroactive. It can only investigate and prosecute crimes committed after July 1, 2002. It is hard for the ICC to act in a country that has not ratified the *Rome Statute* unless the state where the crime has been committed accepts its jurisdiction. When a crime constitutes a threat to international peace and security, the UN Security Council can refer the case to the ICC. The Council also has the authority to postpone any investigation.

In its actual practice, the ICC is not mandated to prosecute authorities in power. Such prosecutions can be taken as a violation of the principle of national sovereignty. Given today's system of international relations and the UN structure, it is hard to expect the UN Security Council to activate the ICC for the prosecution of ruling tyrants. Such decisions can be vetoed by a permanent member of the Security Council if it has close military, economic and political ties with the ruling power in question.

Universal Jurisdiction

UNIVERSAL JURISDICTION CAN be defined as the competence of national courts to prosecute a crime of international law that has been committed outside the country. The philosophy behind universal jurisdiction is that the crime is so heinous that its consequences go beyond any national border. It shocks the conscience of every human being and, therefore, any state has the jurisdiction to prosecute its perpetrators.

It is unfortunate that with the exception of New Zealand, no country in the world has meaningful universal jurisdictions against the perpetrators of torture, genocide, war crimes and crimes against humanity. The following are attempts by different western countries in addressing the problem of impunity for torturers and perpetrators of other heinous crimes.[12]

Canada

THE *War Crimes and Crimes Against Humanity Act* came into effect on October 23, 2000. Only those perpetrators who live in Canada can be prosecuted under this legislation. While the RCMP can start an investigation at any time, there is a need for approval by the Attorney General of Canada to prosecute. On the occasion of President George W. Bush's visit to Canada on November 30, 2004, Vancouver lawyer Gail Davidson filed torture charges against him on behalf of Lawyers Against the War (LAW). She based her charges on the provisions of the *Canadian Criminal Code* as well as the *UN Convention Against Torture* ratified by both Canada and the United States. The charges concerned the well-known abuses of prisoners held by US Armed Forces in the Abu Ghraib prison in Iraq and the Guantánamo Bay prison in Cuba. The charges were accepted by the Justice of the Peace and referred for a hearing to decide whether Bush should be required to appear for trial.

The Attorney General of Canada blocked the charges by referring to President Bush's diplomatic immunity. Judge William Kitchen had no choice but to declare the charges "a nullity."

United States

THE US CONGRESS has adopted a criminal torture law, allowing for prosecution. The legislation is prospective only, post-1994, because of the e*x post facto* clause in the US constitution.

United Kingdom

IN THE UNITED KINGDOM, there is universal jurisdiction for torture. The *Criminal Justice Act* of 1988, in sections 134 to 138, criminalizes torture. It is not retrospective before September 1988.

Unlike mandatory requirements of the ICC, the UK system is basically a discretionary one. Extradition is a combination of court orders and government decisions. The court decides whether a person can be extradited and the government decides whether the person will be extradited. With the exception of Pinochet, there has been no request for extradition of torturers from the UK. Apart from pursuing criminal prosecutions, courts may propose other measures like imposing fines or seizing bank accounts.

Switzerland

SWITZERLAND RATIFIED THE *UN Genocide Convention* in September 2000 and incorporated it into its December 2000 legislation. There is no statute of limitations in Swiss legislation. Enactment of the universal jurisdiction requires that the perpetrator be on Swiss territory.

Switzerland has ratified the *Rome Statute for the ICC*. Human rights advocates praised the Swiss contribution towards addressing the problem of global impunity in its prosecution of modern war crimes. Switzerland initiated the investigation of 20 cases of war crimes, 6 from Rwanda and 14 from the former Yugoslavia. Of those who were prosecuted, two were referred to the ICTR, one was acquitted and one, a former mayor in Rwanda, was sentenced to life imprisonment, later commuted to 14 years.

Sweden

SWEDEN HAS RATIFIED most international instruments relevant to war crimes and terrorism, including the *Rome Statute for the ICC*. The prosecution of international criminals is carried out by six regional prosecution authorities with 14 units working under them. They work independently without the involvement of the Ministry of Justice. Sweden is a civil law country. Prosecutors and courts do not apply international instruments. They apply Swedish law.

All crimes are subject to a statute of limitations of 25 years for serious offences. This created a controversial problem in 2001 when Sweden released a naval officer who was a suspect in a case of kidnapping in 1977, in Buenos Aires. Sweden asked Argentina to extradite this Swedish-Argentinean co-citizen who had never lived in Sweden. The accused officer disappeared. In 1986 the military Supreme Court in Argentina acquitted the accused on the basis of the statute of limitations. Sweden issued an international warrant that resulted in the arrest of this notorious person. He spent only one month in Swedish detention and was released, because 25 years had lapsed and the statute of limitations had come into effect.

Netherlands

THE COUNTRY HAS torture legislation to punish crimes committed after 1984 with no statute of limitations. This law only applies to those within the country. Universal jurisdiction is enacted only if the person is in the Netherlands at the time of apprehension.

Germany

IN GERMANY UNIVERSAL jurisdiction exists for genocide, torture, and crimes under any of the four *Geneva Conventions*. Germany has a strict approach to *nullum crimen sine lege*: the crime must be in a German statute. The only ICC core crime now in German law is genocide. The Federal Supreme Court of Germany has developed a theory of universal jurisdiction that needs a German link to be effective. There is a central office charged with the investigation of war crimes.

Germany has maintained a collaborative approach with regards to the ICC by providing assistance to it at different levels. The German government can enforce the personal appearance of a witness before the ICC as well as before a German court. Upon the request of the ICC, it may freeze assets. It has shown a strong willingness to accept the conviction of sentenced persons.

Since June 1993, there have been 140 investigations into genocide in the former Yugoslavia and the German police have questioned 4,500 witnesses. There have been four trials of Bosnian Serbs with life sentences applied in two cases. At present, Germany is conducting 20 investigations from the former Yugoslavia. Africa and Asia are not on an equal footing. So far, there have been preliminary examinations but no investigations for cases from Eritrea, Ethiopia, Rwanda, and Sri Lanka.

Belgium

BELGIUM RATIFIED THE 1949 *Geneva Conventions* and incorporated it into its law in 1952. A separate legislation dealing with war crimes was passed in 1993. It applies to both civilians and military personnel. A new legislation in 1999 expanded the law to crimes against humanity and the crime of genocide. The law can be applied to non-international armed conflicts.

According to Belgian law, anyone who can prevent a heinous international crime but omits doing so has committed an offence. Until, recently every Belgian court was competent to try an international law case. A statute of limitations does not apply to international crimes. The 1993 law recognized the universal competence of Belgian courts regardless of where the crime had been committed. Perpetrators did not have to be found on Belgian territory. Victims could initiate a prosecution, without the interference of the prosecutor.

The practical implementation of the law of 1993 was in the trial of 4 Rwandese in Belgium in the year 2001. They were accused of participation in the 1994 genocide in Rwanda. All of the accused had a link with Belgium. The trial process continued for almost eight weeks, from April 17 to June 8, 2001. The court heard testimony and convicted the defendants to long-term imprisonment of 12 to 20 years.

Universal competence of the Belgian courts encouraged political as well as human rights groups to file law suits against statesmen at the apex of power. Following heated debates in Belgium and elsewhere concerning immunity, the Belgian parliament changed the law and ruled that the accused had to be a Belgian or presently in that country.

National Prosecutions Based on Universal Jurisdictions

IN RECENT YEARS, attempts to exercise universal jurisdiction in the prosecution of perpetrators of torture and other crimes of international law have ushered in a new era in addressing the global problem of impunity. Universal jurisdiction for international crimes has provided courts with judicial power and a mandate to prosecute. The significance of universal jurisdiction can be assessed in the ruling of a court in the US that regarded torturers as pirates and slave traders, as *hostis humani generis,* the enemy of all humankind.[13]

Attempts to prosecute Augusto Pinochet in the UK (and later Chile), Henry Kissinger in France and other countries, and the former Chadian dictator Hissène Habré in Senegal are unprecedented in human history. These attempts, although haphazard, will encourage the international community to act in the future. Here is a summary of the Pinochet case.

In response to petitions submitted by Chileans of Spanish descent who suffered under Pinochet, the Spanish National Court initiated judicial investigations against the former Chilean dictator in February 1997. In early October 1998, when Pinochet was in the UK, two Spanish judges filed an official petition with the UK authorities to question him. On October 16, 1998, he was placed under police custody in London. After a series of court hearings, in March 1999, the House of Lords – the highest UK court – ruled that Pinochet had no immunity for his crime of torture after the ratification of CAT in the UK, Spain and Chile on December 8, 1988. This ruling paved the way for the extradition of Pinochet to Spain to face trial. It took less than one year for the UK government to intervene in March 2000 with legal proceedings in response to extradition requests from Spain and three other countries. Authorities in the UK found Pinochet unfit to stand trial. Mr. Pinochet left for Chile the same day.

In Chile, courts removed Pinochet's immunity as a Senator for life. Survivors of torture and their families filed more than 2,000 criminal complaints against him. Prosecution of the former Chilean dictator could not continue, as the Second Chamber of the Chilean Supreme Court of Justice ruled in July 2002 that he was not mentally fit to stand trial.

Despite its discontinuation, attempts to bring Augusto Pinochet to justice encouraged human rights advocates in other countries to use the principles of universal jurisdiction to prosecute torturers and war criminals in national courts. The indictment of Augusto Pinochet outside Chile was a great step forward in addressing the problem of global impunity. In its daring supposition of extraterritorial judicial power for prosecution, this case revolutionized international law. It reiterated the principle that crimes against international law must be prosecuted with no arbitrary limitations. Pinochet managed to escape prosecution outside and inside Chile. This was certainly a step backward in addressing the problem of global impunity. However, it was at the same time a step forward in the sense that Pinochet is now officially labelled an insane person. As a "mentally incapable" individual he is removed from the Chilean political arena for the rest of his life.[14]

The Pinochet case has made Henry Kissinger extremely cautious about leaving the US due to his fear of arrest and prosecution overseas. As the US Secretary of State under Richard Nixon and Gerald Ford, Mr. Kissinger sent US armaments to the Pakistani regime to use against the people of Bangladesh. He supported the Indonesian dictator General Suharto in waging his bloody invasion of East Timor and initiating the subsequent genocide there. By expanding the war in Vietnam into Cambodia, Kissinger paved the way for the Khmer Rouge to seize power and initiate its reign of terror and genocide. He masterminded coups in Chile and Cyprus and supported the 1970 Latin American network of state terrorism called Operation Candor. His unconditional assistance of Jonas Savimbi and his rebel group Unita fanned the fire of a bloody war in Angola for 25 years where the death toll was more than 500,000.[15]

While in Paris, a French judge, encouraged by the provisions for universal jurisdiction in French law, summoned Kissinger to answer questions regarding his information about French citizens who disappeared under Pinochet, as well as the notorious network of government-sponsored assassins, Operation Candor. Kissinger hurriedly left France and asked the US embassy to use its diplomatic influence to terminate further actions against him. Since then he has been summoned by judges in Chile and Argentina; his trip to Brazil was cancelled in 2001, and there are cases filed against him in Washington, D.C. and in London, UK.

Mr. Kissinger has shown no sign of remorse and in a well-publicized article he has openly challenged the concept of universal jurisdiction. He has warned against ICC interventions: "The danger lies in pushing the effort to extremes that risk substituting the tyranny of judges for that of governments."[16] It is ironic that US President George W. Bush has assigned Mr. Kissinger the task of looking into the shortcomings of the US Intelligence Services.

The concept of universal jurisdiction has left its impact in Europe too. Universal jurisdiction that was previously enshrined in Belgian laws encouraged some activists to file applications for prosecution against well-known figures like US president George W. Bush, the Iranian cleric Mr. Rafsanjani, the late Palestinian leader Mr. Arafat, and Israeli Prime Minister Ariel Sharon. The case of genocide against Mr. Sharon went to the Supreme Court, which accepted his prosecution in principle. It was ruled that the process could be started when Sharon no longer held the office of Prime Minister. The Belgian Senate overturned this historic ruling and laid the foundation for the destruction of the universal jurisdiction provision in Belgian legislation.

Despite its failure, attempts to prosecute Pinochet left a positive impact in Africa. Following Pinochet's arrest in London, survivors of torture and tyranny in Chad organized themselves into the Chadian Association of Victims of Political Repression and Crime. They presented cases against the former President of Chad Mr. Hissène Habré to a truth commission that had been appointed in 1991, after he was overthrown. The truth commission found him responsible for killing 40,000 people and torturing 200,000.

Habré has lived in exile in Senegal since his downfall in a French-backed coup in 1990, after ruling the country with an iron fist for eight years. He had the full support of the government of the US, which regarded him as a buffer against Mr. Gaddafi of Libya. Seven human rights groups filed a criminal complaint on behalf of thousands of people victimized under his reign of terror.

Habré's case opened in a regional Dakar court on January 28, 2000. He was charged with 97 cases of political killings, 142 cases of torture, and 100 disappearances. The former United Nations Human Rights Commissioner Mary Robinson praised Senegal's action in indicting a former head of state for complicity in torture. She referred to Habré's trial as a "further confirmation that torture is an international crime subject to universal jurisdiction."[17]

On July 4, 2000, the Chamber of Dakar's Court of Appeals dropped the case against Habré, ruling that Senegalese courts had no jurisdiction to pursue crimes that were not committed in Senegal. The victims immediately appealed the decision to the Supreme Court of Appeals (*Cour de Cassation*). On March 20, 2001, the *Cour de Cassation* upheld the decision and terminated the process of prosecution of Habré in Senegal. In the meantime, Belgium asked for the extradition of Mr. Habré to be prosecuted there for his role in the torture and persecution of Belgian citizens. Mr. Habré is still in Senegal with no prospect for his prosecution.[18]

Truth and Reconciliation Commissions

SINCE 1974, MORE than 30 Truth and Reconciliation Commissions (TRC) have emerged worldwide to address the problem of impunity with the intention of revealing the truth, healing wounds and laying the foundation for national reconciliation.[19]

TRCs have proved their effectiveness in some countries in their reinterpretation of history and in acknowledging the gross violations of the dark past. They have, unfortunately, been ineffective in other countries and, in many cases, have acted as substitutes for national courts. Here is a historical glance at the successes and failures of TRCs in selected countries of the world.

DURING THE *Dirty War* in Argentina (1976-1983), some 30,000 dissidents were kidnapped by the repressive army and later disappeared. The country's nefarious warriors were granted amnesty in 1987. Today, they live among their traumatized victims with total impunity, sparing no time to obfuscate the truth.

THE PROBLEM OF impunity could not be addressed effectively in Haiti during the transitional period under Aristide due to threats and retaliatory measures against survivors, lawyers and witnesses on the one hand and the lack of state protection on the other.

THE GOVERNMENT OF El Salvador spared no effort in obstructing the Truth Commission from addressing the problem of impunity during the period of transition. The Commission, however, withstood government pressure and published the names of over forty top officials as perpetrators of torture and other international crimes. The then President of El Salvador pre-empted this action by granting a blanket amnesty to all perpetrators. Five days after the publication of the Commission's report, with the full support of the army, the new government passed the *Law of National Reconciliation,* which granted amnesty to many of those responsible for human rights abuses since 1980 (*Legislative Decree 486,* March 20, 1993).

THE SERIOUS CRIMES Unit in East Timor initiated the prosecution of those responsible for masterminding the 1999 rampage. The indictment included military officials of the highest rank. Acknowledgement, restitution and reparation of victims were the main goals of the Truth and Reconciliation agency in East Timor that was named the Commission for Reception. It required perpetrators to reveal their past crimes voluntarily. Perpetrators were asked to enter into reparation agreements with their victims or be referred to courts for prosecution.

THE AFRICAN NATIONAL Congress opposed the idea of blanket amnesty and agreed that amnesty be granted only to individuals upon their requests. A Truth and Reconciliation Commission was set up. The intention was to replace retributive justice (or legal punishment) with a restorative justice based on the needs of survivors and their participation in the process. Survivors were allowed to speak publicly about their past experiences and ask for reparation.

Amnesty was, more or less, a pre-condition for transition to a post-apartheid political system in South Africa. The Truth Commission supported some forms of amnesty to individuals in exchange for revealing the truth. It was granted to 7,000 applicants who gave information about their crimes of the past. Amnesty as such exempted perpetrators from criminal prosecutions and civil suits. This was probably a better option for this poor country, given the fact that the trials of two cases dealing with the crimes of apartheid in 1996 had cost $8 million.

IT SHOULD BE noted that the changes of regime in many countries have not led to structural change in the functioning of the state apparatus. Perpetrators remain active in the army and Intelligence and use their influence to block the road to justice. Despite these limitations, Truth Commissions have tried their best to reveal the crimes of the dark past with the help of tools such as the uncovering of mass graves, reviewing secret files of the army and security forces, hearing and analyzing testimonies of survivors, witnesses and perpetrators, etc. They have contributed towards healing and empowering survivors. They have tried to engage in a series of efforts to compensate for the harm inflicted upon survivors and their families (reparation). They have also contributed towards the restoration of victims to their original situations before the occurrence of torture or crimes of a similar nature (restitution).

There is no doubt that addressing impunity through Truth and Reconciliation Commissions is the first step on the spiral road of establishing a holistic peace, which can be achieved through national and international solidarity. Joan Simalchik, the former Executive Director of the CCVT, has emphasized the need for national solidarity to overcome the problems of impunity:

> "After cataclysmic natural disasters, such as floods and earthquakes, communities come together to commit resources, direct rebuilding efforts and learn from their mistakes. 'Unnatural' disasters require similar acknowledgement on a national level, the same psychological rebuilding and efforts to learn."[20]

There is a need for a holistic approach to the problem of transitional justice. Truth, reconciliation (amnesty), reparation and rehabilitation must come together. Victims should be compensated financially as well. This will help victims whose lives are destroyed to re-establish themselves. There is also a need for ongoing counselling and trauma intervention combined with physical and psychological treatment. The process of justice and accountability should be comfortable and safe in the eyes of victims. The participation of victims is imperative. Their voices must be heard through testimonies and in written submissions. Other essential measures include apologies, restoring legal rights, and revising history books to challenge rhetoric and reflect the truth.

The Role of the US

SINCE ITS ASCENDANCE to power, the Bush administration has shown a unilateral approach to the question of international justice and has applied a utilitarian and arbitrary interpretation of international law. Erma Paris, the Toronto-based author and scholar, has illuminated the role of the US in this respect:

> "I am beginning to believe that the emerging clash between newly born institutions of international accountability and the growing reality of unopposed and pre-emptive American power may mark the twenty-first century in ways we can hardly begin to grasp."[21]

The US administration is openly against the International Criminal Court. It has entered into more than 50 bilateral agreements with different countries - including Israel, Afghanistan, Rwanda, and Sri Lanka – with the mutual obligation that they do not extradite each other's citizens to face international justice. This goes against the fundamental philosophy of the ICC, which is the extension of justice to the entire war-trodden world. The US fear of the ICC and global justice can only be imagined, and is reflected in a bill passed into law that permits the US invasion of the Netherlands to "free" US nationals if they remain subjected to international prosecution.[22]

In an attempt to block the ICC, the US government has utilized its influence at the UN Security Council. On July 12, 2002, under the influence of the US, the UN Security Council adopted resolution No. 1422, which exempted peacekeepers from prosecution by the ICC for a renewable period of one year. Amnesty International opposed this dangerous and precedent-setting decision immediately:

> "By attempting to block countries who are party to the treaty from fulfilling their legal obligations, resolution 1422 strikes at the heart of the principles of justice embodied in the ICC."[23]

Following this decision, Canada reacted positively and even called the legality of the Security Council into question. At the Preparatory Committee of the ICC sessions in New York City, the Canadian representative, Mr. Paul Heinbecker, made the following remarks: "Canada is deeply disturbed by the discussions currently underway in the Security Council concerning a sweeping exemption from national and international jurisdiction for peacekeepers." According to Mr. Heinbecker, "what is now at stake is not the ICC *versus* peacekeeping. In fact, fundamental issues of international law and international relations are in jeopardy." He raised concern that the proposed resolution "would undermine the treaty-making process" and "would dramatically alter and weaken the *Rome Statute*." It "would send an unacceptable message that peacekeepers are above the law." And "when the US acquitted itself of its obligations to investigate, and if necessary prosecute perpetrators, as it would, the Court would be blocked." The resolution may "place the UN Security Council in the untenable position of risking a return to impunity for genocide, crimes against humanity and war crimes."[24]

Under US pressure, the European Union in its decision of September 30, 2000 accepted a compromise decision with regards to the problem of impunity. While the decision prohibited member states from entering into bilateral treaties with the US, it was worded in such a way that some states could use it as an excuse to enter into agreements that would give US citizens and others impunity for international crimes in the ICC or any other courts.[25]

The US government not only plays a negative role with regards to the *Rome Statute* and the ICC, it lacks a consistent policy to deal with torturers and other international criminals internally: "US policy towards torture has long exhibited a paradox of values."[26]

According to the Center for Justice and Accountability, a human rights NGO committed to track human rights abusers in the United States, some 7,000 perpetrators of torture and other international crimes are in that country. Among these perpetrators is a former colonel in the Haitian military junta of 1991, Carl Dorelien, and two former generals from El Salvador – Carlos Eugenio Vides Casanova and Jose Guillermo Garcia.[27]

Torturers and international criminals can be prosecuted in the US on the basis of universal criminal accountability provisions of the *Convention*

Against Torture (specifically Article 6 of the CAT) and the US criminal legislation of 1994. But, provisions of this legislation only apply to perpetrators who have committed the crime of torture outside the US after April 30, 1994, when the legislation was enacted.[28]

The US government vetoed the extension of the UN Mission in Bosnia and Herzegovina (UNMIBH) at the UN Security Council on June 30, 2002 because it was not receiving immunity for its troops from the jurisdiction of the ICC. This decision is interpreted by some human rights activists as the manifestation of the US arrogance in putting itself above international law and beyond the system of global justice.

The Bush administration withdrew the US signature on the ICC treaty in May 2001, and has been conducting a campaign to undermine the Court. Recent developments have proved that the ICC can continue without US support. But it is hard to imagine a viable ICC faced with the active opposition of this dominant superpower.

Forgiveness

THE CONTEMPORARY South African novelist Gillian Slovo has marvelously resolved the dilemma of forgiving the torturer or killer of one's close relatives during the period of transition. Her mother, Ruth First, was assassinated by the security forces of the apartheid regime. Years later, her father, Joe Slovo, contributed to the creation of the Truth and Reconciliation Commission in post-apartheid South Africa that considered granting amnesty to the assassin of Gillian's mother. Let us learn from Gillian's personal reflections:

> "The reconciliation that I experienced was with what happened, not with the perpetrators. And this for me is the important thing about TRC that it helps a whole society reconcile itself to its past without ignoring or denying it."[29]

It is easy to grasp from Gillian's experience that her idea of justice is by no means retributive. Punishment should serve objectives such as correction, deterrence, rehabilitation, reformation, reparation, and healing. These objectives are accompanied with the ultimate idea of forgiveness, extended even to the perpetrators of the most heinous crimes, both at the individual and social levels.

The dilemma of forgiveness stems from the fact that many culprits ask to be pardoned, and once pardon is granted, may repeat their actions. Therefore, forgiveness must be attached to certain conditions. The perpetrators should be compelled to expose their past vices in all their dimensions and be willing to pay their debt to their victims and to society as a whole.

It is impossible to reform perpetrators until and unless they acquire a new conscience. This new understanding must guide them to care for survivors more than they do for themselves. They need to feel remorse and accept punishment in order to achieve emotional peace. According to the Bosnian scholar and linguist Professor Smail Balic, "evil cannot be offset by good when there is no genuine remorse."[30] There is no doubt that remorse and repentance serve no purpose if not accompanied by practical measures by perpetrators to reform themselves and compensate their victims.

There is a need for the victims and society as a whole to develop the idea of ultimate forgiveness. We need to have both retrospective and prospective attitudes. The idea of looking back to the crime should serve the purpose of looking forward to the future of society. The great Indian political leader and theorist, Jaya Prakash Narayan, always pushed authorities to reform criminals. I came to know about him during my first trip to India in 1977. In those days there was a well-known criminal and smuggler in Bombay (now Mumbai) by the name of Haji Mastan who used to run a gang of organized criminals. The late Jaya Prakash Narayan tried single-handedly to reform the notorious lawbreaker by meeting and talking with him frequently. Haji Mastan, encouraged by JP, closed down shop and reduced his criminal activities. The people of Bombay heaved a sigh of relief.

I agree with the Nobel Prize Laureate Wole Soyinka that the "capacity to forgive an enemy is based on love, at least a certain doctrine of love."[31] The transitional society that has emancipated itself from the regime of hate and terror must develop a new and all-embracing perspective of love. Loving the enemy has a powerful healing impact both on victims and on the entire society.

Notes

1. For more information on impunity, see Amnesty International, *End Impunity: Justice for the Victims of Torture*, AI, London (UK), 2001.
2. For more information on the Mennonites' persecution, see John S. Oyer, *They Harry the Good People Out of the Land: Essays on the Persecution, Survival and Flourishing of Anabaptists and Mennonites*, Mennonite Historical Society, 2000.

3. For more information on the Armenian genocide, see Abraham H. Hartunian, *Neither to Laugh Nor to Weep: An Odyssey of Faith: Memoir of the Armenian Genocide*, Armenian Heritage Press, 3rd Edition, November 1, 1997.
4. www.cbc.ca/stories/2004/04/21/canada/armenia040421.
5. *The Santiago Times*, the English Newspaper of Chile, Santiago, August 10, 2004.
6. Maggie Helwig, "Tribunals and Justice," in a collection of articles entitled "Crimes and (no) Punishment," from *A Symposium on Impunity and International Justice* moderated by David Webster. See *maisonneuve*, Issue 4, Summer 2003, pp. 47-48.
7. Out of 24 defendants indicted by the Nuremberg tribunal, one committed suicide and one other was found psychologically unfit for trial. Out of 22 Nazi leaders who stood trial, 11 were hanged, 7 were sentenced to long-term imprisonments, 3 were acquitted and one took his own life.
8. For more information about the Nuremberg Trial, see Ann Tusa and John Tusa, *The Nuremberg Trial*, Atheneum, New York, 1984.
9. *The Autobiography of Bertrand Russell, The Final Years: 1944-1969*, a Bantam Book, published by arrangement with Simon and Schuster, New York, 1970, p. 239.
10. Ibid, pp. 314-15.
11. The list goes on and on. For a detailed account of acts of war crimes see article 8 of the *Rome Statute for ICC*.
12. Information provided in this section is based on unofficial minutes taken from presentations given by various experts at the following events: 1) a conference hosted by the Department of Justice, Government of Canada on April 22 and 23, 2002, Ottawa; 2) Seminar on Human Rights and Impunity, Canadian Ecumenical Justice Initiatives, September 12, 2002, Toronto; 3) Conference on "Searching for Justice: Comprehensive Action in the Face of Atrocities," York University, December 4-6, 2003, Toronto; 4) a conference hosted by the Department of Justice, Government of Canada on December 8-9, 2003, Ottawa. The author actively participated in the last 3 events.
13. As cited in Amnesty International, *Combating Torture, A Manual for Action*, 2003, p. 314.
14. Ariel Dorfman, the Chilean novelist in exile, has illustrated fictitiously the rise and fall of Pinochet, in his book *Exorcising Terror: The Incredible Unending Trial of Augusto Pinochet*, Open Media, August 1, 2002.
15. For more information see Christopher Hitchens, *The Trial of Henry Kissinger*, Verso, June 1, 2002.

16. Henry A. Kissinger, "The Pitfalls of Universal Jurisdiction," *Foreign Affairs*, July/August 2001.
17. As quoted in a report entitled "Human Rights Activists Inspired by Pinochet Case" by the BBC West Africa correspondent Mark Doyle, Saturday, February 5, 2000, at 10:45 GMT.
18. For more information see Human Rights Watch, Chad: "The Victims of Hissène Habré Still Awaiting Justice," *Human Rights Watch Reports*, Vol. 17, No. 10 (A), July 2005.
19. Truth and Reconciliation Commissions have worked with various degrees of effectiveness in the following countries: Afghanistan, Angola, Bolivia, Bosnia-Herzegovina, Cambodia, Chad, Chile, Colombia, East Timor, Ecuador, El Salvador, Ghana, Guatemala, Haiti, Indonesia, Jamaica, Kenya, Liberia, Mexico, Morocco, Nepal, Nigeria, Panama, Peru, Philippines, Serbia and Montenegro, Sierra Leone, South Africa, South Korea, Sri Lanka, Uganda, Uruguay, Venezuela, and Zimbabwe. For detailed information, see Library and Links, "Truth Commissions Digital Collections" at http://www.usip.org/library/truth.html.
20. Joan Simulchik, "Impunity in Chile," in Footnote No. 6, p. 53.
21. Erna Paris, "Impunity and Accountability," in Ibid., pp. 46-47.
22. Maggie Helwig, "Summing Up," Ibid., p. 54.
23. From the Press Release of July 12, 2002, issued by Amnesty International USA. See http://www.amnestyusa.org/ainews.html.
24. Remarks by H.E. Mr. Paul Heinbecker, Ambassador and Permanent Representative of Canada to the United Nations at the tenth session of the Preparatory Commission for the International Criminal Court, Wednesday, July 3, 2002.
25. For more information, see Amnesty International EU Office (Brussels), *EU Compromise On US Impunity Agreements a Setback for the International Criminal Court* (30/9/2002).
26. William J. Aceve, *United States of America: A Safe Haven for Torturers*, Amnesty International USA, New York, 2002, p. 49.
27. Del Quentin Wilber, "Rights Abusers Can Find Haven," *Baltimore Sun*, Tuesday, 29 August, 2000.
28. For more information, see World Organization Against Torture, *Memorandum*, Washington DC, April 4, 2000 (www.woatusa.org).
29. Gillian Slovo, "Truth and Reconciliation in South Africa," in footnote No. 6, p. 50.
30. As quoted in Simon Wiesenthal, *The Sunflower: On the Possibilities and Limits of Forgiveness*, Schocken Books, New York, p. 111. Prof. Balic's remark is in response to the following question put before him and other contributors by the book's author, Simon Wiesenthal: "You are a prisoner

in a concentration camp, a dying Nazi soldier asks for your forgiveness. What would you do?"

31. Wole Soyinka, *The Burden of Memory, the Muse of Forgiveness,* Oxford University Press, New York, 1999, p. 98.

9

Canada Against Torture

WITHIN THE CANADIAN population there are thousands of people who carry the historical scars of physical and/or psychological torture. The following are some examples of populations, who along with many others, escaped torture, tyranny, war and subjugation:
- Loyalists fleeing the American Revolution
- African-Americans escaping slavery
- Scots from the Highland Clearances
- Jews escaping persecution in various countries, especially during and after the Holocaust
- Thousands of people from the former USSR and Eastern Europe escaping Stalinist torture and state terrorism

Since World War II, Canada has accepted approximately 1 million refugees – more than 30 percent of whom have experienced various forms of torture.

Two chapters of this book deal with the suffering of non-citizens in Canada as a result of living in limbo due to gaps in Immigration legislation and policies. This chapter deals specifically with the negative and positive policies and practices of the Canadian government *vis-à-vis* the scourge of torture within and outside Canada.

Legal Obligations

CANADA HAS RATIFIED most of the international legal instruments related to the prevention and eradication of torture, including the *UN Declaration of Human Rights* and the *International Covenant on Civil and Political Rights* (ICCPR). On June 24, 1987, Canada ratified the *United Nations Convention Against Torture and Other Cruel, Inhuman or Degrading Treatment or Punishment* (CAT). Canada has also accepted the competence of the UN

Human Rights Committee and the Committee Against Torture to consider communications from individuals who feel that their rights (as enumerated in the ICCPR and CAT) have been violated without domestic redress.

As was mentioned before, the *Optional Protocol to the Convention Against Torture* has been available for ratification since February 4, 2003. Canada actively played a leadership role in the working group that wrote the final draft.[1] Canada also voted in favour of the Protocol's adoption at the 57th session of the United Nations General Assembly in December 2002. However, Canada has unfortunately not ratified the Protocol yet.

Delay in ratification of this important document seems to be related to problems of implementation. The primary focus of the Protocol is the regular inspection of prisons and detention centres that are mainly under the jurisdiction of the provincial governments. It is not possible for the federal government to ratify the Protocol without the approval of all Canadian provinces and territories. Negotiations between the federal and provincial governments of Canada have not yet reached any positive outcome. There is an urgent need to break the deadlock, as was done with the *Convention on the Rights of the Child*. Canada cannot play an effective global leadership role in the prevention of torture without the ratification of this crucial legal instrument.

Canada joined the Organization of American States (the OAS) as an observer in 1972 and became a full member on January 8, 1990. The country is therefore subject to the jurisdiction of the Inter-American Commission on Human Rights. The Commission is an autonomous organ of the OAS, created to protect and promote the observance of human rights and to serve as a consultative body of the OAS. The authority of the Commission stems from the *OAS Charter,* the *American Convention on Human Rights,* and the *American Declaration of the Rights and Duties of Man,* its Statute and Regulations. Canada automatically fell under the scrutiny of the Commission by joining the OAS. The Commission can issue study reports and receive individual complaints alleging human rights violations including torture.[2]

In terms of domestic instruments, there are provisions in the *Canadian Charter of Rights and Freedoms* against torture. They include: the right to life, liberty and security of the person (Section 7), and the provision that "everyone has the right not to be subjected to any cruel and unusual treatment or punishment" (Section 12). Section 9 asserts the right not to be arbitrarily detained or imprisoned. Section 32 of the Charter guarantees the rights of private persons against action by the federal and provincial legislatures and governments.

Canada's *Criminal Code* includes the absolute prohibition of torture. Section 269.1 of the Code provides a definition of torture that is similar to the definition contained in Article 1 of the CAT. Section 269.1(3) of the *Criminal Code* is an important tool in the prevention and prohibition of torture, according to which a command from a superior does not justify torture.

There are less significant regulatory and administrative provisions in Canada that can be used against torture. The following are some examples:
- The *Royal Canadian Mounted Police Code of Conduct* offences
- Sections 68 and 69 of the *Corrections and Conditional Release Act* (CCRA)
- The *Penitentiary Service Regulations*

Canada has ratified and incorporated the *Rome Statute* of the International Criminal Court into Canadian legislation. This led to the passage of the *Crimes Against Humanity and War Crimes Act*, which acts as a tool in the prosecution of torturers, war criminals and those who have committed crimes against humanity within or outside of Canada. This Act affirms that any immunities otherwise existing under Canadian law will not block extradition to the International Criminal Court or to any international criminal tribunal established by resolution of the Security Council of the United Nations.[3]

In 1997, the Canadian Forces adopted its *Code of Conduct*, which provides explicit instructions about respect for the *Convention Against Torture*, and the prohibition of torture and inhuman treatment. Rule 6 of the *Code of Conduct* states that all detained persons must be treated humanely. Section 130 of the *National Defence Act* has subjected members of the Canadian Forces to the provisions of the *Criminal Code* and all other Acts of Parliament. They face prosecution if they engage in acts of torture, and can legally refuse to obey an unlawful command from their superiors.

On June 28, 2002, the *Immigration and Refugee Protection Act* was implemented in Canada. This act incorporated Article 1 of the *Convention Against Torture* into its provisions (Section 97, Subsection 1) and has provided protection to survivors of torture and those who might be at risk of torture back home (Section 115, Subsection 1). The provisions helped the quasi-judicial refugee determination body, the Immigration and Refugee Board (IRB), to apply a consolidated decision-making process. The Act mandated IRB to determine not only whether a claimant would face persecution on the basis of the UN 1951 *Refugee Convention* but also whether the applicant would be in need of protection because of a danger of torture or other cruel and unusual treatment or punishment. A person accepted under any of these categories becomes a "protected person."

Canada accepted gender-related persecution as grounds for claiming refugee status. The Immigration and Refugee Board (IRB) has issued guidelines on dealing with cases of female refugee claimants fearing such persecution. Examples of gender-related persecution include rape, domestic violence, female genital mutilation, and persecution due to nonconformity with gender-discriminatory, religious, and cultural laws.

Canada can present its adversarial judicial system as an example to the international community and help other nations develop similar legal systems. In this system, the lawyer and the prosecutor (the Crown Attorney in Canada) contest the matter with each other in a courtroom. Truth is sought in this adversarial system and there is no place for forced confession. This is in contrast to other countries, where, as it is documented, torture is practiced in jails and detention centres by law enforcement authorities in an attempt to extract information or confessions.

It should be stressed that this adversarial system is not to be used during refugee hearings by the Immigration and Refugee Board when they examine refugee claimants and survivors of torture. This is quite understandable, as refugee claimants should not be treated like criminal offenders. Refugees have gone through persecution and torture and have fought for human rights. Canada has correctly decided to give them a full chance to share their stories in a non-adversarial manner. This is necessary because adversarial confrontation could easily lead to the retraumatization of refugees and survivors of torture.

Unfortunately, we have had cases of refugee hearings becoming adversarial as a result of inappropriate, aggressive intervention by panel members, Refugee Protection Officers, and CIC representatives who occasionally attend refugee hearings. We have documented cases of refugee hearings that have become adversarial, leading to the retraumatization of the clients of CCVT.

Under the previous *Immigration Act*, the Minister's representative needed special permission by the Immigration and Refugee Board to attend refugee hearings. The present *Immigration and Refugee Protection Act* has waived such permission. Besides, the Act has provided the Minister with the right to appeal a positive decision of this quasi-judicial body.

The consolidated decision-making process of the Immigration and Refugee Board as well as the new role for the Minister of Citizenship and Immigration speak to the need for the Immigration and Refugee Board to develop guidelines in dealing with victims of torture, war and organized violence with the help of human rights and torture rehabilitation centres. Refugee protection agencies and organizations helping survivors of torture have been calling for the acceptance of these guidelines since 1994, with no success.

Torture Practice

DESPITE THE HEAVY emphasis of the *Immigration and Refugee Protection Act* on removal and detention, and an ever-increasing number of Immigration detainees in Canada, torture is not used in Canadian jails and detention centres as part of a systematic political strategy of repression, and we are fortunate and proud in this regard. In the whole history of the Canadian Centre for Victims of Torture (CCVT), we have rarely faced anyone claiming torture against Canada. Since September 11, 2001, we have accepted only two clients against Canada on the basis of Article 16 of the *Convention Against Torture* (subjection to other cruel, inhuman or degrading treatment or punishment).

The arrest of 19 Pakistanis in Toronto on August 14, 2003 and the subsequent consequences is a matter of grave concern. It can perhaps be attributed to the government's post-September 11 hyperobsession with the danger of terrorist attacks at the cost of human rights in Canada. In their pre-dawn joint raids, the Department of Citizenship and Immigration (CIC) and the Royal Canadian Mounted Police (RCMP) arrested 19 Pakistani men, between the ages of 19 and 33 in Toronto.

The arrests were made on the "grounds" that the Pakistanis might pose a threat to Canadian national security. To our knowledge, neither CIC nor the RCMP produced adequate evidence to warrant such massive arrests. One of the reasons for suspicion came from the fact that the men lived in "clusters of four or five" and kept a "minimal standard of living." One of the men was enrolled in flight school to become a commercial pilot. The men's place of origin, the tumultuous province of Punjab, could have also played a role in their arrest.

Without being formally charged with a crime, the arrested Pakistanis were detained in the Maplehurst Correctional Centre in Ontario. Their detainment was made possible due to the current *Immigration and Refugee Protection Act* that allows the federal government to detain non-citizens indefinitely without laying charges. In the course of time the detained Pakistanis were released on bail. Two of them were referred by their lawyers to the CCVT.

We found that the arrest and detention had left a devastating effect on the aforementioned clients. One of them told us that enforcement officials raided his house before dawn while he was sleeping. They searched the entire house and led him away in his night clothes. While in a police cruiser, he pleaded without success for an opportunity to use the washroom. He was allowed to go to the washroom forty minutes after his first request. He reported that in the interrogation, his interrogator approached him, stared into his eyes and began his interrogation with insults and threats. In the evening, with his hands cuffed and his legs chained, they took him to Maplehurst Correctional Centre. There was no *habeas corpus* and no hearing for eleven days. He told me about his experience of harassment in jail. His jail-mates spared no time in calling him a terrorist and beating him physically.

It has been difficult for these Pakistanis to live a normal life in the community since their release. Due to the high level of publicity about their arrest, people recognize them in shops and on the street and point fingers accompanied by comments associating them with terrorism and Al-Qaeda.[4] One client told me that the news about their arrest and detention had reached Pakistan through print, visual media, the internet and word of mouth.

To the best of my knowledge, two of the detainees, Mr. Mohammad Asif and Mr. Fahim Kayani, have been deported to Pakistan. I have come to know that upon his arrival in Pakistan, Mr. Asif was arrested without charge, unlawfully detained and interrogated, and had his passport seized by Pakistani officials. We have no news of Mr. Kayani and there is no way to learn about him.

Such actions violate the right of every person not to be subjected to cruel, degrading and unusual treatment or punishment, as stated in Article 16 of the CAT and Article 12 of the *Canadian Charter of Rights and Freedoms*. There is a need for Canada to define cruel, inhuman, or degrading treatment or punishment and to develop mechanisms for the accountability and prosecution of officers who commit such offences.

Police violence is another increasing concern in Canadian society. I have received complaints from my clients about being beaten by police while in custody. One client reported that police officers beat him to the point where he became unconscious and was transferred to hospital. Another gentleman reported that the police stopped his car and mistreated him as a suspected terrorist. He reported that when he complained against police violence, the police charged him with a series of crimes that he had never committed. What is at stake here are people's civil and political rights. Lacking in Canada is an effective complaint mechanism against excessive police measures and violence. An internal committee investigates complaints against individual police officers. While it is important to have an effective and powerful police force in Canada, that power must be subject to independent civilian supervision.

Non-refoulement to Torture

ARTICLE 3 OF the *UN Convention Against Torture* speaks to the principle of *non-refoulement*, i.e., that under no circumstances should a person be returned to a country in which s/he will be at risk of torture. This is regarded by human rights and torture rehabilitation centres as an absolute that cannot be balanced with such considerations as danger to the public or risks to national security.

Canada has, unfortunately, failed to comply with this Article. There are hundreds of non-citizens in Canada who have ended up with removal orders due to the inadmissibility provisions of the *Immigration and Refugee Protection Act*. What is disturbing is the prolonged inaction and indecision. This is illustrated at length in chapters in this book dealing with limbo.

Among refugees in limbo, the case of Mr. Suresh has received nationwide attention. Mr. Manickavasagam Suresh, a Tamil citizen of Sri Lanka, entered Canada on October 5, 1990 and was accepted as a Convention refugee on April 11, 1991. In the summer of 1991, Mr. Suresh applied for landing in Canada, but his application was suspended as a result of a joint certificate issued by the Solicitor General of Canada and the Minister of Citizenship and Immigration classifying him inadmissible to Canada on security grounds. It was stated that during the initial 5 years of his stay in Canada, Mr. Suresh had been involved with the World Tamil Movement (WTM) and its fundraising activities, and had acted as a coordinator for the

Federation of Associations of Canadian Tamils (FACT).

Mr. Suresh was detained on October 18, 1995 and spent two years in an Immigration detention centre before being released on bail.

The Suresh inadmissibility certificate was based on the opinion expressed by the Canadian Security Intelligence Service (CSIS) that he could be a member of the Liberation Tigers of Tamil Eelam (LTTE), an alleged terrorist organization.[5]

In 1998, the Minister of Citizenship and Immigration reviewed his case and signed an opinion that he was a danger to the security of Canada pursuant to section 53(1)(b) of the Act.

Pursuant to subsection 40.1(3) of the *Immigration Act*, a hearing was conducted in the Federal Court of Canada, and on August 29, 1997, the judge held that the issuance of the certificate was "reasonable" and the return of Mr. Suresh to torture neither violates the international law nor the Canadian Charter. The court ruled that it is not acceptable that "the right under international law to be secure against torture is absolute and binding on Canada."[6]

The Federal Court of Appeal confirmed the decision. Suresh's lawyer, Barbara Jackman, sought leave to appeal the case to the Supreme Court of Canada and was granted permission to do so on May 25, 2000. Many human rights agencies, including the CCVT, showed interest in intervening with the Supreme Court of Canada in the case of Suresh. The widespread optimism for a positive decision from the highest court turned to bitter despair with the terrorist crime of September 11, 2001 in New York and its aftermath.

In its ruling of January 11, 2002, the Supreme Court allowed Mr. Suresh to stay in Canada pending a new deportation hearing under the *Immigration Act*. The Court ruled that "Determining whether deportation to torture violates the principles of fundamental justice requires us to balance Canada's interest in combating terrorism and the Convention refugee's interest in not being deported to torture."[7]

The Supreme Court's ruling is a matter of grave concern. The Court's decision has serious national as well as global implications for the life and security of torture survivors who are in similar situations. It can set a dangerous legal precedent in the protection of torture victims and may provide governments with the green light to return people to torture. This ruling is contrary to the decisions of the UN Committee against Torture[8] and the European Court of Human Rights in different cases. The UN Committee

Against Torture, in its decision on Cecilia Rosana N. Chipana vs. Venezuela, has confirmed: "The Committee considers that the test of Article 3 of the Convention is absolute."[9] The Committee against Torture has advised that Canada should "[c]omply fully with article 3(1) ... whether or not the individual is a serious criminal or security risk."[10]

A European example is Chahal v. the United Kingdom (November 15, 1996), in which the European Court of Human Rights held that the decision to deport a Sikh separatist to India for national security reasons violated Article 3 of the *Convention for the Protection of Human Rights and Fundamental Freedoms.*[11]

It was reiterated that there could be no derogation from Article 3 even in times of national emergency.

The Supreme Court of Canada has underestimated the special significance of the *Convention Against Torture* and its focus on human rights principles as the foundation of protection. It is widely accepted that torture, in many cases, is worse than death. It is surprising that the Supreme Court of Canada opposes extradition of suspected criminals to a place where they may face the death penalty, but refuses to confirm the absolute right of *non-refoulement* to torture.[12]

The Supreme Court's decision may deliver a heavy blow to the prohibition of torture as "one of the most basic principles of human rights" that is "compared to the most fundamental rights, such as the right to life or the prohibition of slavery."[13] The absolute nature of Article 3 of CAT "allows for no exceptions, reflecting the special and serious nature of the prohibition against torture in international law."[14]

It should be noted that the principle of non-derogable right of *non-refoulement* to torture goes beyond individual protection. The purpose is to deprecate torture in the most straightforward and absolute manner and to send a clear-cut message to the international community that torture is a human vice that must absolutely be condemned and whose use or existence can never be justified under any circumstances. Canada is reluctant to accept this principle due to its preoccupation with deportation and its lack of political will.

There is a serious concern that, in their task of enforcing immigration legislation, immigration officials apply the Suresh exception in an overly broad fashion to send genuine refugees back to torture. The passage of Bill C-36 into the *Anti-Terrorist Act* on December 18, 2001 and the subsequent Bill C-42 into *Public Safety Act, 2002,* which received Royal Assent on May 6,

2004, may also lead to the intensification of enforcement measures.

Under the *Anti-Terrorist Act* police can arrest and detain people without warrant. This can happen under "exigent circumstances" even without the consent of the Attorney General, the minister responsible for police forces. Police may also enter a dwelling without such a warrant. Terms such as "believes on reasonable grounds" and "suspects on reasonable grounds" are not defined by the *Anti-Terrorist Act*. These provisions leave police with tremendous power to arrest and detain people without due process. The Act suffers from lack of transparency and encourages secret trials.

The Canadian government may boast that "to date, Canada has not deported anyone to a country where the person was determined to face a substantial risk of torture."[15] This is, however, far from reality. Canada has used the "Security certificate" as a powerful tool in removing people to an unknown fate. A certificate is issued under IRPA against a permanent resident or any foreign national who is deemed to be inadmissible in Canada on grounds of security or criminality suspicions.

There is no due process in issuing the certificate, as IRPA allows for it to be signed by members of the executive, the Minister of Public Safety and Emergency Preparedness Canada (PSEPC), and the Minister of Citizenship and Immigration Canada (CIC). On December 10, 2004, the Federal Court of Appeal reiterated in the Charkaoui decision that the certificate process is constitutional and is in accordance with the *Canadian Charter of Rights and Freedoms*. The UN Committee Against Torture has criticized Canada for

> "the blanket exclusion by the Immigration and Refugee Protection Act 2002 (97) of the status of refugee or person in need of protection, for persons falling within the security exceptions ... "[16]

Out of 2,050 admissibility hearings that were concluded in 2003-2004, only 4 percent were permitted to remain in Canada.[17] In a 12-month period ending on March 31, 2005, the Canada Border Service Agency (CBSA) removed 11,845 people from Canada.[18] A breakdown of this number is not easily available and there is no monitoring system in Canada for returnees from human rights agencies of the countries of removal. These agencies are under tremendous pressure and are obviously incapable of getting any information from their tyrannical governments.

Protection of Canadian Citizens Overseas

ARTICLE 9 OF the *UN Convention Against Torture* is about the cooperation of the state parties in the process of prosecution of torturers. I believe that it will be against the spirit of this Article if states parties to CAT refuse to protect their citizens against torture by other states or, even worse, facilitate torture against their citizens under any guise or excuse.

Since the tragedy of September 11, 2001, the fundamental human rights of Canadian citizens overseas have increasingly come under attack. A tragic example is the death of Canadian photo-journalist Zahara Kazemi under torture in Iran on July 12, 2003. This was followed by the testimony of William Sampson about his experience of abhorrent tortures during his 31 months of imprisonment in Saudi Arabia. Following that, Mr. Maher Arar testified that despite being a Canadian citizen, he was deported to Syria by the US authorities to face torture and other cruel, inhuman and degrading treatment there.

Both Mr. Sampson and Mr. Arar have mentioned the inadequate support from the Canadian government to protect them as Canadian citizens. Mr. Arar even made an allegation about possible collaboration between the Royal Canadian Mounted Police (RCMP) and the Canadian Security and Intelligence Services (CSIS) on the one hand and US and Syrian authorities on the other. The UN Committee Against Torture has criticized the alleged roles of the Canadian "authorities in the expulsion of Canadian national Mr. Maher Arar, expelled from the United States to Syria where torture was reported."[19]

It should be acknowledged that the government of Canada took some measures in the cases of Ms. Kazemi and Mr. Arar. The consistent and effective Canadian protests forced the Iranian government to initiate an investigation into Ms. Kazemi's death under torture. However, despite recent hair-raising exposures by the Iranian Dr. Shahram Azam on March 31, 2005 of the rape and deadly tortures of Ms. Kazemi, Canada has so far failed to explore national and international procedures to secure the prosecution of Ms. Kazemi's torturers.

Canada, unfortunately, has not come up with a firm and consistent policy for the protection of its citizens abroad. It has normally been lenient towards violations of the human rights of Canadian citizens by our neighbour to the South.

Impunity

CANADA HAS ALWAYS been at the forefront of the global campaign against impunity for torturers and other perpetrators of international crimes. From the very beginning, Canada played a significant role in efforts that led to the adoption and later enforcement of the *Rome Statute* and the establishment of the International Criminal Court.

Canada took practical steps and contributed to a United Nations trust fund and to NGOs enabling poor countries to participate in the negotiations that led to the adoption of the *Rome Statute* for the International Criminal Court (ICC). Canada signed this important document on December 18, 1998 and introduced the *New Act to Implement International Criminal Court* on December 10, 1999. On June 29, 2000, Canada became the first country in the world that incorporated the *Rome Statute* for ICC through its comprehensive *Crimes Against Humanity and War Crimes Act*. The adoption of this Act paved the way for Canada to ratify the *Rome Statute* on July 7, 2000. Canada is among the few countries in the world that has legally accepted universal jurisdiction in the prosecution of perpetrators of torture, war crimes and crimes against humanity.

It is encouraging that Canada has also demonstrated its willingness and ability to conduct investigations into allegations of torture against Canadian perpetrators. During the Canadian peace-keeping mission in Somalia (1992-93), Canadian soldiers shot from behind at two Somali youths who were allegedly trying to steal supplies from the Canadian base. A second incident involved the torture and killing of a Somali youth. There were some reports about a cover-up by higher officials.

The government of Canada conducted a thorough investigation that continued for two years. The members of the airborne regiment responsible for the torture and killing of the Somali teenager Shidane Arone were prosecuted. A private was convicted of manslaughter, and a sergeant attempted suicide before facing trial. The Commission of Inquiry admitted that the peacekeeping troops were ill-prepared for their mission and unclear about their mandate. The Commission made a series of constructive recommendations to the Canadian army and the United Nations to reform the system that governs their peace-keeping mandate.[20] This sent a positive message to the Canadian as well as the world community on the zero tolerance of the Canadian government in accepting the crime of torture.[21]

While Canada should be credited for its leadership towards the establishment of the ICC, it should also be noted that Canada is not free from blemish in addressing the problem of impunity. It was expected that the Canadian government would prevent the participation of the Chilean tall ship Esmeralda at the International Tall Ship Festival in Halifax, on July 21, 2002. This notorious ship visited Quebec City for four days (July 30 to August 2). Esmeralda was stained with the blood of thousands of innocent people when the military junta, under Pinochet, used it as a detention and torture centre following the 1973 coup in Chile.

It is also upsetting that the Canadian government has always approached deportation as a substitute for punishment without considering the possibility that the deportation of perpetrators of torture and other international crimes may lead to their further impunity. The establishment of the War Crimes Unit in 1996 strengthened the Canadian government's tendency towards deportation. In terms of criminal prosecution, thus far only one case has been prosecuted, and that case was lost. The most recent case of the government's pre-occupation with deportation was that of Dejan Demirovic.

Mr. Demirovic is a former member of a Serbian reserve police unit called "The Scorpions." He was indicted in Serbia and Montenegro for his alleged role in a 1999 massacre of ethnic Albanians in Kosovo. He fled to Canada in the summer of 2001 and was arrested in January 2003 on an Interpol warrant but later released on bail. He applied for refugee status.

The government of Canada has chosen to deport Mr. Demirovic instead of considering options such as his prosecution in Canada or his surrender to the International Criminal Tribunal for the former Yugoslavia (ICTY). The war crimes lawyer Leo Adler, who is involved in the case, has shared his frustration about Canada's inaction: "Canada has always been very reluctant – and this goes right back to the end of World War II – it has been very reluctant to get involved in the war crimes process."[22] Mr. Demirovic is still in Canada pending a ruling on his appeal against a deportation order.

The lack of attention given to criminal prosecution is justified by high costs, and by the technical difficulties of obtaining evidence and bringing foreign witnesses to Canada as well as getting permission to enter the offending country to conduct investigations.

Among various anti-impunity measures, due attention should be paid to extradition. On June 17, 1999, Canada's new *Extradition Act* came into force. The Act permitted the surrender of persons sought to states and to entities like the International Criminal Tribunals for the former Yugoslavia and Rwanda.

The *UN Convention Against Torture* could also be used as a basis for extradition. It is positive that the Canadian government is presently cautious in considering the option of extradition. It is crucial for Canada to ensure that the subject of extradition receives a fair trial after extradition. It is a fact that there is rarely any functioning judicial system or viable witness protection program in place in countries that suffer from war or generalized violence. Another problem is the close connection between the judiciary and effective powers in these countries. Politicians as well as police and bureaucratic authorities can assert influence over the outcome of particular investigations or prosecutions. Given these limitations, the best remedy is the prosecution of torturers and other perpetrators of international crimes in Canada.

Amongst NGOs working against impunity in Canada is the Canadian Centre for International Justice (CCIJ). The CCIJ was founded as an independent not-for-profit organization in 2000 by a group of Canadians and some organizations. Its mandate is to ensure that any persons living in Canada accused of committing atrocities abroad such as war crimes are brought to justice, and their victims supported and compensated.

Despite the recognition of universal jurisdiction in the prosecution of torturers, Canada has failed to take effective measures in this respect. There are people who have been tortured in their countries of origin and in the course of time have become permanent residents or citizens of Canada. It is almost impossible for these torture survivors to ask for compensation from the governments responsible for their torture. The case of Dr. Houshang Bouzari is a manifestation of the Canadian failure in this area of struggle against impunity.

Dr. Bouzari experienced horrible tortures in Iran in 1993.[23] He arrived in Canada in 1998 and in the course of time became a Canadian citizen. The Ontario Court of Justice dismissed his lawsuit against the Iranian government in 2002. Rejection of Bouzari's claim was based on a provision in the *State Immunity Act* that has granted immunity to foreign states from the jurisdiction of the Canadian courts. Mr. Bouzari argued at the Ontario Court of Appeal (December 2003) that the *Canadian Charter of Rights and Freedoms* carved out an exception to the *State Immunity Act* for torture. The court refused his argument.

The UN Committee Against Torture has recently criticized Canada for "the absence of effective measures to provide civil compensation to victims of torture in all cases." The Committee has recommended that Canada ensures "the provision of compensation through its civil jurisdiction to all victims of torture."[24] The *State Immunity Act,* according to the Canadian human rights lawyer David Matas, "needs a specific exemption for torture."[25]

Conclusion

ALTHOUGH CANADA HAS made sincere efforts towards the prevention of torture and the rehabilitation of survivors, there is much further work to be done for the achievement of such challenging goals. As a democratic country, Canada needs to create a balance between the global campaign against terrorism and the protection of civil and human rights of Canadian citizens and non-citizens. The implementation of the *Anti-Terrorist Act and Public Safety Act, 2002* and the use of the Security certificate against non-citizens pose serious concerns. There are provisions in these documents that limit fundamental rights, and can lead to the imposition of cruel, inhuman or degrading treatment against non-citizens.

Canada must do more to address the principle of *non-refoulement* to torture. There is a need for reforming Canadian domestic legislations and regulations with regards to refugee determination, detention and removal. Human rights agencies are particularly concerned about prolonged detentions and keeping non-citizens in Immigration limbo indefinitely. Enforcement officials must be accountable and accessible. Canada should come up with more resources for human rights training of all levels of personnel involved in enforcement, interrogation and correctional activities. There is also a need for public education about the scourge of torture, the rights of survivors, and the urgent need for the prevention and eradication of this human plague.

Canada has hardly engaged in pristine measures in the struggle against global terror. Ratification of legislations with restrictions on civil liberties does not, in my opinion, prevent terrorism. In her speech to the Biennial Conference of the International Commission of Jurists in Berlin on August 27, 2004, Ms. Louise Arbour, the former judge of the Supreme Court of Canada and the present UN High Commissioner for Human Rights, made the following remarks:

> "I firmly believe that terrorism must be confronted in a manner that respects human rights law. Insisting on a human rights-based approach and a rule of law approach to countering terrorism is imperative."[26]

While I agree with Madam Justice Arbour, I feel that Canada should go beyond enforcement and legislative measures against terrorism. As a first step, Canada needs long term pro-active measures to address the socio-economic, political, psychological, and cultural roots of present-day terrorism. The second step is an exploration of the peaceful means of pacifying terrorism. It is only by a deep alternative approach to the evil of today's terrorism that Canada can contribute to the global effort towards its prevention and eradication.

The government of Canada must accede to the *Optional Protocol to the Convention Against Torture*. That would be a significant step towards Canadian global leadership in the prevention of torture and organized violence. It is also to be expected that, as one of the initiators of the UN Fund for Torture Victims, Canada will increase its contribution to this world institution for the global rehabilitation of torture survivors. Canada's contribution is minimal today ($60,000) in comparison with other industrialized countries. Canada should also allocate more resources for rehabilitation services at home.

There is also a need for Canada to overcome "practical difficulties" and introduce legislations that would specifically prohibit trade or production of weapons and instruments that are specifically designed to inflict torture. It is distressing that there is no provision in the Canadian *Criminal Code* for such a prohibition.

Finally, Canada should be commended for its refusal to join the war against Iraq and for its international peace-making efforts with the involvement of Canadian forces. Such efforts challenge the atmosphere of global violence that is the source of all kinds of terror, torture, cruelty and atrocities. There is a dilemma showing its ugly face here: Canada is one of the main parties in the international arms trade. Without a satisfactory resolution of this dilemma, Canada cannot meaningfully engage in cooperating with other nations in creating a culture of peace and non-violence at the global level.

Notes

1. For more information, see Ezat Mossallanejed, "Canada and the Global Prevention of Torture," *The First Light,* CCVT, Toronto, Spring 2000.
2. For more information, see UNHCR, *Collection of International Instruments Concerning Refugees,* Geneva 1990, Part Two, Section II, Americas, pp. 207-268.
3. For more information on this important instrument see *Government of Canada, Fifth Annual Report: Canada's Crimes Against Humanity and War Crimes Program, 2001-2002,* Minister of Public Works and Government Services Canada, 2002. I would also recommend *Canada's Crimes Against Humanity and War Crimes Act,* International Legal Resource Centre, 2001.
4. A wide variety of media covered the story for many weeks. See, for instance, the following: *The Toronto Star,* Saturday August 23, 2003, p. 25; *The Markham Economist and Sun,* Thursday August 28, 2003, p. 5; *The Saturday Star,* August 30, 2003, front page; *The Toronto Star,* Wednesday December 10, 2003.
5. I have explained the Suresh case and the intervention of various Canadian NGOs in Ezat Mossallanejed, "The Suresh Case and the Principle of Non-return to Torture," *The First Light,* Summer 2000.
6. Manickavasagam Suresh and the Minister of Citizenship and Immigration the Attorney General of Canada, *Reasons for Judgment,* Docket A-415-99, Date 2000/01/18, p. 23.
7. *Suresh vs. Canada* (Minister of Citizenship and Immigration), January 11, 2002, file No. 27790, section 47.
8. Examples are the 1996 decisions in *Paez v. Sweden* and *Chipana vs. Venezuela.*
9. UN Committee Against Torture, Communication No. 110/1998.
10. See UN Committee Against Torture, *Conclusions and Recommendations of the Committee against Torture: Canada,* CAT/C/XXV/Concl. 4, at para. 6(a).
11. See European Court of Human Rights Case of *Chahal v. the United Kingdom,* 70/1995/576/662, Strasborg,15 November 1996.
12. The Supreme Court of Canada decided in the case of alleged murderers Burns and Rafay that to order their extradition to the US without obtaining assurances that the death penalty would not be imposed would violate the principles of fundamental justice. See *United States v. Burns,* [2001] 1 S.C.R. 283, 2001 SCC 7 (CanLII), Parallel citations: (2001), 195 D.L.R. (4th) 1; [2001] 3 W.W.R. 193; (2001), 151 C.C.C. (3d) 97; (2001), 39 C.R. (5th) 205; (2001), 81 C.R.R. (2d) 1; (2001), 85 B.C.L.R. (3d) 1, Date: 2001-02-15, Docket: 26129.

13. As quoted in Deborah E. Anker, *Law of Asylum in the United States*, Refugee Law Center, 1999, Chapter Seven, "Protection from Return to Torture: International Legal Protections and Domestic Law."
14. Ibid.
15. CANADA'S RESPONSES TO THE LIST OF ISSUES, PRESENTATION OF THE FOURTH AND FIFTH REPORTS, COMMITTEE AGAINST TORTURE, MAY 2005, Canada's response to Question 4 of the Committee, p. 7.
16. CAT/C/CO/34/CAN, Committee Against Torture, 34th session, CONSIDERATION OF REPORTS SUBMITTED BY STATES PARTIES, UNDER ARTICLE 19 OF THE CONVENTION, Conclusions and recommendations of the Committee against Torture, Canada, section 4-c.
17. DPR 2003-2004, Immigration and Refugee Board, p. 23, http://www.tbs-sct.gc.ca/rma/dpr/03-04/IRB-CISR/IRB-CISRd3401_e.asp. Date accessed: July 28, 2005.
18. Canada Border Service Agency National Statistics (2004-2005) at http://www.cbsa-asfc.gc.ca/newsroom/releases/menu-e.html.
19. Footnote No. 16, section C-4 (b).
20. See the *Report of the Somalia Commission of Inquiry* at: http://www.dnd.ca/somalia/somaliae.htm.
21. See United Nations, Committee Against Torture, *Convention Against Torture and Other Cruel, Inhuman or Degrading Treatment or Punishment*, Committee Against Torture (CAT), Dist. General, CAT/C/55/Add.8, 9 January 2004, sections 82, 85, 86, 163, 165.
22. For more information on Demirovic see "Massacre at Podujevo, Kosovo," *CBC News*, March 29, 2004 at: http://www.cbc.ca/news/background/balkans/crimesandcourage.html.
23. For more information about Dr. Bouzari's torture in Iran and his subsequent efforts in Canada, see Houshang Bouzari, "How to Find the Courage to Bring Your Torturers to Justice," *Searching for Justice: Counteracting Hate, Torture, and Crimes Against Humanity*, co-hosted by The World Organization to Investigate the Persecution of Falun Gong and International Coalition Against Torture in Montreal, Saturday, June 19, 2004, pp. 49-51.
24. Footnote No. 16, section C(g) and section D(f).
25. David Matas, "Bringing Kazemi's killers to justice," *National Post*, Thursday, April 28, 2005.
26. Louise Arbour's speech is available at: http://www.unhchr.ch/huricane/huricane.nsf/view01/3485B28EDDA173F0C1256EFD0035373C?opendocument.

10

Limbo as a Technique of Torture

> One Moment in Annihilation's Waste,
> One moment, of the Well of Life to taste –
> The stars are setting, and Caravan
> Starts for the dawn of nothing – Oh, make haste!
> – Edward Fitzgerald, *Rubaiyat of Omar Khayyam*

LIMBO IS A term from the Latin *limbus* meaning hem, edge, margin or border. It is normally used to denote any place or condition of uncertainty, instability or being taken for granted. It is the most tormenting state of human life in which the victims lose themselves and suffer endlessly. In this chapter, an attempt will be made to portray the effects of living in limbo on human life in general, and on the lives of torture victims in particular.

Limbo in Literature

AS A CONCEPT, the condition of being in limbo has been expressed in various literary forms. In Greek mythology, Damocles, courtier of the king Dionysius, the tyrant of Syracuse, had been extremely preoccupied with the luxuries of the king's seemingly carefree existence. One night, amidst a royal banquet, Damocles looked up and realized there was a sharp sword hanging by a thread precariously dangling over his head. The tyrant had planned this well, to show the condition of danger and precariousness attached to the statesman's attempts to maintain his power.[1] The story of the Sword of Damocles illustrates that even a stable life does not offer immunity against future threats. The sword is an apt metaphor depicting the vulnerability and uncertainty that being in limbo represents.

Middle Eastern literature defines limbo as an intermediate abode between hell and heaven where people are desperately waiting for resolution. Such people live in a state of permanent wandering and bear the tremendous agony of oblivion and neglect.[2]

The 15th century Iranian poet Hafiz has illuminated, in an artistic way, an inherent limbo that is common in the lives of mortal human beings:

> "Within life's Caravanserai[3]
> What brief security have I
> When momently the bell doth cry
> Bind on your load the moment is nigh."

The British novelist Daniel Defoe found the state of living in limbo as one of the worst punishments deserved by the devil:

> "Satan, being thus confined to a vagabond, wandering, unsettled, is without any certain abode; for though he has, in consequence of his angelic nature, a kind of empire in the liquid waste or air, yet this is certainly part of his punishment, that he is ... without any fixed place, or space, allowed him to rest the sole of his foot upon."[4]

Limbo is sometimes used to explain the situation of captivity, incarceration, or segregation, and occasionally is taken to illustrate jail or jail conditions.[5]

In addition to classical literature, the torture of limbo is illustrated in hundreds of folkloric myths and stories. The following is a myth I remember from my childhood:

> Once upon a time, a king became so furious with his chancellor that he sought an excuse to kill him. He weighed a lamb and gave it to his chancellor telling him to bring it back after forty days weighing exactly the same. The shrewd chancellor used a tactic of limbo against the poor lamb. He purchased a wolf from a hunter and kept it in a cage in his pasture. He then started grazing the lamb. Within a few days, when the lamb had put on weight, he placed the restrained wolf where the lamb could see it. The threat of being devoured by the wolf made the lamb so terrified that it stopped eating and drinking. The chancellor repeated his experiment of limbo a few times, first letting the lamb graze without threat and then using the wolf. At the end of the forty days the lamb had neither decreased nor increased its weight.

Limbo is a state of contradiction, as depicted above. You are confused, uncertain and unstable about everything. You are unable to evaluate your situation and cannot understand where you stand. Being in limbo, you feel lost about who you are and what will happen to you. Limbo is a place for people who are forgotten and cast aside for an indefinite term. Thus, people in limbo feel totally out of time, out of place and out of themselves.

Limbo as a Religious Punishment

THE PUNISHMENT OF keeping a believer in limbo exists in almost all religions of the world. According to various religious doctrines, limbo is a place or a state succeeding the present life, serving as an ordeal to endure to achieve moral purification. In Catholic theology, purgatory is a place in which souls suffer, because they need purification. Hindus, Sikhs and Jains believe in reincarnation. There is an endless round of being reborn in different manifestations. This cycle of uncertainty in which the soul is trapped continues until the soul can break free and reach the state of perfect peace called *moksha*.

Like Hindus, Buddhists believe that the soul is trapped in an uncertain and unpredictable cycle of life that can go round endlessly like a wheel. It can take millions of years for the soul to reach the stage of *nirvana* – enlightenment.

According to an old Chinese religious doctrine, the soul, after death, travels and goes through the ordeal of uncertainty to make reparation for past misdeeds.[6]

The Old Testament reflects the agony of living in limbo in the story of Jonah. Yahweh punished Jonah for disobeying his commands, by placing him in the darkness of limbo. Jonah set out on a voyage at sea. The sea became tumultuous with a wild storm. His friends cast him overboard. "Now the Lord had prepared a great fish to swallow up Jonah. And Jonah was in the belly of the fish three days and three nights."[7] From the belly of the fish he prayed to Yahweh: "Thou hadst cast me into the deep, in the midst of the seas; and the flood compassed me about ... The water compassed me about even to my soul; the depth closed me round about."[8] When Jonah had almost lost hope within the abyss of limbo, the whale disgorged him.

Dante Alighieri illuminates the Catholic concept of limbo in his *Divine*

Comedy through the biblical image of purgatory. According to Catholic teaching, purgatory (from the Latin, *purgare*, to make clean, to purify) is a place or condition of temporal punishment for those who are not entirely free from forgivable sins, or who have not fully paid for their transgressions. Purgatory, therefore, is designated as an abode between heaven and hell where people live in uncertainty while they undergo purification. St. Augustine comments in his book *City of God* that the less virtuous have to go through the ordeal of purgatory to "pay the last penny." While the nature of suffering in purgatory is uncertain, some churches believe in a purging fire more tormenting than any kind of temporal suffering.[9]

Muslims believe that the soul remains in limbo for thousands of years until the Day of Resurrection (*Ghiamat*). On this doomsday, the angel, Esrafil, blows his whistle bringing the dead back to life. Billions of people appear before Allah, the Ultimate Judge. Another limbo starts at this point that is the most unbearable one of all. Given the number of people to be judged, this Day of Ultimate Judgment will take 50,000 years. The body and soul of each human has to withstand harsh ordeals. The Holy Quran illustrates the condition of this endless day as follows:

> "When the sun ceases to shine ... When the stars fall down and the mountains are blown away ... when the seas are set alight and when the records of men's deeds are laid open ..."[10]

According to traditional belief in Saharan Africa, the body must be buried immediately after death or the soul will wander in perpetual limbo. Thus, according to some African traditional religions, the tribulation of living in limbo is among the most tormenting ordeals in human life and afterlife.

The religious and literary renderings of limbo, as illustrated above, reflect the reality of an alienated humanity across the world and through the course of history. It implies that in all times and in all places, people have suffered in limbo and have aspired to be rid of it. Under tyrannical regimes, torturers have used this bitter experience of human life as a means of making their tortures more effective.

Towers of Forgetfulness

IN ALMOST ALL historical epochs, tyrannical regimes have used their strong castles as state prisons for actual or potential leaders of the opposition. They have kept them in chains with hardly any communication with the outside world. This was a tactic to make the whole world forget about them and vice-versa. Here are some classical examples.

THE CELEBRATED ORIENTAL pantheist and Sufi leader, Hallaj, was locked in a tower of forgetfulness. Hallaj is considered the Middle Eastern champion of social justice and enlightenment. This semi-legendary figure, like the Greek, Prometheus, was a victim of the most severe torture and a hero of superhuman resistance. He suffered a tormenting limbo before his horrible torture in 922 AD. Prior to this, he travelled extensively to India, China and a part of Asia Minor leading an enlightened socio-political movement against the unjust rule and the dogmatic attitudes of the Islamic ruling clique. The powerful emperor of the Islamic world, the Caliph of Baghdad, issued a warrant for his arrest. Hallaj escaped by moving from one place to another, calling on people to struggle against the Caliph and his puppet clergy. He was arrested in 914 AD. His torturers tied him to the gallows for a number of days and then chained and imprisoned him. He withstood unspeakable torture and cruel treatment in jail for eight years during which time the Caliph tried repeatedly to get a verdict of execution against him from the clergy. During this period, servants of the Caliph suppressed his movement and killed his close friends and disciples. They kept him *incommunicado* in the hope that people would forget him. However, the movement, with him as its spiritual leader, continued to gain momentum.

In his desperate attempt to suppress the movement, the Caliph decided to execute Hallaj. He finally assembled the clergy and obtained a religious verdict from them. They attested to Hallaj's blasphemy and passed a death sentence against him. After eight years of suffering in limbo in prison, withstanding torture and awaiting his execution, finally on March 26, 922 AD the Caliph's guards took him to the execution site where they ordered a huge crowd to stone him to death. The next day they burned his body and threw his ashes into the river Tigris.[11]

THE FRENCH MONARCH Charles V built the Bastille as a prison and citadel about 1370 AD. It was used for more than 400 years as a lockup for persons of high rank who had displeased the king and his associates. They were confined with a *Lettre de Cachet* (warrant of arrest), a direct order of the monarch, that the person be held until further notice. These arrests were arbitrary and confined persons of public profile so long that they were entirely forgotten by the public. On July 17, 1789, with only seven prisoners remaining, an armed Parisian mob released all prisoners from limbo and destroyed the tower. The next day, they captured the Bastille. The fall of the Bastille is now celebrated in France as the end of torture and tyranny in that country.

ON APRIL 17, 1534, Sir Thomas More, the English statesman, was imprisoned in the Tower of London. He was charged with betraying the king. The Tower was originally built as a palace and castle and was later turned into a state prison known as the "Bastille of England," "Traitors Gate," and "The Bloody Tower." According to English historian Thomas Babington Macaulay, there was no sadder place on earth than this sordid tower: "Death is there associated with whatever is darkest in human nature and in human destiny."[12] Many state prisoners of high rank were brought through the tower to face a torturous death. Sir Thomas More suffered a nerve-racking limbo "in this close filthy prison … shut up among mice and rats."[11] He languished in this tower of forgetfulness for more than a year until his trial in 1535, and his mounting of the scaffold a few days later, where he was beheaded.

KEEPING PRISONERS IN limbo waiting for extermination, in their notorious towers of forgetfulness, was an infamous method of torture in Nazi Germany:

> "At Treblinka the victims almost always knew that they were to be exterminated, while at Auschwitz we endeavored to fool the victims into thinking that they were to go through a delousing process. Of course, frequently they realized our true intentions and we sometimes had riots and difficulties. Very frequently women would hide their children under their clothes but of course when we found them we would send the children to be exterminated. We were required to carry out these exterminations in secrecy, but of course the foul and nauseating stench from the continuous burning of bodies permeated the entire area and all of the people living in the surrounding communities knew that exterminations were going on in Auschwitz."[13]

TOWERS OF FORGETFULNESS are not limited to the historical cases mentioned above. Today, tyrannical governments across the world keep their political opponents in custody without *habeas corpus* and with no prospect of being tried. In Nigeria, for instance, under the military regime, hundreds of prisoners, political or not, were kept in jail with no trial for years. During the transitional government of General Abubaker, I attended an international conference in Lagos for the protection of survivors of torture, in November, 1998. I met one of these unfortunate prisoners there. He was young when the military government arrested him. Authorities kept him in jail without a trial for seven years and then they sentenced him to twenty-one years of imprisonment. He was released after eighteen years when he was already an old man. Upon his release, our sister organization in Lagos, Prisoners Rehabilitation and Welfare Action (PRAWA) rushed to help him. PRAWA provided him with a carpentry workshop on its premises. He described how his sentencing, even though it was harsh, was a great relief to him because at least he could gear his life towards his known fate. He shared his suffering during the time of being in limbo with me as follows:

> "Every day I moved from one extreme to another – from absolute hope to total despair. Any time a guard called my name, I saw both freedom and death on the horizon. I felt that I did not exist and the whole world had forgotten me. The psychological impact of such a vast margin is horrible."

I have seen many clients at the CCVT in similar situations. They have recounted their suffering in a state of limbo that was used as a technique of torture, before getting their final sentence.

The Limbo of Torture and the Torture of Limbo

THOSE WHO HAVE survived torture know that limbo is both a direct method of torture and its baleful by-product. Torturers throughout the world use different types of limbo to break the morale of their victims in the process of torture and during the time they keep their victims in custody. Let me share some examples based on the experiences of CCVT clients, others and myself.

Limbo During the Act of Torture

LIMBO IS USED as an actual technique of torture by torturers, war criminals and perpetrators of genocide. Some survivors tell stories of being arrested by police or authorities and being blindfolded and brought to detention. Instead of taking them directly to torture, the torturers stop outside the torture chamber where the screams of the person being tortured within can be heard. The torturers tell the victims that this will be their fate so that the victims live in terror waiting for the moment when they are brought to this chamber. The prisoner is made to wait in anguish, remaining in a state of terror, not knowing when the dreaded event will occur. Following is the testimony of Mr. Mahmoud Khavar, an Iranian political prisoner who languished in Islamic Republican jails for years:

> "I saw somebody with a blindfold. They had tied his hands behind him to a steel chair under the burning summer sun with no breeze to reduce the tormenting heat. He was sitting there waiting for his interrogation."[14]

This prolonged waiting is part of the victim's torture. By the time the victimizer arrives to take them to the torture chamber, the prisoner's morale is often broken. This is an intentional method of torture to break the victim's power of resistance.

When I was in jail, there was a saying among fellow-prisoners: "There is no trend. Nothing is a sign of anything." You could never predict what would happen to you next or what plans they would have for you. Sometimes they would unlock your cell, call your name and then disappear. They may order you to get ready and wait for them to return without coming back to you. The use of a blindfold during torture or while moving within the jail is a method of keeping prisoners in a state of total ignorance about what is happening in their surroundings and what will happen to them next. I will never forget when I was in Evin Jail and SAVAK agents kept me blindfolded by a brick wall in front of the torture chamber. I heard the sounds of blows and the screams of victims with the feeling that my turn would come sooner or later. In my subconscious, I preferred to be tortured rather than waiting in the torture of limbo. Torturers sometimes force their victims to witness torture *en masse*. Here is the testimony of a political prisoner:

> "We sat there for five hours with blindfolds on, in front of the wall. If anybody moved a little bit, a guard would beat his head with a stick."[15]

Another form of limbo used as a technique of torture is when the captors severely torture their prisoners and then constantly remind them that this will happen to them again. The prisoner is told this every day but the torturers rarely take them to be tortured again. This is a psychological game that keeps the prisoner living in perpetual fear, and with the agony of not knowing when or if the torture will be repeated.

Let me share a personal recollection. After torturing me for hours, the torturers took me to their office to let me know they were preparing to use another method of torture against me. "We are now preparing to burn your body and send boiling water into your rectum," the chief interrogator said. It was around 2:00 a.m. My soles and legs were bleeding as two soldiers took me underground to the torture cellar to wait in limbo for hours. It was almost dawn when the same soldiers carried me away and locked me in a cell.

There was another type of limbo that continued for a few heartbreaking minutes. When they wanted someone brought to be tortured, they sent a guard inside the public cell. The guard never called the person by name when he entered. Instead, he asked each and everybody's name till he reached the person whom they wanted. From the very first moment the guard entered the cell everybody's heart was thumping, as nobody knew who was going to be taken.

Another particularly base form of limbo used as torture was the punishment of *rations*. "Rations" refer to a set number of beatings or lashes that a prisoner would receive each day. I still remember my cellmate of March 1973 in Evin Jail, Mr. Majid Moini, who had a "ration" of twenty lashes per day. He lived in a painful limbo because he did not know when Mr. Hosseini, a notorious torturer, would next come to inflict his daily ration. It could be first thing in the morning, or when the prisoner was sleeping or eating. The uncertainty of not knowing when the torturer would appear ensured that every second of the day became an agonizing torture for Mr. Moini. One day, he told Mr. Hosseini:

> "Stop your damn ration! If you think I am left with any further information, take me to the dungeon and torture me to death. If there is anything, it will come to the fore."

The torturer laughed, gave him a slap, insulted him and responded: "You will be better off with daily rations. No other torture for the time being."

Under interrogation, you are always in a state of limbo due to your own obsession about your ability to resist. The following is the testimony of a woman survivor of torture that was shared with the author.

"I did not know whether I could stand their horrible tortures. They used all their dreadful techniques against me to get information about my friends. Any attempt to save my body from their torture was tantamount to a shameful spiritual death. What was the use of life if I provided them with information that enabled them to arrest my comrades? Although I was only sixteen, my hair turned white during the process of the torture."

Limbo in Jail

TYRANNICAL REGIMES NORMALLY keep their political prisoners *incommunicado* to give them a feeling that nobody in the world cares for them. Life in prison is like living like a vegetable: you can hardly initiate any change. As a helpless prisoner, life is so monotonous that you welcome any minor event like receiving and eating food. I will never forget my awful loneliness when after a dreadful day and night of torture my torturer opened the cell door and started threatening me. I rejected his threats, but insisted that he stay and continue talking. The torturer, who sensed my loneliness in solitary confinement, shut the iron door with a loud bang and left.

Prison authorities spare no effort in order to make life useless and tedious for their captives. Here is a personal recollection. I was imprisoned in an open jail, called Ghezel Ghaleh, in Tehran, from January to August in 1974. There was a huge weeping willow tree in the jail's compound. It was a source of beauty for everybody. Poets among us were inspired by the tree and composed verses about its glory and charm. The Chief of the Jail, Colonel Vaziri, came to know about it. In the gloomy afternoon of May 28, 1974, he locked all forty prisoners in their cells and ordered some sixteen guards led by a chief sergeant to enter. They cut the tree down with a huge saw and thick wires. "This is not a hotel," he said later. "Each of you should feel that you're a captive."

We were confined in our dark, suffocating cells. There was only a small window that connected us to the outside world. Seeing not more than two colours bored us: dark representing night and bright representing daytime. We sometimes felt that the torturers had left us to ourselves to rot. The Shah's secret police, SAVAK, used this infamous technique against the famous Iranian political prisoner Mr. Yahya Rahimi. They tortured him almost to death without being able to extract any information from him. Then they locked him in solitary confinement in a small cell for thirty-three months while inflicting ongoing torture and degrading treatment. He withstood the ordeal. They had nothing against him. They sent him to a martial court and sentenced him to life imprisonment.[16] It happened frequently that torturers transferred their victims to a new cell and left them there with no information. Was it a simple transfer? Death row? A new torture chamber? The cell for release? One could never guess. They kept you in a state of uncertainty for weeks.

Let me share another personal experience. On a summer day, a guard came to my cell and asked me to get dressed. He blindfolded me and took me to the jail's office. They body-searched me and left me for a long time. Then they blindfolded me again and took me into a vehicle. I was apprehensive that they had arrested someone with new information about me. "Could I stand the torture this time? Who had been arrested? Had they killed anybody? Were they going to kill me?" I had no answer. I prepared myself for the worst. After driving a long time, the driver stopped and a guard took my hand and guided me into another jail. It was a temporary detention centre named "Committee" that was run by the Intelligence, police and gendarmerie. They threw me into a solitary cell with no blanket. The next day I began talking to my neighbour by tapping on the wall using Morse Code:

"Salaam!"

"Salaam!"

"My name is Ezat."

"My name is Fazel."[17]

"I have heard your name in Evin. You were there. Why here?"

"They tortured me here again. They are going to send me to martial court."

"What sentence do you expect?"

"Execution or life imprisonment."

"They transferred me yesterday. I don't know what they are going to do with me."

"Be prepared! They will for sure torture you here."

They left me without attention in my new jail for almost fourteen weeks. One night my interrogator threatened that he would torture me to death the next morning under Apollo.[18] But it did not happen.

There were cases where political prisoners had no information to provide or the torturers failed to obtain necessary information or a confession from them. In such cases, they kept the victim in jail, under the condition of interrogation, with no trial. I suffered in this unstable situation for a year under the Shah of Iran. They kept a fellow inmate, Mr. Mehdi Saamei, an engineer from the Faculty of Polytechnics in Tehran, in a similar condition for three and a half years. We were all worried that they would shoot Mehdi at any time, and so were kept in limbo about his fate.

Another method of torture was giving bad news to victims to add to their uncertainty. It did not matter whether the information was true or false. What the torturers were aiming for was the demoralization and the mental breakdown of their victims. Here is the testimony of a torture survivor in conversation with the author:

> "One day a guard entered my cell. In an unusual way he greeted me and asked me to go with him. He did not use the blindfold. On our way to the interrogators' office, the guard spared no time to comfort me. When I entered the office, the interrogators stood up, shook hands with me and offered me sweets. After a short conversation about the absurdity of human life, they told me that my father was dead. I did not want to cry or show my feeling of extreme sadness, as they took it as a sign of weakness. I thanked them and told them that death was the ultimate destiny in human life. They sent me back to my cell and left me in psychological doubt for many days. I did not know whether the news was true or false. For days and nights I was plagued with doubt. I got some comfort when I decided to accept my father's death and end the limbo of uncertainty. Two years later, when I received my sentence, my father visited me in the central jail."

The condition of political prisons was aggravated in Iran in an unprecedented way under the clerical regime of Ayatollah Khomeini. Limbo penetrated all aspects of the prisoners' lives. Prisoners were left with no sense of security for a single moment. Jail authorities sent spies to identify them. Prisoners were put to death on a regular basis. This is an excerpt from the memoirs of Dr. Ghaffari, who spent years in Islamic Republican jails:

> "At night, the entry of guards into the cells made everybody panicky. Mr. Lajvardi (the jail's president) stared carefully at each and every prisoner. He used to ask one or two questions about the accusations against them and their political activities outside. He then picked some prisoners at random and sent them outside the jail. Guards wrote their names and their dates of birth on their right legs. Nobody ever saw them again. They sent the group to their eternal journeys ... During

these night invasions, Mr. Lajvardi asked some prisoners whether they would agree to participate in the act of execution and shoot the last bullet. He executed people who dared to say no."[19]

Another technique of torture is forcing victims to languish in a grave-like confinement for an unlimited time. Here is the testimony of a gentleman who spent five years in various Iranian jails:

"In Ghezel Hessar jail, the guards and penitents[20] had built a place they called the 'cow-pen' and we, the prisoners, called it 'resurrection.' It was a cell divided into small portions. The width of each portion was the span of a prisoner's shoulder. They put prisoners in this grave-like confinement blindfolded in a sitting position. The victim was absolutely alone without being able to see and without hearing any voice. Guards gave them their meals and vanished immediately. Prisoners were strictly forbidden to take off their blindfolds – even in the middle of the night ..."[21]

The experience of living in the "Grave" had a highly devastating impact on the victims. According to an eyewitness, some of the victims completely stopped talking to other prisoners weeks after being released from their boxes. The following is a testimony:

"It seems that Mahin cannot get rid of the habits she developed in her Grave – the habit of not speaking to others. Sometimes she sits near the wall. I like her. I love to speak with her, but it seems that she does not want anybody to disturb her."[22]

Torturers never keep their victims in a stable condition. Victims cannot predict what will happen to them next. To keep political prisoners alternating between conditions of hope and despair, jail authorities change their situation repeatedly and transfer them to new places from time to time. The psychological impact of uncertainty as such is devastating. Here is an excerpt taken from the testimony of a woman prisoner:

"It was night. They changed my location. From time to time they transferred us in an attempt to prevent us from getting familiar with our surroundings. They moved us all the time from one spot to another. Even in conditions of absolute uncertainty, they did not like us to get used to a plot of land that connected us together."[23]

Transfer to a new place in the jails of the clerical regime of Iran was almost equal to going to the regime's slaughterhouse. The following is an excerpt from the testimony of a political prisoner:

> "They tightened our blindfolds and handcuffs and pushed all of us inside a minibus. It moved towards an unknown destination. From the very first moment I resolved the problem of death for myself. I was sure that this time they would execute me. After some time the minibus stopped and they ordered us to get off. At first I thought it was the shooting site. We came to know later that we were at the headquarters of the Revolutionary Guards. That day they threw everybody in a solitary cell ... After dinner, we overheard the telephone conversation of a guard who was telling his colleague that we had been transferred there to be executed ..." [24]

This is consistent with the testimony of Dr. Ghaffari:

> "A guard appeared in our cell and called the names. He was reading hurriedly. He read fifteen names. I was eighth. 'Pick up your belongings,' he said imperatively. 'Don't forget your blindfolds. We leave the cell in five minutes.' I wondered what my fate would be: firing squad? torture in cell 209? transfer? Twenty-five people were to remain in the cell. I had only five minutes to wrap up and bid farewell to my cellmates. I was either going to my execution which meant that I would never see them again, or if I ever did come back, they may all have been executed. I was filled with panic and couldn't think properly. I suffered a sense of disassociation with my surroundings. After languishing in the jails of the Islamic regime for years I had become accustomed to an unpredictable life. Nobody knew what would happen from moment to moment. The prisoners had no comfort and remained in a constant state of total anguish and uneasiness. I said goodbye to my remaining cellmates and kissed them."[25]

Subjecting victims to physical hazards and leaving them in an unknown and dangerous place for a long time is another sinister technique of torture. The following is the experience of living in a "blood-stained cell" shared by a woman survivor of torture:

> "It was sunset. The warder asked me to follow him. I was overjoyed. I was going to live with other prisoners. I would no longer be blindfolded

twenty-four hours a day. I would start a new life. In the middle of the ward there was a smaller corridor with four cells. The guard opened a cell door and asked me to enter. I took off the blindfold. He shut the door. I was locked in a small cell, 1.5 x 2 meters. Angry at being in solitary confinement, I carefully looked around ... I looked at the walls. I could hardly breathe. I was overpowered by my horror. The walls were stained with blood. At first I thought it was dirt. But, then I saw blood-stained hand prints ... Had they killed somebody here?"[26]

Living with the Feeling of Death

AS A COMPONENT of their tortures, the butchers of tyrannical regimes keep their captives under the permanent threat of death. Prisoners live in the moment. The bloody monster of death spreads its sinister clutches over their gloomy jails all the time. At any moment their torturers can include their names in the doomed group they take out for execution. An Iranian man of letters, Dr. Parviz Owsia, was among the first political prisoners. He was touched by the feeling of death at the dawn of the change of regime in Iran. Here is his testimony:

"The news of each execution demoralized everybody for a couple of days. Everybody, alone or in talking to others, cross-examined himself about the possibility of being killed: 'Do you think that they will kill us?' ... My bed ... was a cradle of unknown death. I did not know whether the person who slept in my place a couple of nights before had already been executed or would be executed tonight or was on death row waiting for the next night. The feeling of not knowing caused me to shiver when I wrapped the blanket around myself. I made a great endeavor to avoid thinking about this in order to get rid of this feeling. Despite the cold weather, removing the blanket from around my body or getting up and walking in my cell was the way I tried to escape sleeping in the same bed with the plague of death. It was as if I felt its infection within my living body.[27]

"You were aware that you had formed a close friendship with somebody who would most probably be executed. But, you did not know how long you must carry this heavy load of probability. This was coexistence with death that had its nest in a living person beside you. Sometimes you imagined the dead of tomorrow moving today. The dimension of survival, in this imagination, drove you from skin and muscles to bone and skeleton and removed the smile from your lips ... Touching death from such a close distance is another dimension of life: metamorphosis of the existence. What strange dimensions human beings possess!" [28]

Following Dr. Owsia's release, it took less than a year for the situation in the jails to become completely barbarous, as the Iranian clerical regime crossed all bounds of human decency and resorted to the massacre of its opponents. Here is the testimony of Dr. Ghaffari and his feeling about death:

"One night I heard a dreadful sound in Evin and the valley surrounding the jail. The sound was repeated in the nights that followed ... At first I thought it was the sound of unloading iron beams to build a new jail. Soon, I learned what that sound was. First there was a horrible sound and then I counted 100, 200, 300 subsequent sounds. These were the sounds of the last bullets to execute prisoners designated for that night. The first sound was that of the machine guns and the next sounds belonged to the last bullets. After, a deadly silence prevailed over the whole jail. Every night, all ten to fifteen thousand prisoners of Evin used to count carefully the sounds of the last bullets in order to know the number of people who had been executed that night." [29]

This situation kept the helpless prisoner in a state of permanent panic. What follows is taken from the memoirs of a woman prisoner:

"A guard called from the loudspeaker for all the inmates of ward number three to go out with their veils and blindfolds. We asked one another, 'Is it our turn? Are they going to kill us right away?' Nobody had an answer." [30]

In his brilliant book, Mr. Mahmoud Khavar has explained that even while enjoying fresh air in his jail's compound he had the feeling of the Sword of Damocles dangling over his head:

"Those days, they took us out for fresh air twice a week, each time for two hours ... The guards, who were mainly criminals and executioners, used to go to the roof with guns in their hands. They gathered political prisoners in a corner and pointed their guns at them. They threatened to shoot and sometimes they touched the trigger. In this way, they turned the venue of fresh air into a torture chamber. We were uncertain whether we would live until the next moment or not. Survival during fresh air was accidental. We had no hope that we would ever go back to our cells. That day, they had installed a huge anti-aircraft machine gun to be used against Iraqi warplanes. They pointed it at us. Had they killed us all nobody would have called them into account, because they had stigmatized us as anti-revolutionaries, American spies and anti-theologians. Once a guard threw a 20 kilogram block of cement on one of our inmates and on another occasion, a guard shot a non-political prisoner. They had made our outdoor fresh air time so torturous that we found our accursed suffocating indoor cells a safe haven."[31]

Mr. Khavar is telling us about his torturers who spared no time in keeping their victims in an uncertain situation on the borderline of survival and death. The following is an excerpt from his recollections:

"After dinner a warder appeared behind the iron bars, called five names, and asked them to be ready for death. It was their turn. Silence prevailed everywhere. Nobody uttered a word, as if everybody was dead. At last the gates opened and all five said good-bye, smiled and left ... Moments later, from the cell's window that opened to the execution site, we heard the voice of the executioner who read the verdict. He began with the name of God to make Him an accomplice to the crime. Then he referred to victims as 'corrupted on the earth and combatants against God and His Prophet.' Then there was a short silence and the sound of bullets from machine guns that pierced the hearts of the lovers of freedom. A few minutes later, they took all the prisoners out to see how heavy the price for freedom was ... The chief warder who had shed the blood of these innocent youth stared at the prisoners and said: 'You have a deadline until tomorrow to confess. Otherwise, you might be executed like them.'"[32]

Mr. Khavar has illustrated further the agony of living in limbo:

"With their cruel and incessant killings, in this clerical hell, there was no distinction between life and death. There was no criterion for executions. We were not certain whether after breathing in we could let it out. We did not know whether God's attorney on earth would let us take in our breath ... There was no basis for their verdicts – even for the clerical apparatus itself. It was possible that they might give you a sentence of three years imprisonment tonight and the next night they would put you before a firing squad."[33]

Finally let me share the experiences of a woman activist who is presently my client at the CCVT:

"I was arrested in March 1981, in Iran. Jail conditions became tense as a result of an armed struggle outside. In my jail, executions used to take place on Monday evenings. They executed political prisoners at random. They did not spare children or even inmates who had already been sentenced to short-term imprisonment. On the nights of executions, we learned the number of those executed from our cell through the reduced numbers of dishes of food already assigned to the cell. We looked at one another's faces to read whose turn had come.

Our torturers kept us intentionally in a state of limbo. On the night of execution, they took us out handcuffed, with a blanket over our heads, to a van. We could not see and did not know where they were taking us. It was a long zigzag drive inside the jail's compound. Their final destination was the execution site. There, they separated one third of the group (normally eight out of twenty-four) for execution, and took the blankets off our heads. They forced us to watch the execution of our friends and jail-mates. You felt the breath of death and heard their last words and helpless cries or screams. You could also hear the sound of bullets and the laughter of the executioners that followed.

They forced us to witness this sinister limbo of death many times. On one of the nights of execution, they called me at 11:00 p.m. At that hour, it could not be for anything else except execution. I felt myself hanging between heaven and earth. I tried to tie my shoes, but I couldn't. My hands could not reach my shoes. I was disassociated with the outside world. They took me out blindfolded and made me wait against a wall for a long time. Death was hanging over my head. At the end, a guard called me and told me that I had passed my examination and he gave me the school report sheet my mother had brought to the prison office. They could have given it to me during the daytime. In an attempt to demoralize me they had deliberately chosen that time and those circumstances.

The psychological impact of limbo as such was awful. Each time they took us out for execution I began to menstruate. I soon lost my hair. I could not normally sleep. On rare occasions, when I got a little sleep, I had nightmares. One night I saw in my dreams that they were executing me. I screamed and wakened all my cellmates. Guards also rushed to our cells.

The limbo of death was not only against prisoners; it was against the prisoners' families as well. I came to know later that following my trial my torturers had called my mother informing her about my execution. My old mother had rushed to the prison asking for my corpse. They had denied the news and had told her that I was alive and living there. They had, however, refused to let her visit me. In the meantime, they transferred me to a jail in the city of Qam. My mother lived in the agony of limbo for fifteen days until she got news about me from the city of Qam.

The worst period of my life was while I was in limbo in jail. This kept my cellmates in limbo as well. They were in limbo with me and because of me. Their best hope was that I would get my sentence so they could heave a sigh of relief. 'Each night,' they told me later, 'when you covered yourself with your white sheet, we imagined you being wrapped in your shroud.'"

Mock Execution

MOCK EXECUTION IS another infamous method of torture. I have heard terrible stories from clients who have experienced this kind of fatal limbo. Mock executions happen in different ways. Sometimes, the torturers prepare their target while they make an attempt to observe precise formalities. Then they transfer the victim to a special cell to wait for upcoming death that may take weeks or months or never happen at all. On other occasions the torturers blindfold their victims, take them to the execution site, call a so-called clergyman to pray for their souls, ask them to prepare their last will and say their last words. Then they tie them to a post and prepare for the shooting. At the last moment, a guard might intervene by saying that the implementation of the sentence was postponed. Sometimes they would shoot in the air. The following is a terrible experience shared with me by a friend, a wonderful Iranian woman who spent six years in jail:

"It happened in Dastgerd Jail, Isfahan, Iran. I was under torture and interrogation there for nine months. One day, guards entered our cell and took me and two other girls out. I was sixteen and they were sixteen and seventeen. They tied us to a huge old tree. It was raining heavily. They left us there for some time without blindfolding us. Our clothes became wet. Water was flowing down our bodies. The guards came back and started whipping us. A senior guard stopped them and protested that they should not waste time and must finish the job immediately. With open eyes we faced our executioners. When I saw them ready to kill us, they looked to me to be the ugliest and most dreadful beasts in the world. My heart was in my mouth and I thought this would be my last breath. The senior guard gave the command for execution. The guards stood in a row and turned their guns toward us: 'One, two, three, shoot!' I felt paralyzed in death. The guards had shot in the air, but my brain did not understand that and for a few seconds I thought I was dead. They laughed and said that it was an exercise for our upcoming execution. Then they took us back to our cell. One of the girls told me that she was thankful for the rain. 'I urinated,' she said."

A client of mine at the CCVT has gone through the agony of mock execution four times. He told me that throughout the period of his interrogation, and even after that, he expected his execution to happen at any time. "Any noise," he told me, "made me jump, and any sound resembled the sound of bullets."

In the Limbo of Death Row

THIS AGONIZING LIMBO relates to the time after political prisoners exhaust all legal remedies and get their final death sentence, until the implementation of the death penalty. This waiting period may take a few days to a few years. During this time, executioners may use different tactics to maximize their victims' fear. In an attempt to demoralize other prisoners, the torturers may choose to keep their targets in public cells among other prisoners. Or, they may lock them in solitary confinement to make each and every minute of their lives miserable.

Let me share my recollections, along with reminiscences of my fellow prisoners, about the upsetting case of Mr. Abbas Jamshidi Roodbari. While he was on death row under the Shah of Iran he belonged to an armed group called the Organization of People's Fedaii Guerillas. The Shah's security forces shot him with a machine gun during a street battle. His comrades escaped and reported him dead to the other guerillas. The next day, the mainstream media reported him killed by security forces. Convinced about his death, his comrades did not change their secret locations and their places of hiding. Mr. Roodbari was half dead when, that same day, the Shah's SAVAK sent him, by special plane, to a hospital in London, England. After several operations they sent him back to Iran. SAVAK agents extracted information from him and arrested most of his comrades. Mr. Roodbari recovered from his wounds, but he was a person who was officially dead. They kept him in a solitary cell in the Committee Jail for a long time. Every day, when bringing his meals or sending him to the toilet, the guards asked him a standard question: "You're dead. Why are you alive? When will you be executed?" There was no answer – only a bitter smile. They kept Mr. Roodbari in this condition for months before they shot him, this time with no formal announcement.

In Qasr prison in Tehran, I witnessed a conversation between two teen-aged political prisoners. The first one had served all but forty days of his term. The other one had got confirmation about his execution in the first court and in his appeal court as well.

"I will be released within forty days."

"I will also be released hopefully within forty days."

"Good! We'll be free together and who knows perhaps we'll have a cup of tea in a tea-shop on our way home."

"Could be. But, for sure not in this world. I was sentenced to execution in the first court and the appeal court confirmed the sentence. I hope they won't keep me more than forty days in this agonizing death row."

I could not remain with them. With tears in my eyes, I left them while thinking about the psychological tension resulting from the state of living in the limbo of imminent death.

One of the most cruel and inhuman conditions of the limbo of death row belongs to pregnant women political prisoners who are sentenced to death. They have to wait until after delivery and sometimes beyond that until they finish nursing their babies. The Iranian writer and ex-political prisoner M. Raha shares a tragic story. The following is an excerpt from her testimony:

> "She had been given the news about the execution of her husband in
> jail. She was in love with her husband and was tolerating her torment-

ing pain by paying a heavy price. One could see the shadow of a deep sadness in her eyes and in her young face. She was sentenced to execution, but they had postponed the implementation of the sentence possibly because of her child ... She preferred to be alone, perhaps because of her concern for others; she did not want to transfer her tensions to them."[34]

To keep their victims in a condition of permanent limbo, some tyrannical governments have invented the sentence of "conditional execution." They sentence their victims to death, but, instead, they keep them in jail for life. A slight change in the behaviour of the prisoner or the policy of the government may persuade prison authorities to implement the sentence. Conditional execution is like a shadow of death haunting the minds of political prisoners at every moment of their lives.

Limbo After Serving the Sentence

UNDER TYRANNICAL REGIMES where there is no rule of law, it happens frequently that authorities keep their opponents in jail for unlimited periods of time after they serve their sentences. On March 2, 1975, for example, the Shah of Iran officially dissolved Iran's four puppet political parties to set up Hezb-e Rastakhiz (National Resurrection Party) as the sole legitimate party in Iran. In his speech for the establishment of this party he mentioned that his opponents had no choice but to either go to jail or leave the country. Following this, the Shah's SAVAK stopped releasing political prisoners who had served their terms. I was one of them. After serving a three-year-term, they transferred me to a new jail. For one year, my family had no news about me whatsoever and we, prisoners in the limbo of release, did not know what would happen to us the next day.

The above episode was repeated after the Shah's downfall, when the new regime was in the early process of establishing itself. The following is the testimony of one of the first political prisoners of the new regime:

> "I heard from several prisoners that the investigator or interrogator had given them the statement of release. They had left the ward and gone up to the outer gate of the jail. But the jail authorities had then returned them to the ward."[35]

This happened later, as well, when the new clerical regime felt itself well established. M. Raha speaks of an old apolitical woman who was called "Mother" by her jail-mates and who was arrested at random. They kept her in limbo in her cell, because she refused to sign a statement of regret:

> "In cells No. 4 and No. 6 there were people who had finished serving their sentences years ago. They were still languishing in jail, because they had not accepted to be interviewed (by media endorsing the regime). The 'Mother' served her sentence. She was called to the office for freedom. They asked her to write a statement of regret and agree to be interviewed. She refused. They asked her what her motive was. 'I am against you,' she told them frankly. Her braveness and frank language surprised the jail authorities. 'But, you have done nothing,' they told her. 'Mother' told them: 'When you arrested me I was indifferent to you, I neither supported nor opposed you. But, when I witnessed the truth in jail, I turned against you.' When 'Mother' told us the story we all laughed. This was precisely the opposite of what she was supposed to tell them. They expected her to say, 'By seeing the truth in jail, I came to know about the legitimacy of the Islamic Republic.' However, because of her forthrightness, 'Mother', like many others, languished in the limbo of jail for years."[36]

This cowardly tactic is symptomatic of the tyrannical government's inherent fear of the grass-roots population. Tyrants do not respect their own rules at times of abnormalities or when they feel all-powerful or completely powerless.

Limbo After Release

THE LIMBO IMPOSED by tyranny during torture and detention extends its far-reaching tentacles to agonize victims even after their release from jail. Let me share my experience about my release from the Shah's custody.

After my release, I went to our neighbouring city of Shiraz, met a relative there and inquired about the survival of other family members. I came to know about my uncle's death. It took me some time to digest it. The next challenge was to let my family know about my release, as they had taken me for dead and the news that I was alive could have been a shock to them. My relative helped by informing them step-by-step though indirect telephone calls. I stayed in Shiraz for one day and the next day I went to my small town, Jahrom. Another period of limbo started after a week or so. I was being shadowed from dawn to dusk. They were controlling all my movements. Were they going to assassinate or re-arrest me? I did not know.

This limbo could drive its victims crazy; make them hypervigilant and hypersensitive with devastating lifelong effects.

Limbo Against Families

TORTURERS EXTEND THEIR sinister limbo to families of their victims. During the Second World War, Joseph Stalin imprisoned wives and children of those who were captured by Nazis as Prisoners of War. They languished in limbo as long as there was no news about their dear ones. Their release was an accursed one, as it meant the death of their beloved husbands or fathers on the war fronts.

I have clients at CCVT who were taken as hostages because of the activities of their husbands. It happens under some tyrannical regimes that the authorities take parents, siblings, wives or children of fugitive political activists, as hostages. They keep them in indefinite limbo (sometimes torture or rape them) in an attempt to force their opponents to surrender themselves. In this way, torturers keep both the activists and their closest relatives in conditions of an agonizing limbo. While the activist is concerned about her/his relatives, those who are taken hostage continue to suffer from the anxiety about the fate of their beloved. Any mistake, or even no mistake, may lead to a perpetual guilty conscience. "I preferred," a client told me, "that they kept me in jail forever than to release me, for that meant that they had either killed or captured my husband."

In cases where the torturer does not dare or choose to physically harm the families of their victims, they keep them in tormenting psychological limbo. They either deny any information to families or provide them with wrong or contradictory feedback. In these circumstances, victims' families swing between two extremes. It has happened in actual practice that after months or years of waiting, the families have either come to know about the execution of their imprisoned loved ones or have got them back unharmed. The most tragic situation was in Iran when the guards approached families of their victims to let them know that they could claim the corpses of their loved ones if they reimbursed them for the bullets they had used for their execution.

There had been cases in Iran in the 1980s where a guard knocked on the door of old parents to let them know about the rape of their daughters before execution. The guards conveyed this ghoulish news in their own savage way. They took a box of chocolates or candy as a wedding gift to parents. The following is an example of what the philistines would tell the bereaved parents:

> His Holiness married your daughter to me before her execution. I performed my religious duty of removing her virginity. You know that the execution of virgins is not sanctioned under the holy rules of Islamic sharia. I have now come to visit you as my parents-in-law.

The military and despotic governments keep families and communities in tragic limbo by kidnapping their young members and making them "disappear." The cases of disappeared children are among the most tragic ones. In the North of Uganda and South of Sudan, for instance, the Lord's Resistance Army (LRA) has kidnapped 6,000 children. In the course of the International Conference on War-affected Children in Winnipeg, in September 2000, I met with Angelina Atyam, a staunch leader of the Concerned Parents of Uganda, whose daughter had been kidnapped from her school. After more than three years of suffering in limbo, she came to know that her daughter was alive in the bush. A warlord had married her and she had a baby out of this forced marriage. Angelina was lobbying with the international community to get her daughter back. "When I get her back, I will take care of her baby and let her continue with her studies," she told me. At the same conference, I had the honour of having lunch with a wonderful grandmother, Estela Barnes de Carlotto, from Argentina. She is a founding member of the grandmothers' association for retrieving kidnapped children called *Associacion Abuelas de la Plaza de Mayo*. She shared her suffering in limbo with me. She was condemned to perpetual limbo by the military regime of Argentina. After more than twenty-one years, she was still waiting for her granddaughter, Laura, to come home one day.

The acute anxiety resulting from the disappearance of one's loved ones never goes away. The following is the observation of the Latin American psychologist Marta L'Hoste about the reflections of an Argentinean mother on the fate of her son:

> "Has he been able to outlive torture? He was never good at suffering physical pain ... If they've tortured him, how have they left him?

Mutilated? Crazy? Perhaps he has been able to escape and he is now wandering from one place to another without knowing ... No, sometimes I would prefer he were dead, instead of suffering the way he must be suffering."[37]

The sudden disappearance of beloved children may drive parents crazy and make them hallucinatory for the rest of their lives. Here are reflections of some mothers with regards to their disappeared children, observed by Marta L'Hoste:

"As I was walking today at the march, I saw J ... It was incredible. I had to come back home to convince myself that he wasn't there," some Mothers say. "I thought I had seen my son, only he was a little slimmer." "I was walking down the street, when I suddenly saw her. She looked a bit crazy, but she looked just like her. When I drew near, she was already gone." "A friend of ours told us he had seen E. accompanied by a man who seemed to be a military man ... everything is a bit weird, I cannot find a thing." "We cannot move from this house, because perhaps ... she may come back and not find us."[38]

The family of the person who has disappeared feels a deep vacuum and a tormenting psychological confusion. Their beloved one is neither dead nor alive. Tyranny has condemned them to a forced absence that could cease at any time or last forever. The secrecy and unforeseeable nature of disappearances keep a vague hope in the heart of family members despite their painful doubts. Here is a mother's reaction:

"If my son had been killed in an accident, or had suffered any illness, I would be able to understand it. But in this way, it is simply something I can't understand. There is always something that makes me keep on waiting."[39]

An Old Iranian proverb describes the anguish of absurd waiting as follows: "Waiting is more painful than the tooth-ache; waiting is more agonizing than the death pang." The thirteenth century Persian romantic poet Nezami Ganjavi spoke about the dreadful pain of limbo when the lover waits desperately for the disappeared beloved to return:

Thine heart is burst asunder
Thou art desperate for her return

> There's no distress beyond thine.
> Though life's full of grievances,
> No pain is above
> The agony of perpetual waiting.
> This may never happen to anyone.
> To wait in doubt empties the heart
> And erodes the soul.[40]

The restlessness of family members, especially mothers, continues even if they find clues about the murder of their disappeared children. Uncertainty appears and reappears on an ongoing basis and leaves them in a state of perpetual uneasiness. Cruelty as such is well illustrated by Baba Taher Oryan, an eleventh century Iranian folkloric poet:

> My heart is wild and wayward
> It shalt no advice learn
> To air and to fire I cast it
> In air it doth not turn
> In fire it doth not burn.[41]

It has happened that the parents of disappeared children have taken care of their books, notes and personal belongings meticulously and have never changed the decoration of their rooms, as if they were still alive. While this has acted as a defense mechanism for parents and other family members, it has also added to their never-ending anxiety for the beloved one to return one day. I will never forget the day when I returned to my family after a year of disappearance. My father returned to me the money and pen he had collected from my colleagues a few months after my arrest.

Finally, it should be noted that disappearances have socio-political repercussions that go beyond individual families. In his *Open Veins of Latin America*, Eduardo Galeano speaks of disappearances as a component of a strategy of state terrorism. It spreads collective intimidation and anxiety and leaves the community with the feeling that nobody is safe. It aggravates uncertainty among the people and serves as a warning. Eduardo Galeano has put it succinctly: "State terrorism aims to paralyze the population with fear."[42]

By widespread use of such techniques of terror as disappearances and limbo against champions of popular movements, tyrannical regimes keep the whole society in a similar state. Limbo, in this sense, means indefinite postponement of a people's call for their civil, political and economic rights.

Political consciousness has sometimes resulted in proactive grass-roots movements from the most vulnerable sections of the victims' families. The mothers' movement for retrieving kidnapped children in Africa is a vivid example. The movements initiated by the mothers and grandmothers in Latin America, especially mothers of the Plaza de Mayo group in Argentina, are still active and act as sources of inspiration for others to follow.

Concluding Remarks

THIS CHAPTER HAS shown that limbo has always been and continues to be one of the most vicious states of human existence. This has prompted torturers throughout history to the present day to use it as one of their most menacing techniques of torture. While the psychological effect of living in limbo is hard on every human being, it is specifically life-threatening for survivors of torture and trauma. As was illustrated in this chapter, almost all survivors of torture have suffered by existing in limbo in some form during their incarcerations. It is up to the community to which they are released to understand this and not place them in a similar situation that can act as a trigger for retraumatization.

A number of survivors of torturous limbo arrive in Canada as asylum seekers or refugees. Do we understand them? Does our refugee determination system treat them humanely? Do Canadian immigration policies and practices recognize the past traumatic experiences they have endured, or do we keep them in a kind of indefinite immigration limbo here? These questions will be dealt with in the next chapter.

Notes

1. The story is related in Cicero's *Tusculanae Disputationes,* Vol. 61.2.
2. See, for example, *Resslat-ol Ghofran* by Abu-l-Ala al-Ma'arri (937-1058 AD), and *Sanaee Ghaznavi, Seir-al Ebad elal Moad* (*The Journey of Believers to the Day of Resurrection*), edited by Said Nafissi, Tehran 1316 (1937).
3. The closest synonym for caravanserai in English is "inn." In olden times, the state or philanthropic people built buildings (usually of stone) in the middle of the wilderness to lodge caravans temporarily (usually for one night). Travellers had to leave the next day, just before dawn, to reach

their destination faster on the one hand, and leave rooms for fellow travellers, on the other. They announced their departure with the sound of a big bell called *jaras*.

4. Daniel Defoe, *The History of the Devil*. As quoted in Salman Rushdie, *The Satanic Verses*, Viking Penguin Group, London, New York 1988, p. 1.
5. See, for example, Milton, *Paradise Lost*, III, 495.
6. For the concept of limbo and heaven in different religions see Anita Ganeri, *Encyclopedia of Heaven*, Element Children's Books, 1999.
7. *Old Testament*, Jonah 1: 17 and 2: 3 and 5.
8. For more information on Purgatory see Martin Jugie, *Purgatory and the Means to Avoid It*, 1949.
9. *The Holy Quran*, Surreh Resurrection (81), Verses 1 to 14.
10. See Ali Mir Fetrous, *Hallaj*, Farhang Publication, France, Germany, USA, 1984.
11. As quoted in *Consolidated Encyclopedia*, Vol. X, Consolidated World Research Society Ltd., London 1946 (under "More, Thomas").
12. Prescott, *Mary Tudor*, p. 327, as quoted in Will Durant, *Story of Civilization, The Reformation*, Simon and Schuster, New York, 1957, p. 527.
13. William L. Shirer, *The Rise and Fall of the Third Reich, a History of Nazi Germany*, Simon and Schuster, New York, 1960, p. 969.
14. Mahmoud Khavar, *Jomhoori Jenayat (The Republic of Crime)*, Summer 1379 (2000), publisher unknown.
15. Dr. Reza Ghaffari, *Khaterat-e Yek Zendani as Zendamhaye Jomhoori Eslami (Recollections of a Prisoner from the Prisons of the Islamic Republic)*, as translated by A. Saman, Arash Publication, Stockholm, March 1998, p. 101.
16. Mr. Rahimi was transferred later to a small jail in the City of Zanjan. Along with his friend and jail-mate Mr. Abbas Samakar, he waged a hunger strike that continued for 86 days. No one has thus far survived such a prolonged hunger strike. A popular movement just before the downfall of the Shah released Yahya. Islamic guards shot him dead in Kurdistan a few months after Khomeini's ascendance to power.
17. Mr. Fazel Masslehati was sentenced to life imprisonment under the Shah of Iran. He was released by the people before the Shah's downfall only to be executed later by the Islamic Republican regime.
18. "Apollo" was a torture machine in SAVAK named after the American spaceship that landed on the moon.
19. Reza Ghaffari, op.cit., p. 93.
20. Penitents (*Tawabs* in Arabic) were a large group of prisoners in Khomeini's jails who had been brainwashed into accepting the official

theology and repenting their sins. Like Capos in Nazi Germany, they were extensively used against other prisoners.

21. D. Alborz, *Az Evin ta Pasila* (*From Evin to Pasila*), *Memoirs of prisoners inside and outside of Iran* (1981-1989), pp. 103-104.
22. Nasrin Parvaz, *Zir-e Booteh-ye Laleh Abbasi* (*Under the Bush of the Marvel of Peru*), Nassim Publication, Sweden, February 2002, pp. 115-116.
23. Shekoufeh Mobini, *An Isolated Window to Life in the Nasser Mohajer, Ketab-e Zendan* (*The Book of Prison*), Vol. 1, USA, 1377 (1998), p. 130.
24. Mahmoud Khavar, op.cit., pp. 170-180.
25. Reza Ghaffari, op.cit., pp. 99-100.
26. Nasrin Parvaz, op.cit., p. 27.
27. A. Paya, *Zendan-e Twohidi*, Baz Tab Publisher, West Germany, Summer 1368 (1989), pp. 295-296.
28. Ibid., p. 296.
29. Reza Ghaffari, op.cit., p. 84.
30. Nasrin Parvaz, op.cit., p. 238.
31. Mahmoud Khavar, op.cit., pp. 36-37.
32. Ibid., pp. 49-51.
33. Ibid., pp. 52-53.
34. M. Raha, *Haghighat Sadeh* (*Simple Truths*), *The Memoirs of Women's Prisons in the Islamic Republic of Iran*, Book II, Hanover, Germany, Winter 1374 (1995), p. 72.
35. A. Paya, op.cit., p.114.
36. M. Raha, op.cit., p.106.
37. Marta L'Hoste, "Disappearance: Psychological Effects on Mothers," in Diana Kordon and others, *Psychological Effects of Political Repression*, sponsored by Rehabilitation Centre of Torture Victims (CRT), Argentina, 1988, p. 126.
38. Ibid., p. 127.
39. Ibid., p. 128.
40. From the "Anguish of Shirin" in Nezami Ganjavi's *Khosrow va Shirin*, translated by the author.
41. From *Quatrains of Baba Taher Oryan* as translated by Heron Allen in 1902.
42. See Eduardo Galeano, "Open Veins of Latin America: Seven Years After," *Monthly Review*, December 1978, p. 32.

11

Limbo in Paradise

Introduction

CANADA IS OFTEN declared to be a paradise on earth. It is reputed internationally to be the best country for refugees and immigrants. In the words of one refugee in immigration limbo:

> "We came to know that Canada had obligated herself to protect refugees by all possible means. On hearing this, my friend danced happily and exclaimed: 'Oh Canada! Beloved Canada! You protect the people who have remained unprotected.'"

This reputation was not earned overnight. Canada has a long history of refugee protection. It also has a painful history of closing its doors to genuine refugees and keeping non-citizens in a condition of limbo. In this chapter, after a glance at the past, I will study different types of limbo produced and reproduced by the Canadian immigration system. Following this, I will attempt to examine the effects of living in limbo upon different categories of non-citizens living under this appalling condition.

I have been working with survivors of torture living in immigration limbo for the last six years. For more than three years, with the help of funding from the Maytree Foundation, I have coordinated a special project at the Canadian Centre for Victims of Torture (CCVT) to help people in limbo. In this chapter, the human tragedies I will share with you are accurately recorded stories of my clients at the CCVT who continue to live in unresolved conditions.

A Glimpse at the Past

THE HISTORY OF Canadian immigration reveals two trends that continue to this day: on one side of the coin, there has been a strong tendency towards protection, based on the Canadian humanitarian and compassionate tradition. On the other side, there has been rejection and expulsion, based on bureaucratic interests, racism and xenophobia, attitudes that exist in Canada and in many other countries as well.[1]

On the positive side, for example, during the American war of independence, Canada extended its protection to a group of British settlers called the United Empire Loyalists. Among these British loyalists, who fled northwards to Canada, there were genuine refugees like the Mennonites, Quakers and other non-conformists who were persecuted by the newly established American regime.

From 1840 to 1860, many Canadians organized an informal humanitarian network for the protection of fugitive slaves escaping from the United States. Some 30,000 blacks arrived in Canada during this time. The Canadian government, unfortunately, failed to provide a safe haven for fugitive slaves and slave hunters kidnapped and returned most of them to their Southern slave owners. Still, individual Canadians played a very positive role by accepting the risks involved in giving them refuge at their safe houses and shelters.

The period of industrialization, from 1896-1914, witnessed the settlement in Western Canada of Doukhobors, Mennonites and Ukrainians escaping from Russian persecution. The Hutterites, a sectarian group like the Mennonites, were forced into frequent migration because of their beliefs. They escaped from Czechoslovakia to Hungary, Romania, Tsarist Russia, the US, and ultimately to Canada. During the course of their mass migration to Canada, they were protected from American persecution and given safe refuge. Indeed, the Canadian government followed an open door policy to all migrants except blacks and Asians. This policy continued up to the Great Depression of the early 1930s.

The booming economy and its subsequent need for labour persuaded Canada to play a receptive role following World War II. The Canadian government assisted with the resettlement of thousands of refugees from Europe and played an active role in the newly established United Nations High Commission for Refugees.

On the negative side, there are recorded cases of the Canadian government's rejection of uprooted people in desperate need of protection. There are also many historical examples documenting that Canada has kept refugees and non-citizens in painful limbo. The construction of the transnational railway chronicles the tale of thousands of migrant workers who were exploited as a pool of cheap labour. They suffered in an indefinite limbo and withstood painful discrimination. Despite government promises, the protection and well-being of these immigrants was sorely neglected, and the implementation of the *Immigration Act* in 1869 kept thousands of people in a state of uncertainty. The majority of Asian workers, especially the Chinese, enjoyed very few rights. They lived in shantytowns with no status and hardly any access to the privileges and rights of their Canadian-born, non-Asian co-workers.

The presence of Asian workers provoked xenophobic sentiments, especially in British Columbia. The province adopted a series of legislations severely restricting the rights of Asians in an effort to discourage their resettlement in Canada. When the railway was completed, the federal government quickly passed the highly discriminatory *Chinese Immigration Act,* in 1885. This group was singled out and subjected to higher taxes, more stringent medical requirements and tighter documentary restrictions than other groups of immigrants. Provisions such as these kept thousands of Chinese in limbo for years.

The racist characteristics of immigration legislation added to the plight of the black and Asian workers. Any person whose race was deemed by cabinet to be "unsuitable" to the climate or requirements of Canada was added to the list of inadmissible elements. This requirement forced many newcomers to live in a state of limbo if they were already within the country and fell under the definition of "unsuitable." The power to exclude on the basis of race remained with the cabinet until 1976. Cabinet was also given broad deportation powers during this time. An immigrant could be deported within two years for reasons such as being unemployed, hospitalized, being an activist in the labour movement, or for committing a criminal offence. The circumstances were so dire for many people of colour wishing to remain in Canada that they had to go underground to avoid deportation, thus living a life of precarious limbo. During this period, the government also raised the head tax for Chinese immigrants.

During World War I, immigrants from countries that Canada and Britain were at war with were labelled "enemy aliens." As the war progressed, the Canadian government was instrumental in provoking public opinion against them and eroding their fundamental human rights. Tragically, over

8,579 internees were detained in nineteen prison camps from coast to coast. Of this number, 3,179 were prisoners of war. The remainder were innocent civilians arrested under the *War Measures Act*. Internees had no legal rights, as they were declared prisoners of war under the Order-in-Council of October 28, 1914. This was one of the darkest episodes in Canadian history. Thousands of "enemy aliens" were imprisoned for indefinite periods of time, not knowing if or when they would be released or whether they would be allowed to remain in Canada. It was not until February 27, 1920, that internees were released from the camps and then deported.[2]

Following the war, immigration policy was again liberalized, but only for agriculturists. The economic downturn of the 1920s brought renewed calls for restrictions to Asian immigration because they were viewed as competition for the low-skilled labour sector. Provincial racist legislation was rampant at this time and the *Chinese Immigration Act* was revised to effectively stop any Chinese immigrants from entering Canada. These exclusionary revisions served to create a terrible indeterminate state for many Chinese in Canada by splitting families in half. Chinese labourers were literally prohibited from having their wives and families join them. Between 1924 and 1930 only three Chinese people were permitted entrance into Canada.

The period of the Great Depression was the most restrictive period in Canadian immigration history. By 1931, immigration to Canada was restricted to British nationals and Americans. Deportation proliferated in this period. Hundreds of immigrants were deported in the 1930s for receiving public assistance, being outspoken labour advocates or simply being unemployed. The threat of deportation drove many immigrants underground to live an uncertain life in a state of perpetual insecurity. By the end of the 1930s, the economic hardships had lessened, but the government still continued its restrictive immigration policies.

Prior to World War II, the Canadian immigration policy was guided by the anti-Semitic stance of Charles Blair, the Director of Immigration. During the gloomy years of the 1930s, when German Jews sought refuge in any country, Canada closed its doors. Countries with fewer resources hosted far more refugees than Canada. During these years, Canada reluctantly admitted only 4,000 Jewish refugees from Germany, compared with 240,000 hosted by the US, 85,000 by Britain, and 25,000 each by China, Argentina, and Brazil.[3] According to Irving Abella, "xenophobia and anti-Semitism permeated Canada during this period, and there was little public support for and much opposition to the admission of refugees."[4]

One particularly tragic episode of limbo for a group of Jewish refugees was the story of the "Voyage of the Damned." In the spring of 1939, 907 Jews escaped Germany on a boat bound for Cuba. Upon reaching Cuba, the Cuban government refused to grant them entry. Appeals were made to several Latin American states and all were denied. Canada also rejected the refugees on the basis that "the country could not take all the refugees in Europe." The boat was forced back to Germany where its passengers faced what they had fled from in the beginning: the horror of Nazi persecution.

Canada continued with its restrictive policy after the war and it was not until 1969 that the country adopted the United Nations' 1951 *Geneva Convention Relating to the Status of Refugees.*

Following the suppression of the 1956 Hungarian uprising against the USSR, under consistent pressure from religious and ethnic groups, the government of Canada accepted 38,000 refugees from Hungary. They were resettled with the help of Canadian voluntary agencies. This positive step was taken, among other initiatives, as part of a Canadian ideological campaign against the USSR.

In the aftermath of the 1968 Soviet invasion of Czechoslovakia, Canada accepted 11,000 refugees from this country. In 1972, a large number of Asian technological experts were resettled in Canada after escaping the tyrannical regime of Idi Amin in Uganda. Around this time, a smaller number of Tibetan refugees were also resettled.

In 1973, a historical test was put before Canada, as a country of protection and resettlement of refugees fleeing torture and execution. Following the September 1973 *coup d'état* in Chile, hundreds of Chilean and other Latin American refugees desperately sought protection from Canada as a "country of immigrants." Canada contributed towards keeping these refugees in orbit by closing its door. According to one writer, "fearing that most of these political refugees were too left wing, and not wishing to alienate either the American or the new Chilean rulers, the Canadian government took only a small number. This is in sharp contrast to Canada's humanitarian behaviour during the Vietnamese 'boat people' crisis."[5]

During the Vietnamese war, US war resisters (the so-called "draft dodgers") refused to serve in the war. They fled to Canada where they resettled.

Canada's *Immigration Act* was revised in 1976 and is still in effect. Under the new Act, for the first time in Canada, the government recognized refugees as a distinct class from immigrants. The Act obligated the Canadian government to protect refugees. The refugee definition of the

UNHCR was generously incorporated into Canadian legislation.

The Canadian public set an example for the international community to follow by sponsoring the Vietnamese, Cambodian, and Laotian "boat people" from 1975 to 1978. The government admitted between 70,000 and 100,000 refugees from these countries who had been sponsored by individual Canadians.

ON APRIL 4, 1985, the Supreme Court of Canada handed down a historical decision that refugee claimants in Canada deserve the same standard of justice under the *Canadian Charter of Rights and Freedoms* as all others in this country. This was a happy ending to the suffering of a group of seven Sikhs from Punjab, India, most of whom shared the surname Singh. They appealed the rejection of their refugee claims to the Immigration Appeal Board who had refused to hear their case, and the Federal Court of Appeal upheld the decision. Having exhausted all legal remedies, the Singhs were faced with deportation without even having had an oral hearing to determine the merit of their case. Finally, the case was brought to the Supreme Court in 1984. The court ruled in favour of the refugees and against the practice of deciding refugee claims on the basis of written transcripts. An oral hearing was granted to all refugee claimants. This ruling, known as the *Singh Decision,* raised the standard of fairness that refugee claimants receive in Canada. It led to the establishment of the Immigration and Refugee Board (IRB), as a quasi-judicial body to determine refugee claims made in Canada.[6] Since then, April 4th is celebrated by refugee and human rights advocates all over Canada as *Refugee Rights Day.*

The *Singh Decision,* along with the commendable Canadian record of sponsoring South Asian refugees, encouraged the United Nations High Commissioner for Refugees to take an unprecedented measure in awarding the Nansen Medal to Canada in 1986. It was the first time that the medal was awarded to an entire nation.

A year after receiving the prestigious medal for refugee protection, Canada played a negative role by refusing to extend its protection to East Indian, Sri Lankan and Latin American refugees. The Canadian government passed restrictive legislations that left many asylum seekers or refugees unprotected or in orbit. The most tragic case was the *Backlog Clearance Program* that will be dealt with in the next section.

This summary of Canada's immigration history reveals the practices of the Canadian government with regard to refugee resettlement. It has been open and protective on some occasions and restrictive and discriminatory at other times. These contradictory trends in Canadian Immigration history illustrate the tendency of Canadian immigration policy to keep people in limbo. Many have suffered in silence as a result of a deep-rooted bureaucratic tendency within the Immigration Department, the government's economic expediency, racism and the xenophobic hysteria from the general public. The combination of these pressures resulted in a climate where immigrants and refugees were dealt with as if they were superfluous, insignificant objects. This grim historical background set the stage for later government policies that eventually led to refugees becoming mere ciphers in increasingly backlogged files, thus perpetuating the situation of limbo for thousands of them and their families.

The Backlog: A Cruel and Inhuman Treatment

THE PASSAGE OF an amendment to the *Immigration Act* (Bill C-55) and the establishment of a new refugee determination system created a backlog of refugees in limbo. This was accentuated by the passage of another amendment to the *Immigration Act* in 1988 (Bill C-86). The question was how to determine refugee claims of people who had come to Canada under the previous Act (Bill C-55). On December 28, 1988, the then Minister of Immigration, Barbara McDougall, announced that the backlog of approximately 85,000 refugee claims (110,000 people) that had accumulated would not be dealt with under either of the two Acts. She rejected the idea of amnesty, and insisted that all refugee claims would be decided under a special project called the *Backlog Clearance Program*. She declared that the backlog would be eliminated on a case-by-case basis. The process was to begin immediately and would not take more than two years to clear all backlogged cases.[7]

After the implementation of Bill C-86 on January 1, 1989, virtually nothing was done for over eight months in terms of clearing the backlog. The regulations for the new program were not published until August 1989, and the program was plagued with other problems such as poorly-trained and inexperienced personnel. Over one-and-a-half years later, only some 20,000 cases had been processed. Besides these difficulties, there were people already living without status up to four years before the implementation of Bill C-86. In many cases, they waited years longer than that in a state of limbo before being cleared from the backlog.

Living in the limbo of the backlog resulted in many human tragedies that were rarely reported by the media, as these victims had hardly any voice in Canadian society. In August 1990, the Inter-Church Committee for Refugees (ICCR) established a project committee with the help of the Canadian Centre for Victims of Torture. The committee began to document the physical, mental and social impact upon 200 refugees living under the uncertainty and insecurity of the backlog. The ICCR presented the results to the UN Human Rights Committee in Geneva in a report named *Civil Rights and Refugee Claimants Backlog*.[8]

The report revealed that fear and distress ruled the lives of these refugees. Symptoms similar to survivors of torture and war were documented: fear, stress, nervousness, insomnia, fatigue, lack of concentration, flashbacks, etc.

The refugees surveyed stated they had experienced the following symptoms, in order of priority:

Concern for family safety (76%)
Extreme tension and nervousness (72%)
Depression (70%)
Spontaneous thoughts about their countries repeatedly occurring during the day (70%)
Irritability and/or angry outbursts (62%)
Loneliness (61%)
Brooding about their problems (59%)
Sleeplessness (55%)
Restlessness (55%)
Inability to concentrate (54%)
Headaches or stomach pain (52%)[9]

It was upsetting to learn that 58% of refugees in the backlog reported that their symptoms, including suicidal thoughts, had exacerbated since coming to Canada. When correlated with the year the claim was made, the following percentages of people experienced suicidal thoughts:

1988 – 19% (2 years in Canada)
1987 – 23% (3 years in Canada)
1986 – 30% (4 years in Canada)
1985 – 63% (5 years and over)[10]

The report concluded: "The refugee claim process for people in the backlog is an anti-therapeutic and retraumatizing experience ... The people the procedure has intended to help have become the victims of it. The human price being paid is too high ... The abuse of these people must stop, they must be allowed to have their families join them, and Canada should give them the right to build new lives."[11]

IN THOSE DAYS I was working as a refugee advocate at the Jesuit Centre for Social Faith and Justice. The refugee program of the Centre (Jesuit Refugee Service-Canada) was involved in helping refugees in the backlog. We suffered along with them and shed bitter tears with them. On one occasion, a pregnant refugee woman who had left her husband behind gave birth to her son in Toronto. Her son was four years old and she was still in the limbo of backlog. She told us about the cruel, inhuman and degrading treatment she received from the Immigration officer who was supposed to be helping her. "I went for an interview with my baby," she said. "He started shouting at me and telling me that all refugees abuse the system. He said that I wanted my baby to get automatic Canadian citizenship and to bring my husband here. For one hour, I was crying and my baby was crying ..."

Here is an excerpt from a long letter sent by a refugee in the backlog to the then Prime Minister of Canada, Mr. Brian Mulroney:

> "Mr. Prime Minister, Canada ... has become a limbo on earth for me and thousands of so-called backlogged refugees. We, the reserve army of backloggers, are nothing else but living-dead. As I could be and at the same time could not be regarded as a refugee, I take your kind permission to refer to myself as a defugee for the sake of convenience. Let Canada take pride in adding a neologism to the treasury of human vocabularies."[12]

The limbo of backlog caused tremendous psychological tension, depression and retraumatization for thousands of refugees, especially those who were survivors of war and torture. I will never forget a gloomy afternoon of the year 1991 when, along with a group of colleagues, I attended the funeral of Jesus Seferino Aguilar, a refugee claimant from El Salvador who could not sustain years of torment in backlog and had ended his life. My colleague, Sudha Coomarasamy, a poet of Sri Lankan origin in Toronto, composed the following poem to the memory of Jesus:

Thousands stretched out their hands,
risked their lives and sought refuge
only to be trapped by immigration laws.
Years ate up hopes and dreams,
unanswered questions gnawed their souls.
But so-called diplomats sail smoothly within days
what the common man struggles through years
yet unsolved and unsettled.
Clogged, logged and put on hold,
their life set at pause or freeze.
Running from nightmares and walking to hearings,
their humanness denied and destroyed,
seeing another year slip by – unlived.
Logged lives come alive to shed tears
for another who has decided to die.
Years of inaction speak into action
decision to die than indefinitely hang.

How much more grief can we bear?
How much more proof need we bear?
What will make you believe or decide,
Our mangled bodies or our tortured souls?
As a last resort I beg you and you,
Am I not eligible for even a chance to live?
Disconnect the immigration backlog – now.[13]

The great tragedy of the backlog was family separation. Quite a few refugees had to leave their spouses and children behind when they fled from their countries of persecution. It should be noted that in Canada a newcomer can apply for family reunification only after getting accepted as a Convention refugee or obtaining permanent residence (landed) status; people trapped in the backlog had no status whatsoever. Hardly any family members abroad were permitted to join parents or spouses who were caught in the backlog system. Thousands of people in Canada and overseas suffered in silence for months that stretched into years with no prospect of seeing their loved ones. During this painful process, children suffered most. The government of Canada ignored repeated demands by refugees and their advocates to give priority to families with children who had been left behind.

"It's like a million years that I haven't seen my daughters," said Miriam Garcia, who had fled to Canada with her husband Carlos in 1987. "I cry a little bit for them every night." The Garcias had left their native Guatemala after three attempts were made on Mr. Garcia's life. They had left behind two daughters, aged 12 and 9, to live with a grandmother. "There was no chance to get them out with us," the father remarked, "We left with no passports. We didn't know what would happen to us. We didn't want to risk our children so we left them with their grandmother."

Like thousands of other refugees, Mrs. Morales was tormented by separation from her 14-year-old daughter, Hilda, who lived alone in the city of Carasulia in El Salvador. "She stays in the house, or goes to live with my sister sometimes," said Mrs. Morales, whose father and two brothers had been killed in the war there. "I cry, I feel sick every day, every day."[14]

Despite a well-knitted nationwide campaign by human and refugee rights activists, such as the Canadian Council for Refugees (CCR) and the Inter-Church Committee for Refugees (ICCR), the onerous backlog dragged on well past the expected two-year completion time. It lasted until March 1994, when Citizenship and Immigration Canada officially cleared the backlog and published its final report on the program.

The Current Immigration Limbo

AFTER THE BACKLOG ordeal was over, it was expected that there would no longer be a great number of refugees living in limbo. Unfortunately, the government's policies and practices attested to the opposite. The implementation of the new amendment to the *Immigration Act* (Bill C-86) simply created new types of limbo. Refugees continued to be forced into a state of limbo in different areas and at various stages of their expected integration into Canadian society.

Not yet satisfied with the tough enforcement provisions of the above legislation, the federal government of Canada made another attempt to draft new and tougher legislation. It is worth mentioning that the *Immigration Act* has been amended 31 times in the past 25 years. The problem has become "so complex that it creates serious problems even for experts and those responsible for its enforcement."[15]

The government's new endeavour began in 1995 and the draft amendment to the *Immigration Act* (Bill C-31) was tabled in the year 2000. This bill failed to become law, due to the early election and the termination of Parliament. After winning the election, the Liberal government resumed its previous attempts and drafted a new amendment (Bill C-11). Unlike its predecessor, Bill C-11 got parliamentary approval and was implemented as the *Immigration and Refugee Protection Act* (IRPA) on June 28, 2002. This, among other initiatives, was a "get tough" measure, in response to the internal and external pressures on the government to step up its interdictory and enforcement measures against both potential and actual refugees.

The new Act is supplemented by an alarming number of regulations that are mostly left to the discretionary power of bureaucrats. Of concern in the current IRPA is the power given to Immigration officers to arbitrarily make decisions such as detaining, refusing entry and removing non-citizens (refugee claimants, Convention refugees and permanent residents). The IRPA is inordinately obsessive about eligibility and admissibility criteria that have become stricter and stricter since September 11, 2001. On "reasonable grounds to believe," a non-elected Immigration officer may deem a non-citizen (regardless of her/his status) inadmissible to Canada if the officer entertains the slightest suspicion about the applicant's affiliation with a violent organization, criminality or lack of identification documents. The current Act has produced additional channels to keep more and more non-citizens in Canadian limbo.

Legal and Bureaucratic Backgrounds

NON-CITIZENS suffer in limbo for a variety of reasons, ranging from gaps in immigration policies and legislation to bureaucracy and personal problems. The following categories outline the main reasons for keeping non-citizens in limbo.

1. Lack of Identification Documents

FOR A LONG time, up to the implementation of the current legislation (June 28, 2002), Section 46.04(8) of the *Immigration Act* affected hundreds of non-citizens. It required Convention refugees to have specific identity documents in order to be granted permanent resident status in Canada. In order to obtain landed status, a non-citizen needed to produce a valid passport, travel document or a "satisfactory identity document." If an Immigration officer did not find an identification document satisfactory, the applicant remained in an indefinite state of limbo. Immigration officers were inflexible when enforcing this principle, with little consideration for the exceptional circumstances of refugees who had fled their countries without documents.

This requirement presented an insurmountable barrier specifically for refugees, most of whom left their countries in a great hurry to save their lives. Some of them came from countries with no government to produce identification documents. It was estimated that by the fall of 1998 there were 13,000 refugees living in limbo in Canada because they were unable to produce documents that the Immigration Department considered satisfactory. This number has increased today.

The purpose of the identity document requirement was supposedly to prevent war criminals and people with criminal backgrounds from obtaining permanent resident status in Canada. In practical terms, however, as put by a community leader, it "victimized the victims of war criminals."[16] The requirement of identity documentation also trapped many refugees in a vicious circle: "The authorities' insistence that the refugees present documentation may have the undesirable effect of encouraging those not yet 'landed' to resort to fraudulent papers in order to respond to this requirement."[17] Using false identity documents is common (and most of the time unavoidable) practice for refugees who come from countries which do not issue identity documents due to civil unrest, war, or lack of a central government.

Refugees from certain countries are particularly hard hit by the identity document policy. For all refugees from Somalia (with no government), and many from Afghanistan, Iran and Sri Lanka, it is almost impossible to obtain the necessary documents from the governments that persecuted them.

For years, the Somali community in Canada has been in the forefront of a campaign to remove this main cause of keeping refugees in limbo. In the late 1990s the Somalis began collaborating with the Immigration Department to find a solution to the identity documentation problem. The Somali community called upon the federal government to accept sworn affidavits in lieu of official identity documents, but Ottawa was slow to respond and eventually rejected the proposal. In January of 1997, however, the Department of Immigration implemented the *Undocumented Convention Refugee in Canada Class* (UCRCC) regulation, which stipulated that Convention refugees without identity documents could apply for landed status after waiting a period of five years. The creation of this special class of refugees tended to raise serious issues of discrimination, when compared with the treatment of other refugees in Canada who were granted permanent resident status within a reasonable amount of time.

The five-year waiting period was viewed as unfair and arbitrary to the communities involved. Indeed, the long-term negative impacts of this requirement were devastating to many refugees and their families. "Subjecting the very people who already have experienced horrific abuse and persecution in their country of origin to further discrimination and emotional pain is unfair and cruel."[18] Five years of waiting for permanent resident status also meant prolonged delays of family reunification, lack of access to post-secondary school, and lack of employment opportunities, along with various mental health problems such as "depression, suicidal tendencies, family breakdowns and lack of self-esteem"[19] especially for survivors of torture.

In the winter of 1999, at the biannual conference of the Canadian Council for Refugees, the then Minister of Citizenship and Immigration, Ms. Elinor Caplan, announced that she had reduced the waiting period for the *Undocumented Convention Refugee in Canada Class* from five years, after being determined to be a Convention refugee, to three years.

The latest developments in the identity document saga occurred in December 2000, when an agreement (an out-of-court compromise) was reached between the Somali community and the Department of Citizenship and Immigration Canada. The agreement allowed the *Undocumented Convention Refugee* to provide two sworn-in affidavits attesting to their identity. Although there was no time frame for the processing of landing applications under this agreement, CIC was "obligated to process as expeditiously as possible in all circumstances."[20] The implementation of the new *Immigration and Refugee Protection Act* on June 28, 2002, with its tough identity requirements, did not allow time for this shaky agreement to prove its effectiveness. The obsessive suspicion of Immigration bureaucrats against refugees after the terrorist attack on The World Trade Center in New York on September 11, 2001 hardly left any room for testing the effectiveness of sworn-in affidavits as proof of identity.

The new *Immigration and Refugee Protection Act* has obligated the refugee determination body (the Refugee Protection Division of the Immigration and Refugee Board) to consider whether a refugee claimant possesses an "acceptable" identification document. This is a requirement with respect to the credibility of a claimant. Lack of an identity document at the port of entry has frequently resulted in the detention of refugee claimants without providing them an opportunity to make their claims. Besides this, refugee claimants have only 28 days to register their *Personal Information Forms*, otherwise their claims are considered abandoned. Strict identification requirements have produced a new category of people in limbo under the new legislation, and many of them have spent months under Immigration detention.

2. Security Concerns

UNDER THE CURRENT *Immigration Act*, a Convention refugee could be determined to be inadmissible to Canada due to security concerns regardless of the number of years s/he has lived in Canada. The *Immigration Act* outlines several classes of people who are deemed inadmissible to Canada, one of which includes those affiliated with a suspicious terrorist organization, and this is the most common category encountered.

Subparagraph 34(1) of the *Immigration and Refugee Protection Act* specifically states that a "permanent resident or a foreign national" is inadmissible on security grounds for "being a member of an organization that there are reasonable grounds to believe engages, has engaged or will engage in acts of terrorism."

The problem with this subsection of the *Immigration Act* is that it is highly discretionary. An Immigration officer could target any organization as one involved in terrorism. This makes a Convention refugee or permanent resident of Canada, having even loose or alleged affiliation with such an organization, a risk to the national security and therefore inadmissible to Canada. Inadmissibility as such cannot result in removal, due to situations involving the refugees' countries of origin. Many of them have come from countries ravaged by war or generalized violence. To this, one can add technical problems such as incomplete identification or lack of travel documents.

The end result is either letting the "subject" mercilessly languish in Immigration detention or suffer at large in an indeterminate state. Freedom from detention is only a little better than being confined. Most of the members of this inadmissible class, who are bailed out, have to report to police every month – another source of humiliation! In some cases when suspicion is not backed by adequate documentation to prove affiliation, these people are kept in a state of uncertainty for many years.

It is unfortunate that there is no transparency in this process. Nobody knows on what basis an organization is designated by the CIC as terrorist. It seems that Citizenship and Immigration Canada along with the Canadian Security Intelligence Service (CSIS) have prepared a list of terrorist organizations in the world. Some believe that, justified as inter-governmental collaborations, there is a level of American influence in this area. According to a client of mine, who was interviewed by CSIS, the list is open-ended. A peaceful organization today may be included as a violent one the next. The tragedy is that CSIS or CIC officials usually lack authentic information; furthermore, they are clearly incompetent to make important decisions based upon such information. I have a client who has been suffering in limbo for the last ten years. When he was a teenager, he distributed pamphlets prepared by an organization that was involved in violent activities 35 years ago. His activities were sporadic and the organization had abandoned violence at the time of his casual affiliation. Since then the organization has gone through so many splits that it no longer exists. My unfortunate client has to languish in permanent limbo due to his one-time casual sympathy for a now non-existent group.

It is also not clear what level of affiliation is needed to mark a person inadmissible. In its actual practice the CIC does not make any distinction between a full, active member of a violent organization and a casual, unconnected supporter. Both groups are inadmissible to Canada. During the last six years of working with non-citizens in limbo, I have not known anybody with even the slightest level of involvement with a so-called violent organization to be exempted from inadmissibility provisions.

Before processing Convention refugee applications for landing, Immigration officers go through their refugee narratives. If by sheer chance, a refugee has mentioned the name of a militant organization, s/he would be called for an interview by CSIS. No counsel can help the interviewee. There are poor interpretation services and my clients who have been interviewed told me that security interviews were highly bureaucratic. They are like summary trials where no one is considered a truthful person. It's like, I was told, putting a rubber stamp on the inadmissibility decision already made about the person. It acts as a justification for posing a helpless refugee as a *persona non grata*. It has happened that such interviews have led to the retraumatization of a victim of torture and war.

Interviewing officials usually ask the refugee not to make any attempt to contact CIC after the interview. It has taken up to 4 years for CSIS/CIC to call the person for the second interview. There is no accountability mechanism and nobody is accessible. There are hardly any answers to the letters of support for landing applicants by refugee and human rights groups. Intervention by the person's Member of Parliament, while useful in other cases, is useless in this area. Many MP's refuse to intervene at all. Careful not to disturb the relationship with the government, intergovernmental agencies like UNHCR hardly make any effective intervention.

It should be mentioned that although CIC uses the services of CSIS for security checks, the final decision for landing a non-citizen belongs to CIC. There is no doubt that chronic indecision by CIC/CSIS is a sign of weakness. An efficient organization – especially an intelligence agency – should be capable of investigating the security situations of people and making a decision within a reasonable period of time. It seems that unfounded fear is behind the prolonged indecision of CIC/CSIS.

At face value there are legal and bureaucratic remedies for people in limbo: 1) Making submissions to the Federal Court of Canada, and if the court rules, forcing the CIC to make a speedy decision. This option, named mandamus, is risky. I have frequently advised my clients against it, as there is no guarantee that CIC will make a positive decision about the client's landing application. 2) Applying for ministerial relief. I have witnessed an applicant, after suffering in limbo for many years, experience her/his third or fourth security interview, only to be encouraged by the Immigration Officer to apply for ministerial relief.

Pursuant to subparagraph 34(2) of the IRPC, if the Minister of Citizenship and Immigration decides that a person is a potential security risk to the national interest of Canada, her/his application for permanent residence will be refused. If, on the contrary, the Minister decides that granting permanent residence to Canada would not be detrimental to the national interests of Canada, the processing of the person's application will be resumed.

I have seen clients in security limbo being advised by Immigration officers to have their cases reviewed by the Minister. I have helped them to complete their submission for Ministerial Relief. They have played the rules of the game by signing, dating and returning the *Affirmation* sent to them by a senior Immigration official within 60 days of the date of the letter. They have supported their submissions with positive documentary evidence relevant to the review of their cases. It is upsetting that up to now I have not seen a single case of my clients in limbo being granted *Ministerial Relief*. In a rare opportunity when I wrote letters of follow-up to the interviewing CIC officer, she called me and advised me to encourage my client to remain calm and patient. She said that all submissions and their supplementary documents would be read personally by the Minister, but her extremely busy schedule would not allow her to do that for several months.

In addition to the specific cases of keeping non-citizens in an intermediate state, there is another type of security limbo. According to the *Immigration Act*, all non-citizens must undergo a background security check before being granted permanent residence in Canada. The background check is conducted by the Immigration Department with the help of the Royal Canadian Mounted Police (RCMP) and the Canadian Security Intelligence Service (CSIS). These security checks are, for the most part, routine, unobtrusive and do not cause any unusual delays. However, in some cases, particularly with refugees from certain regions such as Turkey (mainly Kurdish refugees) and Iran, security checks can take much longer. "Little official information is available on the reasons for these delays, though refugee advocates are investigating the alleged links between Canada's foreign policy (e.g. trade, strategic and diplomatic interests) and the use of extended security checks to discourage and delay landing of dissidents from current or potential allies."[21] Whatever the reason for these delays, a number of refugees have suffered and continue to suffer in prolonged limbo while the security checks drag on.

If non-citizens are found to be inadmissible due to security concerns, their dependants included on their application will also be declared inadmissible. Similarly, applicants who are admissible but have dependants on their application who are considered inadmissible would not be processed for landing unless and until they separate their applications from family members with security problems. It is only after a prolonged period of waiting that the CIC officials offer this option to the affected non-citizens.

3. Bill C-44 and Criminality

ON JUNE 15, 1995, Bill C-44 passed and received Royal Assent. The Bill amended the *Immigration Act* in a number of ways:
- It prohibited those convicted of serious crimes (considered to be a danger to the public and punishable by a maximum term of imprisonment of 10 years or more) from claiming refugee status;
- It cancelled the right of appeal to the Immigration Appeal Division

by non-permanent residents certified by the Minister of Citizenship and Immigration and the Solicitor General to be a security risk;
- It forbade admission to Canada of anyone who had two summary convictions for non-serious crimes, regardless of whether both occurred in Canada or elsewhere;
- It prohibited any new immigration inquiries for people who had been ordered to leave Canada;
- For permanent residents under a removal order, it stripped them of their permanent residency.

This piece of legislation was utilized by Immigration bureaucrats as a vehicle to take away independent judicial guarantees for Convention refugees and landed immigrants suspected of criminality. It placed incredible discretionary powers in the hands of immigration and visa officers to pose non-citizens as a danger to the public. Bill C-44 acted as a foundation for still tougher provisions in the *Immigration and Refugee Protection Act*.

Section 36(1) of the Act makes both "foreign national" and permanent residents of Canada inadmissible to this country if they have committed a crime inside or outside of Canada that is punishable by ten years of imprisonment according to Canadian law. We have had people spending several weeks in jails for using a forged passport to travel to Canada. The sole purpose was to join their families. This was considered a serious crime punishable by ten years of imprisonment in Canada. The Immigration department denied the family sponsorship and kept the family members on both sides in indefinite limbo. Section 36(2) of the *Immigration Act* considers any Convention refugee or permanent resident of Canada a danger to the public if s/he has two cases of repeated criminal convictions.

Since the implication of the new Act, Immigration bureaucrats have been quick in their arbitrary decisions to issue "danger to public" certificates to Convention refugees, permanent residents and other categories of non-citizens for offences like drinking and driving, domestic disputes and shoplifting. The discriminatory nature of the criminality provisions of IRPA could be judged by the fact that 5 percent of adult Canadians have had similar sorts of criminal records.

Given the difficulties involved in removing Convention refugees and permanent residents, the criminality provision of IRPA has resulted in keeping hundreds of non-citizens in limbo.

4. Family Separation

IN CANADA, REUNIFICATION of non-citizens with their spouses and children is tied to permanent residence status. Non-citizens who have not been landed cannot bring their families to Canada.

Refugees are permitted to sponsor their immediate family members as soon as they get their Convention status. Refugees' applications in Canada and those of their families overseas are processed simultaneously. Any kind of delay either in Canada or in the country of residence of the spouse/family will postpone landing for both parties of the separated family. A structural problem results from the fact that in some countries there is no Canadian embassy or visa post. In the whole African Continent, for instance, there are four visa posts, and sponsorship applications in many Middle Eastern Countries are processed by the Canadian Visa Post in Damascus, Syria.

Delays in the family reunification process could have serious consequences. These precarious situations cause an elevated level of anxiety for those in limbo awaiting family reunification. More on this later.

5. Processing and Right of Landing Fees

IN 1994, THE federal government implemented a processing fee of $500 per adult and $100 per child on inland refugees seeking permanent residence. This is now increased to $550 and $150 respectively. In 1995, the government imposed an additional right-of-landing fee of $975 per adult – applicable to all categories of non-citizens applying for permanent residence. The effect of these fees was a prolonged landing process for impoverished Convention refugees. This prolonged period a refugee might have to wait while raising the required money also meant longer delays in their landing and family reunification process.

There was, however, a loan program established by the federal government to assist those refugees who could not afford the excessive fees. But the program was problematic in that it required that borrowers prove their ability to repay the loan. Across the country, refugee advocates waged a consistent campaign against right-of-landing fees, calling it "the head tax." This forced the Minister of Citizenship and Immigration, Ms. Elinor Caplan, to waive the right-of-landing fee for Convention refugees applying for permanent residence status in Canada. The non-refundable processing fee ($550) remained for all landing applicants in Canada, including Convention refugees. Such financial requirements are responsible for keeping hundreds of non-citizens in limbo.

One other major obstacle facing Convention refugees is that they must apply for landed status within a six-month period after being accepted by the Immigration and Refugee Board. Many Convention refugees cannot afford the $550 processing fees for themselves and their family members within this time period, so they are relegated to an uncertain life of limbo.

6. Other Bureaucratic Reasons

IT HAS HAPPENED that Immigration has left a person or his or her whole family in a state of uncertainty for unknown reasons. If bureaucrats lose the applicant's file, they never admit to their mistakes and instead take no action and leave the person in orbit. I have dealt with the cases of survivors of torture who have reported the change of their addresses to an Immigration Centre, but the officers have not registered the change properly. After a year or so they received a letter informing them that their landing application was considered abandoned. This was the source of further delays in the processing of their applications.

As was mentioned before, all landing applicants must go through medical examinations and background checks. Both of these expire within twelve months. It has happened frequently that the Immigration Department has failed to complete the landing process one year after the medical examinations or background checks have occurred. It has kept the landing applicants in limbo by requiring applicants to start from scratch.

In the previous *Immigration Act* there was a provision for medical inadmissibility of family members if they imposed excessive medical expenses on Canada. Although this provision is waived under the new act, it takes a long time, sometimes three to four years, for visa officers to issue visas for those family members with serious medical problems. They send them repeatedly for various types of medical examinations without taking any positive action.

All landing applicants, including Convention refugees, who have spent more than six months in a country other than their countries of origin must produce a police clearance certificate from that country. This cumbersome landing requirement has kept many refugees in limbo, as it is not easy to obtain police certificates from the xenophobic police of their first or second countries of asylum.

Non-citizens in Limbo

1. Rejected Refugee Claimants

SURVIVORS OF TORTURE, who come to Canada as asylum seekers, mostly suffer from retraumatization upon arrival. Refugee claimants, in general, face culture shock and are often overwhelmed, unaware and misinformed about the refugee determination process. One of the first sources of misinformation is from "smugglers" who help refugee claimants come to Canada. They give them wrong advice that could affect their claims negatively. I have heard from my leftist clients that the smugglers had told them not to mention their Marxist activities in "a capitalist society like Canada." As a result they never told the Immigration and Refugee Board about their persecution due to their membership in a peaceful communist organization. They never submitted the valid documents and written evidence that could support their claims. The result was their rejection as a protected person in Canada. Another client of mine was told by her lawyer's interpreter to claim that she was a lesbian, even though she was not. It was an attempt by the interpreter to strengthen her claim.

Another source of problems is incompetent lawyers who do not spend adequate time with their clients to reflect the full account of their persecution at home. I had a client who saw his lawyer only at his refugee hearing. Although incompetent lawyers are uncommon in the refugee field, the bad ones create serious problems for genuine refugees and survivors of torture. Adding to this problem is the inadequate amount of money Legal Aid pays the lawyers. Lawyers do not receive adequate compensation for the time that they spend with their clients. We cannot expect all lawyers to do a part of their work on a *pro bono* basis. In some Canadian provinces there is no legal aid whatsoever for refugee claimants. Based on my experience working with refugees for the last eighteen years, bad lawyers and interpreters have been responsible for most of the rejections. Of those who do come forward to make refugee claims, almost 50 percent are denied status. Rejection happens when the refugee hearing panel members feel that the person would not face persecution on the basis of the story s/he has shared. It could also happen because the decision-maker does not believe the story.

Of those refugees who have their claims denied, many choose not to return to their home countries for fear of reliving the trauma they have already experienced. For some of these refugees, it is not a choice to remain underground in Canada but a necessity in order to avoid imprisonment, torture, rape or death, which awaits them in their countries of origin. Unfortunately, under the present immigration system, there is no effective opportunity to appeal a denied refugee claim. The new *Immigration and Refugee Protection Act* has made a provision for an internal appeal to the rejected refugee claims by a body called Refugee Appeal Division (RAD). This provision was never implemented due to an alleged lack of money and human resources.

Following the implementation of the Act, the Minister of Citizenship and Immigration, Mr. Dennis Coderre, during his speech at the Canadian Council for Refugees, promised that the appeal division of the Immigration and Refugee Board would be established within one year. We are far beyond the one-year promise and there is no sign of a RAD. Instead there are talks about the cancellation of that provision of immigration legislation. In the absence of any meaningful appeal, rejected refugee claimants face deportation orders. When the threat of deportation looms, many refugees have little choice but to live underground in Canada. They remain in an uncertain state of limbo with no rights or protection in "paradise."

Rejected refugee claimants who are living underground face various obstacles. They are not permitted to work and have a very difficult time accessing services like healthcare, social assistance, education, and work permits. Under the previous *Immigration Act* a rejected refugee claimant could leave Canada, come back after 90 days and make a new claim. Asylum seekers who had come from the United States could go there and succeed in their new claim by providing new evidence. This provision is eliminated under the new legislation. An asylum seeker can make a refugee claim in Canada only once in her/his lifetime. This has added to their fear and pushed them more deeply underground.

2. Convention Refugees

THE TERM "Convention refugee" refers to asylum seekers who are accepted by the Refugee Determination Division of the IRB as a protected person under the *UN Refugee Convention* of 1951 or *Convention Against Torture*. This category of protected people is only a shade better than refugee claimants. Under normal conditions they can stay in Canada and be protected against return to their countries of origin, but they do not enjoy many rights in Canadian society until they get permanent residence (landed) status. As was mentioned earlier, they can never obtain landed status if they have "improper" identification documents or if they are suspected of being a danger to the public or a risk to national security. Convention refugees from certain countries remain subject to deportation until they get their permanent residence status. I have helped Convention refugees from Tibet whose files were referred to the Enforcement Centre right after their acceptance rather than being sent to the local Canadian Immigration Centre for normal processing. When I asked a senior Immigration officer for the reason she simply answered, "This is a long-standing policy."

Removing a Convention refugee from Canada is not easy. It is contrary to Article 33 of the *Geneva Convention relating to the Status of Refugees*. Canada is a party to it. This article allows removal of Convention refugees under exceptional national security situations. If the protected person is at risk of being returned to torture s/he has the absolute and non-derogable right of *non-refoulement* (Article 3 of the *Convention Against Torture*).

The above guarantees are mostly sacrificed by Citizenship and Immigration Canada upon the altar of the sacred enforcement centres. Despite the provision for *Pre-Removal Risk Assessment* (PRRA) in the new legislation, Immigration bureaucrats hardly look at the balance between the problems posed by refugees to the Canadian public on the one hand and their risk of return on the other. At best, they keep them in limbo and at worst, they throw them into their detention centres to buy time for the full preparation for their removal.

3. Landed Immigrants

I HAVE HAD clients who were stripped of their permanent residence status to be deported from Canada. The removal process takes a long time, as the case must go before the Appeal Division of the Immigration and Refugee Board. The decision made by this quasi-judicial body could also be appealed to the Federal Court of Canada on the point of law (not the merit of the case). When the person is deemed ready for removal s/he could apply for *Pre-Removal Risk Assessment*. All these keep the person in an uncertain condition for a long period of time.

4. H&C Applicants

ACCORDING TO SUBSECTION 9(1) of the *Immigration Act* all landing applicants in Canada should proceed with their application from a visa post outside the country. However, there is an exception to this provision. According to Subsection 114(2) of the *Immigration Act*, Citizenship and Immigration Canada can exempt a person from the requirement of Subsection 9(1) if s/he: 1) faces unexpected hardship upon his/her return; or 2) have developed deep-rooted bonds and have fully established themselves in Canadian society. This recourse is termed "Humanitarian and Compassionate" application or simply H&C review of the file. Some consider this as the only option left to a rejected refugee claimant. Despite its hope-raising appearance, the H&C process is not an effective solution. First of all it does not prevent removal and keeps the applicant in alternating conditions of hope and despair. Secondly, the applicant needs to pay an initial $550 processing fee and then another $975 if they are accepted. Thirdly, s/he needs to have a professional job, good savings, high education and a proper account with Revenue Canada to cherish the hope of acceptance. Fourthly, if accepted under H&C, the applicant has to fulfill all immigration requirements (ID, medical and security check). I have observed H&C applicants suffering in agonizing limbo due either to the indecision of Immigration H&C officers or their inability to fulfill H&C requirements, which in some cases are stricter than normal immigration requirements.

5. People with *Minister's Permit*

UNDER THE *Immigration Act*, the Minister of Citizenship and Immigration is mandated to bring people who need immediate protection to Canada under a special *Minister's Permit*. This is a good provision in cases of refugees and survivors of torture whose lives are in great danger. This could also help accelerate family reunification when a part of a family, in Canada or overseas, could face risk. Unfortunately, this provision is of little help when it comes to its practical implementation.

First of all, the Minister rarely exercises his right to use this protective apparatus. I have witnessed repeated attempts by the Jesuit Refugee Service-Canada, the Inter-Church Committee for Refugees, and the Canadian Centre for Victims of Torture in this direction. They all tried in vain to persuade the

Minister to issue *Minister's Permits* to spouses of refugees overseas to come to Canada and begin her/his landing process here.

Secondly, people who come to Canada under a *Minister's Permit* have no status. They have to extend their permits every year. Failure to do that would lead to the cancellation of their permits. They do not enjoy the protection that Convention refugees do. They are deprived of the rights and privileges of landed immigrants.

Thirdly, people with a *Minister's Permit* have to stay in Canada for five years to be eligible to apply for landing. If their normal landing process takes two years, they have to remain in limbo for 7 years until they can enjoy landed status in this society. In my lifetime, thus far, I have only met one person who was brought to Canada with a *Minister's Permit*. He was an Iraqi businessman whom I met in 1992. He was living between hope and fear in an unnecessary limbo for years.

6. Stateless People

I HAVE SEEN stateless survivors of torture whose cases are symptomatic of the tragic stories of stateless people in Canada. I admit that there are millions of worse tragedies that occur in a global environment that remains a breeding ground for the creation of stateless peoples.

Crucial to the understanding of statelessness is the concept of citizenship. Essentially, citizenship is official membership in a particular state. Such membership consequently entitles an individual to certain rights. In fact, citizenship is described as simply "the right to have rights." Stateless people, of course, are incapable of enjoying these rights.

According to the UN 1954 *Convention on Protection of Stateless Persons*, statelessness occurs when a person "is not considered as a national by any state under the operation of its law." Unfortunately, this definition is purely technical and does not address the plight of people with no effective nationality.

Citizenship is granted usually on the basis of two principles. Under the principle of *jus soli*, persons become citizens if they are born in a state's territory, while the principle of *jus sanguinis* means that persons become citizens if their parents are also citizens of that country. Statelessness can occur when these two principles come into conflict.

Canada enjoys one of the world's most progressive laws of citizenship. It has liberally combined both principles of *jus sanguinis* and *jus soli*. All babies born on Canadian soil as well as those born to Canadian parents abroad are regarded as Canadian citizens.

This liberal approach diminishes when it comes to the protection of stateless people in Canada.[25] Canada has only ratified the 1961 *Convention on the Reduction of Statelessness*. The Canadian government is reluctant to ratify the 1954 *Convention on the Protection of Stateless Persons* that is crucial for the protection of stateless people in Canada. It should be noted that the 1954 Convention deals with granting minimum rights to stateless persons, while the 1961 Convention addresses the root causes of the problem.

It seems that Canada has refused to sign the 1954 Convention in an attempt not to accept further obligations towards the protection of non-citizens and stateless persons in Canada. It is a fact that the 1961 provisions are already in place in Canadian legislation in a more liberal and progressive way. Therefore, ratification of this instrument does not bring much change in the lives of stateless people in Canada. Concrete protection for this vulnerable group could come with the accession to the 1954 Convention.[26]

Three categories of stateless people are easily identifiable in Canada:

> Stateless people who come to our borders and apply for asylum. If all goes well, these people have access to the Canadian refugee determination system and the Immigration and Refugee Board is mandated to deal with their claims. It should not be forgotten that statelessness per se does not provide grounds for getting accepted as a protected person in Canada. The claim should be based on the five grounds of the 1951 *Geneva Convention relating to the Status of Refugees* or the *UN Convention Against Torture*. Under such circumstances, stateless people, like other asylum seekers, must come up with a well-founded personal story of persecution in order for their case to have merit. There is hardly any special attention paid to the condition of people who come from war-ravaged countries with no effective and functioning government in place.
>
> Removable refugee claimants whose countries of origin refuse to accept them. The only alternative open to this category of stateless persons is prolonged and sometimes indefinite detention, jail, maltreatment and torture.
>
> People who have come to Canada as visitors and have become stateless in the course of their stay. The Immigration Department usually issues a removal order against these people and, as there is no country to

accept them, they have to remain in detention centres or jails without having committed any crime.

There is neither any regulation nor any institution to deal with the last two subgroups of stateless persons mentioned above. The only recourse available to these persons is to apply for *Humanitarian and Compassionate* review of their cases. But they have hardly any chance to get a positive answer to their H&C application due to the lack of specific guidelines for H&C officers to deal with stateless people. Moreover, they can hardly fulfill the requirements (e.g. stable employment, regular payment of taxes, money in a bank account) for a successful settlement in Canadian society. Another problem is stateless persons' inability to produce the required identification document or passport.

With the end of the Cold War and the subsequent rise of ethnic conflicts, the problem of statelessness will continue to increase and has the potential of turning into a critical global problem. International legal instruments and institutions to handle this issue are inadequate and ineffective.

Provisions of the 1954 Conventions should be incorporated into Canadian legislation. Canada should go beyond these outdated international instruments and come up with more generous provisions for the protection of stateless people in its upcoming legislation. There is a definite need for an independent and efficient Canadian institution to deal with this specific issue. Stateless people are human beings who have happened to lose their citizenship. It is inhuman to leave no alternative to their statelessness but indefinite limbo, detention or psychological torture in a country that celebrates itself as a paradise on earth.

7. Limbo in Hell

INCARCERATION, WHETHER DETENTION or imprisonment, is one of the most bitter experiences in the life of a human person. You are not only deprived of your freedom – which is the most basic need of human nature – but you also remain helpless in the hands of your detention authorities. It leaves such a devastating impact on one's personality that the bad memories will remain for the rest of one's life. The problem will not be over after freedom from custody. Victor Hugo, in his masterpiece, *Les Misérables,* writes about released prisoners who used to carry a yellow passport in France and be rejected everywhere by everybody.

People are detained in Canadian Immigration detention centres for different reasons:

- Refugee claimants who are suspected of not reporting to immigration officers.
- Refugee claimants who come to Canada with no "appropriate identification document."
- Visitors who are suspected of posing risks for Canada upon their arrival, or later, those whose visas are expired.
- Rejected refugee claimants who have exhausted all legal remedies to stay in Canada and are under removal order.
- Refugees and immigrants who have been found inadmissible to Canada as "a danger to the public" or "national security risks."
- Stateless people who are not removable to any country.

If they are lucky, detainees will be taken to immigration detention centres – in Toronto, the Celebrity Inn. Otherwise, they will be sent to jails and have to live with convicted criminals. There is a detention review after 48 hours of the arrest of the detainee. One week later s/he will have the second review, and following that, detention reviews take place once a month. As there is hardly any change in the situation of detainees, detention reviews could continue, as a formality, for years. In Canada, we have had cases of people languishing in Immigration jails or detention centres, solely for immigration-related issues, for up to four years. For all intents and purposes, I call this type of uncertainty "limbo in hell."

There are reports about maltreatment of detainees by prison guards and their lack of access to medical and psychiatric care. The situation was so bad that a few years ago a detainee from Nigeria named Michael Atkin died because he did not receive adequate treatment for his diabetes.

What follows is taken from the testimony of a Sudanese woman who travelled legally to Canada but was caught up in the deterrence strategy of immigration officers:

> "We were returned directly to the detention centre holding room. I felt very vulnerable as there were three men in the room, and I was left with my hands cuffed behind my back unable to care for myself or my daughters. When the officer returned to uncuff my hands, his face showed that he too found the stench in the room somewhat overwhelming. I was taken outside and the handcuffs were removed. I was then returned to the

holding cell. Just before I was returned I asked for food but was told that I could not have food now. A cleaning woman who heard my request for food brought us 2 cups of milk and 2 juices."²⁷

Following the death of Michael Atkin and complaints to Immigration authorities, the situation was somewhat improved in immigration detention centres. Still, there remain problems. These include lack of access to counsel, proper and meaningful detention reviews (they are done once a month as a kind of formality), no psychological and psychiatric care and the absence of any kind of access to social workers who could prepare the detainees for future participation in social life. Detention, as such, can be very harmful for vulnerable groups like women and children as well as for survivors of war and torture. It can lead to their retraumatization and irreparable life-long mental damage.

I have rarely seen Immigration adjudicators releasing detainees even if there is no reason for the continuation of their detention. In such conditions, they agree to release the person in detention on bail. The Bail Program or friends and relatives who put cash or performance assurances up for them usually bail out detainees. Some of them have to report regularly to police or probation officers. I have clients at the CCVT who have been reporting to police for the last twelve years. They suffer in silence without knowing when the humiliation of unnecessary signature and reports will be over. Similar to convicted criminals, they are constantly supervised by the Bail Program, as the latter is responsible for verifying their addresses and availability to the Immigration officials when the need arises.

In Canada we do not provide people who are released from Immigration detention yellow passports as described by Victor Hugo. Immigration detainees who are released on bail can apparently live like everybody else and enjoy their freedom. However, they are not provided with any kind of authorization and this means that their plight can be worse than Victor Hugo's yellow passport holders. They have no access to employment or to education because they have no permit. As ex-detainees who usually have no status, it is extremely difficult for them to get social assistance. The situation is worse when it comes to housing. They have no money to pay rent and even if they have, landlords do not rent their properties without knowing their tenants or at least having an official letter about their identity. One can go to a shelter, but shelters are always overcrowded. There are no beds and no welcoming hand. The only option is to join the homeless and suffer the agony of living penniless in a big city. "Freedom," as it was put to me by a released detainee, "is not a big deal; it is just being transferred from a small jail to a bigger one, a town without pity."

Detainees who were used to a specific mode of life in detention centres suddenly find themselves in an unwelcoming atmosphere. They have to adapt to their new condition quickly and rely on themselves. This is a source of stress, which could affect the daily functioning of the person. I have seen the continuation of depression after detention was over in the case of victims of torture. One person told me that he preferred to go back to detention rather than being abandoned in a merciless atmosphere. Most of these people are unhappy to report regularly to the authorities. This has reminded them of their torture and persecutions at home. Some of them have to report every week to two or three places. This leaves them no time and peace of mind to work and plan for the future.

An issue of future concern is the possibility of Immigration detention centres being managed by private companies. These companies go only with their profit incentives and, as seen in the US, have a tendency to hide the truth and add to the suffering of detainees.

8. Limbo of Citizenship

IN CANADA PERMANENT residents can apply for Canadian citizenship three years after obtaining their landed status. It has happened in the case of survivors of torture and trauma that they are not able to apply for mental health reasons and occasionally financial problems (the application fee is $200). According to Subsection 5(1)(d) of the *Citizenship Act,* the applicant should have adequate knowledge of one of the official languages of Canada in order to qualify for citizenship. Subsection 5(1)(c) requires that an applicant must have adequate knowledge of Canada as well. I have encountered survivors of torture who have not been able to meet these criteria due to mental health problems. Although Subsection 5(3) has conferred discretion on the Minister to waive these requirements on compassionate grounds, it has never been easy for our clients to get exempted from them. The result has been a limbo of citizenship that could continue forever.

I have two clients who have been in Canada as permanent residents for the last fourteen years. They were both brought to Canada as government-assisted refugees. They have applied for Canadian citizenship many times and have been rejected due to language barriers or lack of knowledge about Canada. They have become so frustrated that they have abandoned the idea of becoming a Canadian citizen one day. What worries me about these clients is their involvement in petty offences due to the state of their mental health. This could lead to their deportation under the *Immigration and Refugee Protection Act*, regardless of the fact that they have put down roots in Canada and have lost their bonds to their countries of origin.

It is unfortunate that living in Canada as a permanent resident does not count from the time of arrival in this country. Subsection 5(1)(c) of the *Citizenship Act* requires that an applicant for citizenship must have accumulated at least three years of residence in Canada within four years immediately preceding the date of her/his application in order to qualify for Canadian citizenship. For all practical purposes this citizenship provision is redundant, unjust, and cumbersome. It is not clear why these are maintained in the Canadian legislation.

Conclusion

SO FAR, THE general trends in Canadian immigration history have been examined, along with the notorious backlog program and the modern-day legal and bureaucratic grounds for keeping people in limbo. All these illustrate several key problems at the heart of keeping non-citizens in limbo. Structural problems resulting from various amendments to the *Immigration Act* – particularly privatization, restriction and control – account for creating a state of limbo for a large number of non-citizens. There is also the problem of unjustified discretionary powers of Immigration and Visa officers, and a total lack of accountability of these officials. The absence of face-to-face contact between people in limbo and Immigration officials often results in a lack of compassion and attention to special individual needs and emergency situations. There are also problems in dealing with the lack of correct information and the inexperience, inadequate training and sheer ignorance on the part of Immigration or Visa officials. Non-citizens also commonly face difficult language and cultural barriers in interacting with the immigration process.

At this point, however, it should be acknowledged that limbo is not exclusively a Canadian phenomenon. Many countries that grant protected status to refugees have a gap between the point at which a refugee makes a claim and the finalization of that case. In fact, at present there are millions of non-citizens living in limbo in Europe, Australia, and the United States of America. There is an Iranian gentleman, for instance, who has been languishing in a jail-like situation in Charles de Gaulle Airport in France for the last fourteen years. The airport in France is considered an international zone. He has been taken for granted not only by French authorities but also by the whole international community. Nevertheless, the nature of limbo in Canada has its own peculiarities. Canada is perhaps the only country in the world that puts non-citizens through an agonizing intermediary stage of limbo for all of the various reasons mentioned in this chapter.

Notes

For a short history of the Canadian Immigration and refugee protection, one can refer to:
    a.   Ninette Kelley, "History of Canadian Immigration and Refugee Policy," in the Jesuit Refugee Service-Canada, *A Guide to Education about Refugees,* Toronto, 1990, p. 12.
    b.   *The Canadian Encyclopedia,* Second Edition, Vol. II, pp. 1044-1048 and Vol. III, pp. 1839-40.
For detailed history, the interested reader could refer to many available books, for example:
    c.   F. Hawkins, *Canada and Immigration,* 1972.
    d.   R. Harney and Harold Troper, *Immigrants: A Portrait of the Urban Experience,* 1975.

1. Barbara Roberts, *Whence They Came: Deportation from Canada 1900-1935,* University of Ottawa Press, 1988, pp. 68-69.
2. See word "Refugees" in *The Canadian Encyclopedia,* Second Edition, Vol. III, p. 1839.
3. Irving Abella in Ibid.
4. Ibid., pp. 1839-40.
5. For more information about the *Singh Decision* see Jesuit Refugee Service – Canada, "The Singh Decision," *Refugee Update,* No. 21, Spring 1994, pp. 11-12.
6. Jesuit Refugee Service – Canada, "The Backlog," *Refugee Update,* No. 2, March 1989, p. 4.
7. All the statistics and quotes are taken from the Inter-Church Committee for Refugees, *Civil Rights and Refugee Claimant Backlog,* brief to the United Nations Committee for Human Rights on the occasion of

Canada's Examination Under Article 40 of the *International Covenant on Civil and Political Rights,* October 1990.
8. Ibid., p. 13.
9. Ibid., p. 14.
10. Ibid., p. 15.
11. Jesuit Refugee Service – Canada, *Refugee Update,* Spring 1991, p. 3.
12. I would like to express my heartiest thanks to Sudha, who made her brilliant poem available to me and permitted me to use it in my book.
13. John Mentek, "Give us back our children, refugees tell government," *Hamilton Spectator,* February 17, 1990.
14. Citizenship and Immigration Canada, *Building on a Strong Foundation for the 21st Century,* Minister of Public Works and Government Services, Canada, 1998, p. 14.
15. See Dr. Mohamed Tabit, "Identity Document and CIC Broken Promises," *Refugee Update,* No. 33, Winter 1997, p. 11.
16. Goodwin-Gill & Judith Kumin, *Refugees in Limbo and Canada's International Obligations,* The Caledon Institute of Social Policy, September 2000, p. 12.
17. Andrew Brouwer, *What is in a Name?: Identity Documents and Convention Refugees,* The Caledon Institute of Social Policy, March 2000, p. 13.
18. Mohamed Tabit, "Update on Identification Documents," *Refugee Update,* No. 42, Spring 2001, p. 13.
19. Ibid.
20. Andrew Brouwer, *Refugees in Legal Limbo,* Caledon Institute of Social Policy, October 1998, p. 5.
21. The Canadian Ecumenical Jubilee Initiative, *A New Beginning, A Call for Jubilee, Action for Redistribution of Wealth, The Campaign for the Rights of Migrant Workers,* Priority Jubilee Campaign for December 1999.
22. Neve, Alex, "There Are Rights Without Status" *Refugee Update,* Spring 1998, pp. 6-8.
23. Jetty Chakkalakall and Alex Neve, "Living With No Status in Canada: Human Rights Underground," *Refugee Update,* Winter 1997, pp. 1-5.
24. For more information on the plight of stateless people in Canada see Andrew Brouwer, *Statelessness in Canadian Context,* UNHCR, Ottawa, July 2003.
25. See Ezat Mossallanejed, "Canada and Protection of Stateless People," *Refugee Update,* Issue No. 39, Winter 1999, pp. 4-7.
26. For a comprehensive survey of the problems and prospects of Immigration detention in Canada, see Joan Simalchick, *Is This Canada?,* Toronto, 1998. A sketchy overview of this comprehensive report is published by Ms. Simalchik in *Refugee Update,* Fall 1998, pp. 3-8.
27. For the full story, see *Refugee Update,* No. 21, Spring 1994.

12

All Is Limbo: No Paradise on Earth

IN THIS CHAPTER, I will attempt to highlight the human aspect of limbo and demonstrate what it is really like to live in this state. On one hand, the stories that follow are illustrative of the toll limbo takes on families and individuals, and on the other, they demonstrate the impact it has on Canadian society.

These cases have been compiled in the course of counselling sessions with my clients at the Canadian Centre for Victims of Torture (CCVT). Working on their cases and facilitating their access to CCVT health, legal and other holistic services has provided me with further information about these people. Details of these cases have been altered or obscured to protect the identities of the persons involved. The stories, however, remain true and authentic in content. These are, of course, the experiences of real people and as such cover a vast range of issues and themes. In order to best understand these, the chapter is subdivided loosely to better guide you through their accounts.

The Outcasts

1. Zhaleh: A Woman in Total Despair

ZHALEH HAD COME to CCVT more than ten years ago with physical and psychological scars of torture. There was credible documentation about how she received these extensive wounds, but the Refugee Determination Division of the IRB did not believe her story and rejected her refugee claim. She soon exhausted all legal avenues of help and her situation became desperate. She became one of the thousands of people in Canada who have no legal status, living "underground," an existence characterized by poverty and unbearable anxiety. Zhaleh is afraid of everybody, even her own shadow. Fear had become ingrained in her psyche and she needed help and support. She was wary of coming to CCVT to utilize our services – especially the debriefing that she needed so badly. She does not have a telephone number and nobody knows her address. She calls me constantly, asking me the same questions: "If they send me back, I'll be killed. Is there any way out for me? Is there any change in the law that could help me?" She left me always with a feeling of helplessness and occasionally with tears in my eyes, as my answers were always negative.

There was one occasion when I saw her eating supper in a restaurant. She was hypervigilant, her eyes darting around the room. When she saw me a look of utter fear crossed her face, her fists clenched and she shrank in her chair. After a moment, she registered who I was and why I was there. For a moment she had mistaken me for an Immigration officer. This exemplifies the fear people in limbo face, and how they are restricted from participating in mainstream society through fear of capture and possible deportation.

Other clients who know Zhaleh have approached me with pleas: "For God's sake please do something for this poor girl. She is dying every day. She is ill to the point of death, she has no money to pay for a doctor. She is even afraid of going to a hospital lest they arrest her." Although I tried my best to be positive, it was difficult for these people, so worried about their friend, to comprehend that there was little I could do. In my anxiousness to help, I consulted with many colleagues, including those of the Canadian Council for Refugees. To this day, nobody has come up with an effective solution. Zhaleh remains in limbo.

2. Mr. Didd: Will He Be Deported Again?

ALONG WITH EIGHT members of his family, Mr. Didd came all the way from an Asian country in search of safe haven in Canada. When he visited me for the first time at CCVT he had two contradictory letters in his hand: A letter of deportation from Immigration Canada and a letter of support from the United Nations High Commissioner for Refugees testifying about his persecution at home. I had a long interview with him through which I learned that he had gone through torture and trauma in his country of origin. He told me about the military forces that raided and burned his house and put him in jail and tortured him because of his affiliation with a peaceful, opposition political party.

He told me that the IRB panel members who heard his case believed his story. However, they rejected him, because his file was linked with those of all his family members. He argued that all his family members were at risk because of him, but the judge refused this plea and rejected all of them together. This occurred four-and-a-half years ago, and shortly thereafter he appealed his rejection in the Federal Court of Canada. However, this kind of appeal is meaningless, because the Federal Court of Canada neither reopens the file nor looks into the merit of the case. It only considers whether the law has been served during the hearing. Mr. Didd's appeal was rejected at its very initial stage. His *Post-Determination Refugee Claim* (PDRCC) was also rejected. He appealed the decision of PDRCC in the Federal Court. It was rejected. He was driven by desperation, and as a last hope he went to the United Nations High Commissioner for Refugees (UNHCR) for support. They interviewed him intensively and found his case credible. His ethnic community also supported him whole-heartedly, but it was too late. Nobody could overturn the decision. He found "a huge gap between law and justice."

Mr. Didd's lawyer made a move at IRB to reopen the case. As was becoming the pattern for Mr. Didd, they rejected the move. The lawyer then went to the Federal court of appeal. It was also rejected. Eventually, Immigration Canada sent a letter to Mr. Didd asking him to leave Canada along with all his family members. It came as a shock to the whole family. In Canada, Mr. Didd and two of his sons had become involved in the media and in political activities against the tyrannical regime of their home country. However, he suffers from multiple diseases and, consequently, received a letter from a doctor explaining that he was unable to be removed from the country because of the possibility of collapse or even death. He sent the doctor's certificate to an enforcement officer expecting a favourable decision from CIC, but soon afterwards enforcement officers raided his house. In what can only be described as a terrorizing situation, about ten CIC officers arrived at his house. He told them that he was sick and had a medical certificate attesting to the fact that he could not travel. Instead of recognizing this fact, or even examining the certificate, they arrested him along with all of his family members who were present at the time. That same day, enforcement officers went to Mr. Didd's children's school and work sites and arrested all of them. No explanation was given to the family except that they were to be detained.

Mr. Didd along with his entire family was deported back to Detroit. (People who come to Canada through the US are deported back there when they are removed from Canada). Despite the fact that Mr. Didd was extremely ill and that his heart was in an extremely fragile state, his hands and legs were bound and cuffed during the process of removal.

Mr. Didd was treated as an object as he was passed from Toronto to Detroit. One Immigration official even asked whether this man was being removed or killed. However, treatment improved and a US officer helped Mr. Didd and comforted him by trying his best to provide him with immediate treatment. The officer called a famous shelter and refugee protection centre in Detroit. The Didd family stayed there and received various kinds of support. Mr. Didd was advised that the US government had developed an excellent relationship with the military regime in his country of origin and his chance of acceptance as a Convention refugee would be next to zero. He had no option but to return to Canada and make a second refugee claim.

So, Mr. Didd returned to Canada. He was allowed in and told that he would have a hearing by the IRB. He was lucky, as he entered Canada just before the implementation of the new Immigration legislation. Unlike others who came after this legislation, he could make a second refugee claim in Canada. His lawyer, following procedure to the letter, submitted a narrative. If Mr. Didd is to have a strong case, he must be able to submit convincing new evidence to the deciding body. At CCVT, I asked him if he had any new evidence. He said that he didn't. His case, therefore, is weak; consequently, his chance of a positive decision is slim. Will he be accepted or will he be forced to go through the same odyssey again?

In Limbo Due to Security Suspicion

1. Nehle: A Bereaved and Benevolent Nurse

I SEE NEHLE almost every day in her usual green skirt coming into CCVT and attending our various rehabilitation programs. She is in her late 30s with a noble face, black hair and a soft, pleasant voice. She has been our client for more than seven years. Nehle is a spiritual being who travels a long way to reach her temple, where she "prays for everyone," but mainly for the loss of her husband, son and two daughters who were killed during a bombardment in her war-ravaged country. The CCVT has intervened frequently to address her traumatized condition. We have used our resources in an attempt to alleviate Nehle's suffering and to promote her coping capacity. She is still feeling the after-effects of torture and war. The emotional and physical scars are deep and are taking an indeterminate time to heal. She has received many marriage proposals since her arrival in Canada and has refused all of them, on the grounds that any man is second best compared to her first and beloved husband.

In the course of counselling, Nehle revealed to me her story of torture. She has also explained her so-called involvement with an organization disliked by CIC. She told me that her involvement was based on humanitarian and compassionate attitudes and an adherence to the *Principles of Medical Ethics*: "As a nurse I had to care for anybody including those who were suspected of being affiliated with guerrilla gangs." Nehle's affiliation with another organization – a supposedly violent one, as she told me – was short-lived. It was a desperate and utilitarian attempt to enable her to escape her war-trodden country. Desperate times often call for desperate measures.

Despite our lengthy and frequent involvement with Nehle over the years, we are not aware of any information that would lead to the conclusion that the admission to Canada of this noble and bereaved lady would be harmful to Canadian interests. Nehle has worked as a registered nurse for many years; she is going through different training programs in Canada to upgrade her knowledge. Her aspiration is to obtain her landed status and work in a hospital. Nehle is now volunteering with a community agency and is serving needy people there. Given the scope of her activities, Nehle will be able to do better if she gets her landed status in Canada.

Furthermore, Nehle has nobody in her homeland. All her family members, including an aunt, an uncle and siblings, are in Canada. She has repeatedly shared with us problems of internal strife, tribal animosity and religious fanaticism in her country, which may lead to her detention, torture and possible death should she return there. Moreover, living in her native country may act as a trigger to remind her of her husband and children and lead to her retraumatization as a victim of torture and war.

Nehle is a Convention refugee in limbo due to CIC security suspicion. At the end of her second security interview, she was encouraged by an Immigration officer to apply for *Ministerial Relief*. With the help of the CCVT Legal Committee, I helped her to write a detailed submission to the Minister of Citizenship and Immigration to obtain her landed status. Three months later, I sent a letter to the concerned officer and asked her to expedite the process. The officer called me recently and told me to ask my client to be patient: "All applications for *Ministerial Relief* are read by the Minister herself. She has a busy schedule. It will take her seven to eight months to read it." This is a long time to wait when you have your future happiness resting in the balance. A lot rides on the decision of the Minister.

2. Heerba: A Chronically Ill Woman

I CAME TO know about Heerba through a friend who is a full-time physician in a Toronto hospital. He called me, sounding terribly stricken as he proceeded to give me the following information:

> "I am desperate. I have a patient who is terminally ill. She has cancer and a chronic infection and is bed-ridden in hospital most of the time. All these could be related to the tortures she has experienced back home. Her last wish is to see her children before she passes away, but there is no action from Immigration Canada."

I requested that the caring doctor send me Heerba's entire Immigration file. Upon reading her file, I came to know that she was a Convention refugee from a war-ravaged country. She was a victim of war and torture and had come to Canada when she was about 30 years old. I went through the narrative she had submitted to the Refugee Determination Division of IRB. She had mentioned her affiliation with a group fighting for her country's freedom and independence. She told me later that the group became the ruling party of her country after the termination of war. This, I could see, was the source of the problem. The CIC officials had categorized the chronically ill woman as a risk to the national security of Canada and had virtually deprived her of seeing her children.

Along with a colleague at CCVT, I visited Heerba in the hospital. Despite her serious illness, she was in good spirits, a strong and resourceful woman, determined to see her family before she passed away. She told us about her children, aged 4 and 9 at the time. They were taken care of by her sister with inadequate resources: too little food, clothing and shelter. She also told us about her husband, who had been killed during the war, right before her eyes. She shared her anxiety with us and asked if we could help her to accelerate the process of her family reunification. Although we told her that we did not possess any decision-making power, our visit gave her a glimpse of hope, something which she desperately needed.

After getting accepted as a Convention refugee in the late 1990s, she sponsored her children to join her in Canada. It took a long time for the Immigration Central Processing Office in Vegreville to send a letter advising her to wait between 12 and 18 months from the date of the approval of her application.

We developed a strategy for her early family reunification. As the first step, I brought the issue to the attention of almost all the members of the Canadian Council for Refugees (CCR) and begged for help. We received some hopeful and positive feedback from the CCR. A life-long refugee advocate, a wonderful woman from Eastern Canada, made personal contact with a senior Immigration officer. I shared the plight of Heerba with the United Nations High Commissioner for Refugees (UNHCR) and received a positive promise. The case was also accepted by a legal clinic, and a sensitive woman there took it upon herself to pursue the case legally.

On our second visit to the hospital we came to know that Heerba had no relatives in Toronto and that her physical condition was rapidly deteriorating. She shared her apprehension with us and the doctors, nurses, and social workers, as to whether she would be able to see her children again in her lifetime: "I have been in hospital for a long time. I want to get better and start my life."

More than six months later Heerba was called for an interview. She attended in a wheelchair. She shared the process of the interview with me, pleased that some progress was being made. However, I came to know by the nature of the questions she was asked, that it was an interview by the CIC/CSIS. It meant the continuation of her limbo for many more years to come. Limbo continued for Heerba for days and nights which passed by in a haze of confusion. None of us could penetrate the fortress erected by Citizenship and Immigration Canada in addressing the plight of this vulnerable human being.

Heerba got frustrated and never contacted me. The process made me wary of contacting Heerba, as I had no positive news for her. I do not know whether Heerba is dead or alive. If she has survived her multiple illnesses, she has been separated from her children for six years now. I do not understand this earthly paradise called Canada. Does a terminally ill woman pose a threat to its national security?

3. Ahmed: Caught in the Whirlwind of Life

HE HAS BEEN a client of the CCVT for the last eleven years. He was accepted as a Convention refugee one year after his arrival in Canada. Like so many others, he is still in a condition of uncertainty.

After becoming a Convention refugee, Ahmed sponsored his wife and four children. In early 1996 he received a letter from CIC asking him to send separate information about his children, and a month later he sent the required information. Two years passed and he received a letter from CIC letting him know that all requirements "had not been met." No further advice or instructions were given to Ahmed until CCVT intervened and activated his file by writing to the local CIC in July 1998. Concerned about the vulnerability of Mr. Ahmed's children and his own risk of retraumatization, the CCVT wrote a letter to the former Minister of Citizenship and Immigration. The CCVT also wrote to his case-processing officer and explained Mr. Ahmed's vulnerable condition.

A senior Immigration officer interviewed Mr. Ahmed in December 1998. The interview lasted for a relatively long time. Mr. Ahmed's lawyer received the text of the interview later through an *Access to Information* request. The text indicated that Mr. Ahmed had also been interviewed by CSIS in 1994. He was asked in the interview whether he knew anything about NLF (a supposedly terrorist organization in his country). He replied that the group was "working for freedom of speech and human rights in my country." He further mentioned that he could not remember anything due to his memory loss and psychiatric problems. In December 1998, he received a letter from an Immigration officer asking him to provide a letter from his physician confirming his mental health condition and memory loss.

Four months later, the CCVT requested the then Minister of Citizenship and Immigration give clear direction to the local CIC to activate Mr. Ahmed's file and immediately issue a *Minister's Permit* to Mr. Ahmed's wife and three children so that they could be reunited with him in Canada. This was of utmost importance, as Mr. Ahmed's family was left with inadequate support and had become quite vulnerable in his country of origin.

Efforts for Mr. Ahmed's landing and family reunification did not produce a positive result. We came to know through his lawyer that he had been categorized as a risk to national security in Canada and, therefore, was inadmissible to this country. It came as a shock to a service organization like CCVT that had served him for eleven years.

Despite all these difficulties, a positive development occurred in Mr. Ahmed's life. With all of his hard work he had made a profitable success in his small business. He established a relatively big and viable business of which he immediately informed the CIC officer who was working on his file. This was one of the rare occasions that I personally spoke with the decision-making officer. She encouraged Mr. Ahmed to apply for *Ministerial Relief*. He did apply and attached all the documents about his newly established business. He used to call me regularly, sharing his hopes with me about his impending status.

Mr. Ahmed's hopes turned to despair, as he lost his business, remained in limbo and continued to be separated from his family. There is no response to his application for *Ministerial Relief*.

Mr. Ahmed is traumatized as a result of torture and other cruel and degrading treatment he underwent in his country and his prolonged – eleven years – separation from his children. This is an excerpt from a report by his psychiatrist:

> "He has felt overwhelmed by all the pressures and frustrations with which he has had to deal. Because of the ongoing nature of his difficulties, I expect his difficulties to continue for some time. However, he would eventually improve once his life becomes more stable and is getting on with his life in a positive fashion. Being able to work and his family support has always been important to him and should greatly help his emotional state."

During counselling sessions, Mr. Ahmed has revealed that the Immigration judgment in classifying him inadmissible to Canada was based on false information and lack of adequate knowledge about his country of origin:

- The term "supporter" in his country's politics does not mean any kind of affiliation. At the time of his political activities, the term was used even for people who had participated once in a demonstration organized by opposition groups.
- NLF should not be evaluated as a terrorist group. It was involved in violence at the time of its establishment in the late 1960s. But in 1978, it changed its strategy entirely and accepted a peaceful means of struggle. Mr. Ahmed's alleged involvement goes back to the years after 1978.
- Over the course of time, the NLF went through different splits and it is almost non-existent today.

I have stopped new endeavours to end limbo for Mr. Ahmed, as he has discontinued coming to CCVT. From time to time he calls me. We both ask each other the same question: "Is there any news?" And the answer is the same from both sides: "No."

4. George: A Man Who Looks Older than His Age

GEORGE'S REFUGEE CLAIM was rejected in Canada almost a decade ago. He was issued a deportation order. He could not go back to his country of origin because of his past participation in a number of demonstrations with an opposition Christian group. He emphasized that his participation in demonstrations was symbolic and did not represent his affiliation with any organization.

In preparation for his deportation, George was detained by CIC and was released on bail. Since then, he has been reporting to the Enforcement Centre every month. He feels humiliated and this has had a retraumatizing impact on him. The constant checks and the insinuation that he is in some way doing wrong by staying in the country was a drain on him emotionally. He was left with no choice but to apply for a *Humanitarian and Compassionate* review of his case. In principle, he was lucky to have his application accepted, as this was four and a half years ago. Instead of receiving his landed papers, he was interviewed by Canadian Security Intelligence Service (CSIS) in connection to his alleged past activities. Since then, he has been living in a tormenting limbo.

George is living under a terrible psychological condition, because he has been vacillating between fear and hope for the last eleven years. He tells me that most nights he does not sleep. If he happens to fall asleep he has nightmares. It has become very difficult for him to overcome his fears. He jumps at any knock on the door, thinking that he is going to be sent back to torture and death. His parents are octogenarians and are chronically ill. He has no status and therefore cannot obtain any travel documents to visit them before they pass away. He has to renew his work permit every year and is incapable of continuing with his studies due to his lack of status.

In the course of his counselling sessions with me, George has assured me that he stopped his political activities many years ago and has had no contact with any political organization since his arrival in Canada. He asked me in a quiet voice: "How long should I pay for nothing?" He is suffering in silence and we suffer because of his suffering. Enough has happened to him. Will the time ever come that he lives a normal life like the rest of us?

5. Pedro: Crime and Punishment

PEDRO USED TO be my frequent client at CCVT. He was classed by Immigration Canada as a dangerous criminal. But in every counselling session I had with him, he appeared to me as a person of integrity and high moral standards. He was in his early 30s when he visited me for the first time at CCVT. Pedro had escaped tyranny and persecution in his war-ravaged homeland. He had arrived in Canada, as a teenager in the mid 1980s seeking political asylum. He was faced with the change of the *Immigration Act* and the possibility of falling between the cracks of the notorious refugee backlog. However, he was lucky and he went through the *Backlog Clearance Program* fast. He got his landed status without going through the normal determination procedure.

Pedro told me repeatedly that, for him, working represented the highest value in human life. He loved to support himself and others through his own labour. In 1988, he was working in a well-known company as a professional industrial worker. Later that year he was involved in an ethnic dispute. Pedro had a squabble with a friend resulting in an assault charge. To date, he insists upon his innocence, and fortunately, before attending court, the complaint was resolved in a friendly manner. The plaintiff gave his consent to have the charge withdrawn.

Unfortunately, the judge postponed the trial and the charge remained. A few days later, Pedro came to know about his mother's serious illness at home. In early 1989, he received a one-month leave of absence from work and returned home to visit his dying mother. The military junta arrested him upon his arrival. He was detained at a military base and severely tortured for several months. They tortured him because of his father's past political activities although they had killed his father during a military raid. Pedro's initial escape and his residence in a foreign country (Canada) added to their suspicions. Following his release in early 1990, Pedro went to visit his mother for the last time, and the guerrillas who fought with the military junta abducted him. They suspected him of being an informer due to his so-called premature release by the army. During more than four years of captivity, Pedro went through all sorts of tortures, and cruel and degrading treatment: beatings, mutilations, burns, water immersion, hanging, whipping, and exposure to physical hazards as well as food and water deprivation. They broke his legs and forced him to witness other people being tortured. Many times he went through mock executions. Harassment, deprivation and solitary confinement were among the ongoing practices of his captors.

One night, during the heavy bombing of guerrilla bases, he utilized the darkness and escaped. Despite tremendous hardship he managed to return to Canada where he shared his entire story. The border officer sent him to a hearing where he was given back his landed immigrant status.

After his second escape to Canada, he went to a professional school and worked simultaneously. A Toronto-based psychiatrist treated him for the physical and psychological tortures he had received in his country of origin. A year later, police arrested him because of his old unresolved court case. He remained in police custody for a few months without trial and was then sentenced to a year of imprisonment.

He served his sentence and cherished the prospect of learning from his past traumatic experiences and building a new life. Alas! He was posed as a "danger to the public" by Immigration Canada and was arrested and transferred to an Immigration detention centre. He languished there for a few months before being released on bail. In total he spent close to two years in confinement. He was released in early 1998, but was still considered "a danger to the public" by the Immigration Department. Following his release, he worked as a full-time technician in a company. At the same time he was utilizing the holistic services of the Canadian Centre for Victims of Torture (CCVT), as he was highly traumatized and panicky at the thought of being returned to torture and possible execution.

Fortunately, there was an avenue available to Pedro before his deportation. It was up to the Appeal Division of the Immigration and Refugee Board to make the final decision. I worked with Pedro's lawyer and provided him with a letter of support sharing the history of our interventions for his rehabilitation. I also referred to Article 3 of the *UN Convention Against Torture* and the principle of *non-refoulement* to torture in my letter. Pedro insisted that I attend his deportation hearing and testify on his behalf.

I went to Pedro's hearing early in the morning. He was pacing anxiously. His lawyer, cousin and the bail officer were also there. I knew all of them because we had already worked together to support Pedro. I came to know through the lawyer that his deportation judge was a close ex-colleague of mine. We used to share the same office working together in a social justice agency many years ago. We had been in the middle of a disagreement when he quit his job and joined the Immigration and Refugee Board. Consequently, we had an unhappy separation. Minutes later, the lawyer informed me that the judge did not want me to testify, but he promised to consider my letter and he permitted me to attend the hearing as an observer.

Pedro's deportation hearing began in an official manner. The judge introduced us to the representative of the Minister of Citizenship and Immigration at the hearing. The judge gave adequate opportunity for everybody to speak. The lawyer called Pedro's cousin and the bail officer to testify. They both spoke well of Pedro. The Minister's representative, however, tried his best to persuade the judge to deport Pedro. His first argument was about the seriousness of Pedro's crime eleven years ago and the negative consequences it held for a peaceful society like Canada. Then he argued that Pedro had one relative in Canada, but two sisters back home and therefore it would be in his best interest to go back to his country of origin. He also questioned Pedro's religious beliefs, querying why a non-Christian was reading the Bible in prison. At this point the judge stopped him.

When it came to the decision I was very apprehensive. My heart was beating fast. The judge started reading his statement. First, he spoke about the seriousness of Pedro's crime eleven years ago and its negative consequences for Canadian society. It took him a long time to present his reasoning, expanding his assertions with details. The tension in the room was extremely high. I felt that the life of a noble person was in his hands. The judge's statement seemed to be going against Pedro, until the last part of his summation when he referred to the support Pedro provided to his elderly cousin and the positive testimony of the bail officer. He also referred to my letter and the "presence of the staff member of the Canadian Centre for Victims of Torture." At last he concluded that despite the seriousness of his conviction, Pedro had reformed himself over the years and he would no longer be a danger to the Canadian public. "He is, therefore, permitted to stay in Canada and get back his landed status."

We all shed tears of joy and shook hands. I embraced Pedro, bowed before the judge, who was preparing to leave, and I left, my faith restored once more in the justice system.

Parting, Cruel Parting!

1. Yusuf: Frustrated but Determined

YUSUF IS A Convention refugee and a survivor of torture. He has been detained and persecuted at the hands of both his government and the paramilitary groups within his country. According to a report of Dr. Donald E. Payne (an experienced psychiatrist affiliated with the CCVT) he "is suffering from symptoms of Post-Traumatic Stress Disorder as a result of political detention, torture and fear for his life in his country of origin." As a Convention refugee in Canada, he applied for family reunification and the Canadian government accepted his application. The Canadian embassy in a neighbouring country to his country of origin was processing his wife's file. His wife was required to go to the Canadian embassy in order to complete the process and to obtain her visa.

It was not possible for his wife to travel outside of their country. They were living under a fundamentalist regime and as such a wife was not allowed to move to a neighbouring country without being escorted by her husband.

Yusuf remained involuntarily separated from his wife for almost five years. It was a time of great anguish for him and the separation from his wife was a great strain. As a Convention refugee, it was not possible for him (under the previous *Immigration Act*) to travel outside Canada. His wife was in a desperate situation for a long time living without any support in her country.

Yusuf applied for a travel document but his application was turned down, as he did not have landed status in Canada (in those days, in the case of family sponsorship, Convention refugees became landed with their families). We tried our best but could not help him to obtain the *Minister's Permit* needed for getting a travel document, because he did not have a passport. He faced a vicious circle. Every route he tried in order to better his situation closed in front of him.

Learning more about Yusuf's plight, we at CCVT appealed for help to the International Organization for Migration in New York and the office of the United Nations High Commissioner for Refugees in Canada. We wrote supporting letters to the Minister of Citizenship and Immigration and contacted authorities of the Canadian embassy and requested their input. Yusuf was very active himself. In desperation to have his wife with him in Canada, he commenced on a frantic tour of advocacy groups, community projects and other organizations, pleading for any offers of help.

Help from these groups was not forthcoming, and although CCVT attempted to help, there was little we could do. However, Yusuf used his substantial network of contacts in his native country and neighbouring countries. Through these contacts, his wife was smuggled out of the country and into Canada. For Yusuf, his state of limbo was over, although for many others without contacts but in the same situation, the outcome is not so positive.

2. Jasmine: A Vulnerable Victim of Family Separation

JASMINE WAS JUST 8 years old when she arrived in Canada in late 1994. She had escaped along with her mother who is a survivor of torture. The child herself had gone through psychological tortures due to her parents' activities. I have provided counselling to the entire family. I have always found Jasmine to be a dedicated and talented child who has worked hard with her family to adapt herself to life in Canada. I was impressed by her endeavours to cope with the ongoing after-effects of persecution and family separation, this not being an easy or pleasant journey to embark upon.

Jasmine is the youngest of her family of five children. While in their home country, the family was in grave danger and lived under daily threats of violence. They escaped from this misery, although their father did not. They had not seen him for five years.

Jasmine and her siblings faced many hardships in Canada. Their mother was extremely fragile, and much of the time she found it difficult to care for her children. Although they attended school and did well academically, the anguish of being separated from their father and the responsibilities they had to take on to care for their mother placed the family under great stress. They were also going through tremendous stress due to their financial difficulties. Much of the time the entire family was living in a one-bedroom apartment. Due to the very limited accommodation, there was no privacy, and living conditions in general were very bad. The heating was inadequate and frequent maintenance problems were left unattended. As clients of the CCVT, the family was able to benefit from the services provided by members of our medical and legal network.

The stress the family endured was compounded by extremely long delays in the family reunification process. As with many refugee cases, the path to a stable and "normal" life is often fraught with complications. After their refugee hearing, they were determined to be Convention refugees, and quickly applied for landing. The first obstacle encountered by the family concerned their identification papers. Citizenship and Immigration Canada determined that the documents provided by Jasmine's mother were "unsatisfactory." She was initially asked to provide a passport, but as is the case with many Convention refugees, it is impossible to obtain a passport from the same regime that carried out the persecution. Eventually, Immigration Canada accepted the family's birth certificates as proof of identification and proceeded with reviewing their landing application.

The family encountered a devastating obstacle when, after three years of waiting for family reunification, their father attempted to travel to Canada on a false passport. This is something that almost all refugees do when no other option is available to them. He was arrested in a European country, and charged and detained for a number of days. It took more than a year for the visa officer to investigate this charge. Finally he decided the charge was serious enough to warrant a ten-year sentence in Canada. Consequently, the Visa officer deemed the father inadmissible, although he had not committed any crime.

During this time, Jasmine and her siblings were under unbelievable stress. The eldest child became suicidal, and numerous emergency interventions on the part of CCVT staff and medical professionals were necessary to save his life. Jasmine was involved in the family rehabilitation process throughout this ordeal. Her elder sister had been studying at university and working part-time to pay for her tuition. She was extremely helpful throughout this period, as she was the only member of the family with the language skills and understanding of Canadian culture necessary to assist with rehabilitation activities. However, even she experienced the injustices apparent so often in these cases. As their family had not received their landed status, she was not eligible for any sort of financial assistance for her university fees. She felt, not surprisingly, that she was being punished for attempting to better her family's situation through education and integration into Canadian society. After five years of being separated from their father, the family finally received good news when a court overturned her father's conviction. The Immigration section of the Canadian embassy subsequently provided him with a visa and the family received their landed status.

The difficulties for the family did not end, however. As they struggled to rebuild what they had lost, Jasmine began to show signs of serious stress. She began to encounter problems at school and her behavior was a cause of concern for her family and the CCVT. Sadly, one incident at school ended with Jasmine being disciplined by school authorities. This acted as a trigger to remind Jasmine of her past tortures and present plights. She felt that she had been victimized as a visible minority and a child without a father. We worked with the school social worker and shared the entire family history and their ordeal in limbo. Jasmine was readmitted to her school and was permitted to continue with her studies. She is doing relatively well and cherishes the hope that she will soon be admitted to university.

Jasmine's situation demonstrates the long-term and far-reaching impact of limbo on every member of the families affected. At a young age, Jasmine endured prolonged separation from her father and took on great responsibilities involving her own rehabilitation and the rehabilitation of her family. When the stress of adjusting to a new culture is magnified by separation from a parent and continual uncertainty about their well-being, the effects can be devastating.

3. Mana: A Young Woman of Integrity

SHE IS 34, a devout Christian, smart and beautiful, escaping death and torture in her country of origin. Whenever she visits me at CCVT she greets me by saying "God bless you!" She is very quiet and does not like to speak about her past. "It would hurt others and myself. I pray that it will never happen to anybody else." Once and only once she told me her story in brief. A hostile tribe tortured her in her homeland because she was the daughter of a peace-loving father. They beat her severely and threatened her. Later, they killed her uncles and cousins. She was an apolitical and innocent target for a warmongering ruling tribe as a survivor of her family. In desperation, she fled her native country for Canada, leaving behind her two small children. She arrived in Canada in mid-1998 and was referred to CCVT to document her torture, three months later. The very first day she visited me at CCVT, Mana shared her anxiety with me about her children. I told her that the first step in this long and painful journey would be her acceptance in Canada as a Convention refugee. Despite her traumatic past, she remained calm and patient. I was highly impressed by the integrity and internal strength of this young woman. Limbo was detrimental to her health. We referred her to our psychiatrist and provided her with our holistic services. We also worked with her lawyer to expedite the process of her refugee determination. She was accepted as a Convention refugee soon afterwards.

We all understand how trying it is for a mother when she is separated from her children for any length of time. However, we can only imagine the desperation Mana felt as she thought of her children still in the country where she herself had been a victim of torture. We did our best to reunite her with her children. We contacted the visa officer overseas and explained her situation: "Please expedite the process. Her children are living with an aunt with inadequate protection. The old aunt is trying to hide the identity of the children, but this can only be successful for a limited period of time. They might be at risk at any time due to their mother's identity and her status as a target for a militant group."

Nearly six months later, the visa authorities questioned the identity of Mana's children. They asked her to go through costly DNA testing. She had no money. I contacted another client Dr. Patan (who is now a successful businessman and whose story will be told later) for help. Dr. Patan agreed to lend her $800. We continued with our support after determining the children's identity. Finally, the children received visas to Canada, but their mother did not have the money to pay for their travel expenses. I asked my friend and colleague, Mary Sanderson, the CCVT Art Therapist, to help. She referred Mana to Jeremiah Field, a church-based foundation that provided her with travel loans.

In July 2003, her children arrived in Canada. They have integrated well into Canadian life and attend day-care while Mana works.

Limbo and Incarceration

1. Rama: Punished, but Still in Jail

WE HARDLY EVER accept collect calls at CCVT. People have called us collect, representing trivial annoyances as torture and asking us to intervene immediately. We even receive collect calls from animal lovers, who think that torture does not exist in human society. They have requested that we receive their pets to prevent their torture.

There is, however, an exception to this general rule: we always accept collect calls from our clients in Immigration jails and detention centres. This is the only way they can communicate with the outside world. Rama is a client from a central African country who makes collect calls to us regularly. He is a youngster who has been languishing in an Immigration jail for the last fourteen months. He has exhausted almost all legal avenues to stay in Canada and is awaiting deportation.

For the last few months Rama has been calling me frequently to receive debriefing and counselling from me. The CCVT youth worker assessed him as a survivor of torture when he was an adolescent. He is now 21. He is under tremendous pressure; his life is a constant struggle for survival. When he calls, I can hear the fear and occasionally his voice is clogged with tears. He has always shared his regrets about his past offences in Canada with me. He has told me that upon his release he will reform himself and will try his best to rehabilitate his personality and make himself a useful member of our society. He has told me that he would use our professional services to make his endeavours a success. He is looking forward to seeing the day when he can compensate for his past. He asks, "Will I ever see the sky outside the jail?"

Rama has also told me about his past tortures and imprisonment. He is very panicky because of his involvement with the movement for the autonomy of his state. He told me that he had suffered in two horrific jails in his country for many months due to his activities to obtain human rights for his people. He shared with me his experiences of different types of physical and psychological tortures there. He told me that his torturers hung him upside down and confined him in a room. They immersed him naked in cold water up to his chest. He could not sit or lie down in his cell. There was no sanitation and sometimes no toilet facilities. He still remembers, he tells me over and over, the way they beat, punched and kicked him.

Rama also shared with me the risk that he believes he would face upon his return to his country of origin. He feels his life would be at great risk because when they released him from jail, the authorities obtained a written commitment from him that he would never involve himself in any kind of opposition activities. Also, the fact that he is an ethnic and religious minority in his country of origin puts him at further risk, should he return.

Rama escaped to his first country of asylum with no passport. After his escape, he told me, they harassed his family back home. Government forces killed his brothers, uncles and many of his cousins. This young man lives with this knowledge every day as he struggles to carry on in jail.

Rama has committed three different minor offences in Canada for which he has been punished by spending two months in jail. This has made him a "danger to the public." After serving his sentence, Immigration enforcement officials arrested him to prepare for his deportation to his country of origin. The Appeal Division of the Immigration and Refugee Board heard his case and his lawyer made a good attempt to save him. In a detailed letter of support I shared the CCVT concerns about him. His appeal was, unfortunately, rejected. This shattered his hopes and gave him no motivation to stay strong or to survive. The only route left open to Rama is the outcome of his *Pre-Removal Risk Assessment* (PRRA).

What will happen to Rama? Will he see the sky outside the jail once more? The answer to this lies only in the hands of the PRRA officer who will handle his case. Allow me to review the number of injustices which have occurred in the short time Rama has been in Canada; Rama has already been punished for the petty crimes he has committed with two months incarceration. He was then detained with no charge and no offence and has languished in Immigration detention for the last fourteen months. If he is sent back to his home country, he will face almost certain torture and death, an experience which has already left him physically and emotionally scarred at the age of 21. It is hard not to ask oneself where the justice lies in this system, and whose interest it serves.

2. Farhad: A Survivor of Multiple Tortures and Detention

IMAGINE A MAN in his early 30s. He has spent all his youth either in jail or in exile, most of the time in a tormenting limbo situation. He is a victim of torture and trauma from Iran. His lawyer brought his case to the attention of CCVT when he was in jail. He had been there for the past eighteen months. I came to know through his lawyer that, following his imprisonment in Iran, he escaped to his first country of asylum. From there he had to flee to his second country of asylum, where he joined an Iranian opposition group. He never involved himself in any military operation and helped the group only with catering and relief activities. In the mid-1990s he escaped to Europe and applied for refugee status, which he failed to obtain. In 1998, he left the opposition group and joined a non-violent left-wing organization. Upon his arrival in Canada, he applied for refugee status and described all of his activities truthfully to the Immigration officer. The officer arrested him on the spot.

A medical assessment was needed for legal reasons, as a supporting document for his *Pre-Removal Risk Assessment*. It was almost an impossible task.

His detention centre was too far and it was difficult to find a physician who could afford to spend the time travelling to the centre, which was more than four hours away.

I approached the CCVT-affiliated physician Dr. Wendell Block, who graciously accepted the job. Dr. Block examined Farhad in early 2003. For the first half hour of the encounter Dr. Block did not have the benefit of an interpreter, but he was able to complete a physical examination. After this, Dr. Block was able to interview him for about 90 minutes while I acted as interpreter.

Through the course of the interview Farhad shared his past tragic life with us. He told us that he was sleeping on the roof of his house with two friends one night in 1985. They were awakened by a loud noise at the entrance to the house. It was a government "Guardian of the Revolution." Farhad and his friends tried to escape while the Guards were shooting at them. He told us that he was hanging from the edge of the roof and was shot in the leg; he fell about ten metres, striking his thigh against the edge of the neighbour's pool, fracturing his left femur. The Guards kicked him, including a kick to his nose, which broke it. He was almost unconscious when they took him away.

He told us that he was taken to an unknown location. After being questioned he was seen by a doctor and transferred to a hospital, where he underwent surgery to repair his fractured femur. After about five days he was transferred back to prison and the interrogations resumed. His torturers slapped and punched him and focused many of their blows on his fractured leg. They kept aggravating his wound as they questioned him about the visitors who had been at his house.

During his subsequent detention there he was subjected to many forms of torture. He described an occasion when, after being kept in solitary confinement, he was blindfolded and then kicked hard enough in the head that he lost consciousness. When he came to, they stripped him and tied him to a bed, where they whipped him with some kind of lash he could not see. He lost consciousness again while they were whipping him. For some time after this he was unable to control his bladder. It was a horrific experience, which has scarred him for life, and he tells of the "flashbacks" he experiences of that night.

They put him in various painful positions. They tied his wrists and then hoisted him from the floor by his wrists until he was suspended. They suspended him horizontally, face down, with his outstretched arms against a wall and only his legs on a table, and then put a heavy weight on his back. (He told us that since then his back "feels like it is in two parts.") They put him in some kind of seated position, with a heavy weight on his shoulder, not allowing him to move his legs as his legs and back became increasingly painful. On one occasion they told him that they were "taking him for a bath." They immobilized his arms, torso and head and then dripped water repeatedly onto his forehead – after a while each drop "felt like a hammer."

He was always blindfolded when taken from his cell or tortured. The rest of the time, for a span of more than a year, he was kept in solitary confinement. There was a period of about three months during which the interrogation and torture was most intense. Because they would wake him up for questioning by kicking him in the head, he became afraid to sleep; he told us that for years afterward no one could touch him while he slept without eliciting a terrible reaction in him. Sometimes they would bring him, blindfolded, to a place where he could hear someone else weeping and crying in pain. They kept him there for a couple of hours, not letting him cover his ears. He told us that on a number of occasions he was told that he had been sentenced for execution; they would tell him to prepare himself, take him to a site, and he would hear the weapons being prepared to shoot him. At that point they would tell him that there was a technical problem, and that they would shoot him next time.

Before he was transferred to the provincial jail, he was told not to tell anyone what had happened to him. He was told, "If we ever arrest you again we will do worse; we will kill you." His experience in jail was psychologically destructive for him. There was a great deal of mistrust between the inmates. He saw fellow prisoners being called out to be shot, and they would not return. Sometimes the prisoners were made to sit in the yard and watch while a guilty verdict was read to another prisoner, and then they were forced to watch him hang. He became so overwhelmed with his feelings that he cut his arms and thighs with the "razor" in a pencil sharpener.

He was released after nine or ten months, after signing a written "agreement." He told us that he was in very bad condition, and stayed home for a long time to recover. He required medication to sleep during that time. One of the other men he was arrested with had been executed, and the fate of the third was unknown. He decided to leave Iran.

The effects of these years have left him with lasting injuries. Farhad told us that he continued to have significant back pain, radiating from his lower back to his right hip. He has pain behind his knees, and still has some pain at the old fracture site in his leg. The surgery was done in poor conditions and, he fears, was not carried out by a sufficiently trained professional. He believes that his leg has been permanently damaged by the operation.

Mr. Farhad also told us that sleeping is a major problem. He often wakes part way through the night and then has difficulty falling asleep again. He has nightmares of being executed. He told us that he feels depressed much of the time. He avoids people and tries to keep himself busy. He tries to do enough physical exercise to tire himself out. In the Canadian prison he did not let anyone see him crying, but he did cry under his sheets. He denied having suicidal thoughts, but did tell us that he would rather die than be sent back to Iran.

Here are the concluding remarks in Dr. Block's detailed assessment: "He startles easily, getting a 'shock in my heart' if surprised. Concentration is difficult for him, his mind wandering after a couple of minutes of trying to pay attention. He has not been able to learn English."

On behalf of the CCVT, I continued seeing Farhad in his detention centre and worked hard with his lawyer to gain bail for him. He was bailed out with a $20,000 cash bond in 2003. He visited me frequently at CCVT and I tried to provide him with our holistic services. But, unfortunately, I could not do much. He had no status and this was often an obstacle when attempting to rehabilitate him. He needed a job, but had no work permit; he liked to study, but was not allowed to do that. These were conditions for his release. He was desperately looking for accommodation, but had no money to pay rent. I tried to send him to an appropriate shelter, but there was no bed. When a shelter became available and I sent him there, he found it unhealthy, worse than his jail. He has to report to the police every other week, something that he finds humiliating. He became so frustrated that he stopped coming to me for quite some time. I did not know where he was and what he was doing. He came back to me again asking for help to make changes to the conditions of his release: "I have to spend a lot of time and money to go and report to the Enforcement Centre which is almost in another city. Do something so that I can go and report every month instead of every two weeks!" We have worked hard on this front with some success at last. Sometimes it is possible to penetrate the cold heart of bureaucracy.

What will happen to Farhad? I cannot guess. He was bailed out, because they could not remove him easily. The best scenario is the acceptance of his *Pre-Removal Risk Assessment* (PRRA) application. It will allow him to stay in Canada, but he will still be considered a security risk. Acceptance under

PRRA does not remove his inadmissibility. It means that his awkward uncertain condition will have to continue for years to come.

A Planet with No Refuge

1. Ali: A Man Who Could Not Be Deported

ALI CAME TO Canada in 1994 after suffering brutal torture in the jails of his home country. His refugee claim was denied because he could not provide documentation of his imprisonment in his country of origin. He was given 37 days to leave the country. He was misguided not to apply for *Humanitarian and Compassionate* review of his file. His friends had told him that he would automatically get Canadian status if he stayed in Canada for five years. During this period, he made an honest, decent living as a truck driver and did not inform CIC of his whereabouts. In September 1998, one of Ali's friends got into trouble with the law and Ali was arrested with him. Immigration came to know about him and he was put in detention, pending his removal. Immigration officials returned him to his country of origin three times while he was in detention. Each time border authorities refused to accept him. Border officials made their position clear to Ali: "Even if they bring you here 20 times, we will send you back." Ali also spoke of the constant maltreatment he received from Immigration officials in the course of these removals: e.g., verbal abuse and threats of being drugged if he did not cooperate. Ali has no criminal record whatsoever.

A community colleague who was helping refugees in detention brought Ali's case to my attention. She asked for our intervention, as Ali had told her that he had been a client of CCVT. I went through her file carefully and visited him at his detention centre. I had an intensive interview with him and came to the conclusion that for all intents and purposes, he was a stateless person although no state or law had recognized him as such. Instead of providing refuge to this stateless survivor of torture, Canada had treated him more like a dangerous criminal, resulting only in his continued retraumatization and deteriorating health. Ali languished in jail for fourteen months, and after great difficulty, community activists bailed him out. He had to report every month to enforcement authorities.

I referred him to a benevolent lawyer who is a member of the CCVT Legal Committee, to help him with his H&C application. She began helping him, but in the process Ali was arrested again. One day when he reported to the enforcement officer, he was accused of not making a genuine effort to get an identification document from his country of origin to allow them to get a one-way travel document and deport him. When he told them that he would never be able to obtain one, they detained him. It took a long time for the lawyer to bail him out again.

2. Daniela: A Woman Who Has Lost Citizenship

IN THE EARLY 1990s, Daniela, a native of a small country emerging out of the collapse of the former Soviet Union, came to Canada with her husband. Her marriage did not last and she and her husband divorced. In 1996, she tried to apply for the citizenship of her homeland, but was rejected due to the new citizenship rules for that recently formed independent republic. Two years later, a driving offence resulted in Daniela's arrest and detention by Immigration officials and a deportation order was issued. She tried once again to apply for her native land's citizenship and was rejected. She also attempted to apply for status in Canada, but she failed to produce the required ID documents. The Canadian government returned her to her native land, only to have the government reject her and send her back to Canada. She remained in jail for quite some time, with her worsening heart problems, filled with despair and frustration. She was unhappy that nobody at the Immigration Department seemed to want to lend a compassionate ear to hear the plight of a stateless person such as herself. She was finally bailed out by refugee and human rights agencies. Daniela remains a person with no status, a confused identity and an increasingly difficult life ahead of her.

3. Mostafa: No Place to Call Home

MOSTAFA IS IN his late 50s. He is caught between two African countries and neither is willing to accept him as a citizen. He has been in limbo in Canada for the last fourteen years. The CIC has kept him in detention for eight and a half months. The CIC's attempts to remove him from Canada have failed, as there is no state to accept him as a citizen and he has no identification document testifying to his citizenship. He was bailed out twelve years ago and since then has been reporting to the enforcement centre every month. He has no relatives in any country, except Canada. After fourteen years of absence, he has lost his natural bonds to both the country of his origin and the country of his first asylum.

Mostafa has established roots and entered into significant relationships here in Canada. His age and health do not allow him to get a permanent job, so there is always financial worry. He has, however, involved himself in many volunteer activities. He is a prestigious and valued member of his Muslim community. As my client at CCVT, I referred him to the Chair of our Legal Committee to get help with his H&C application. Recently an Immigration H&C officer sent him a letter informing him that his application would be considered from scratch under the new legislation. There is always an added concern when the person in question is either very young or very old; Mostafa is of the latter group and as such merits a great amount of support and assistance.

4. Oh, My Beloved Doctor

I WILL NEVER forget the morning of November 13, 1998. It was the first day of my return to work after attending a weeklong conference in Lagos, Nigeria. My colleague Branka, a physician, ran towards me and told me, "We are all waiting for you. I have accepted a doctor as a client, but he was tortured in your country of origin, Iran. It is better that you take care of him." She introduced Dr. Patan to me. The poor doctor was on the verge of collapse: sometimes staring helplessly at me, sometimes sighing, and most of the time crying. He showed me physical scars of tortures he had experienced in jail.

It is always important when dealing with victims of torture that the counsellor allows them to speak at their own pace and lets them willingly participate in any part of the conversation. I allowed Dr. Patan to speak freely to me about his life. I soon came to know that he had been a prestigious doctor of internal medicine practicing in a university-affiliated hospital in Tehran. He was living happily with his wife and two children in a luxurious house in the rich section of the town. He led a relatively normal life; he was happy and financially stable. However, as he put it to me the day of our first meeting, one day the forces of darkness and evil arrested him and ruined his life. They tortured him under the pretext of punishing an alien non-Muslim who had married a Muslim, Iranian woman. The real motive behind his detention and torture was the confiscation of his house and other properties. They murdered his wife and children in jail, covered their bodies with a bed-sheet and told him, "Collect your junk!"

They tortured and degraded Dr. Patan in jail for 42 days and left him on the road with physical and psychological scars. He escaped to Canada in 1998, devastated, in search of refuge and compassion. His story was so horrific and graphic that the IRB members did not believe it and he was rejected as a Convention refugee. The Minister of Citizenship and Immigration sent her special representative to his refugee hearing in an attempt to prevent his acceptance as a Convention refugee in Canada.

Unlike trials in courts, refugee hearings are supposed to be non-adversarial in Canada. When he returned from his hearing, Dr. Patan told me in tears about the highly adversarial nature of his refugee hearing:

> "The Minister's representative ruined my life. He tried to disprove each and every piece of my narrative. He mentioned that I had collected money from smuggling drugs. He asked me to describe in detail my torture and what I saw during the murder of my wife and children. He told the panel that I was a liar …"

Dr. Patan's refugee hearing acted as a trigger to take him back to his traumatic experiences in jail. He was retraumatized to the extent that he totally lost himself. He tried to commit suicide four times. Everybody at CCVT cared for him. We mobilized all our forces to save his life – from the director, to our counsellors, to an art therapist, from staff, to psychiatrists, to the psychologist and CCVT physicians and to many volunteers at the Centre. I would like to extend my sincere thanks to Dr. Rosemary Meier and Mary Sanderson, who went far out of their way to play a vital role in the treatment of Dr. Patan.

I worked closely with Dr. Patan's lawyer, obtained a transcript of his hearing and complained to the Immigration and Refugee Board. Along with my colleague Ann Woolger, from the Inter-Church Committee for Refugees, I met and made several telephone calls of complaint to Mr. John Frecker, the Deputy Chair of the IRB. A few weeks later I met John at the UNHCR conference on "The Stateless" in Ottawa. He admitted that something had gone terribly wrong in Dr. Patan's refugee hearing, but he regretted that he had no jurisdiction to overturn the decision. At this time, the director of the CCVT, Mr. Mulugeta Abai, complained to Ms. Caplan, the then Minister of Citizenship and Immigration, about the traumatizing behaviour of her special representative at Dr. Patan's refugee hearing. Three months later, we received a letter from the Minister saying that her representative had acted professionally.

While Dr. Patan's application for judicial review was in process in the Federal Court of Canada, he was called by the Immigration Enforcement Centre for a removal interview. He was so terrified that he could not go alone. I accompanied him to the interview and explained to the officer that he could not legally deport Dr. Patan, as his application for appeal was pending. The officer accepted this, but still made him complete an application form and apply for a passport from his country of origin. This could facilitate Dr. Patan's removal from Canada in case of the rejection of his judicial review. When the officer took him to the other side of the building to take his photograph he almost collapsed. I accompanied him to the site and fortunately nothing further occurred, although he was in a very fragile and vulnerable state.

Unfortunately, Dr. Patan's application for judicial review was rejected. His lawyer applied for *Humanitarian and Compassionate* review of his file. By this time, Dr. Patan had become a close friend of mine and like a member of my family. He used to call me every night at home, sometimes visiting me, lamenting his irreparable losses and asking me whether he would ultimately be allowed to stay in Canada. It happened that his condition was so precarious that I once rushed to his house to prevent his possible suicide. He was at an all time low and his situation emphasized the detrimental effect torture in Iran and the Immigration bureaucracy in Canada can have on an already vulnerable and damaged person.

A number of weeks later, Dr. Patan was stopped by a traffic policeman for a minor driving offence. After going through the computer system, the officer came to know that he was on the list for deportation. He cuffed him and transferred him to the Immigration detention centre at the Celebrity Inn. It was another traumatizing experience for him. He called me from detention at least five times in the course of one hour crying for help. It was a shock to everybody at CCVT. It took us two days to work with his lawyer and bail him out.

In the latter half of 2001, Dr. Patan's lawyer called and informed me that his H&C application was rejected. The deciding officer had given the lawyer fifteen days to highlight possible mistakes in her rejection statement and to provide new evidence. I rushed to the Director of the CCVT, asking for his full support. He gave it without hesitation.

We mobilized the community. I contacted CCR colleagues and begged for help. We called for an emergency meeting at CCVT. Many dignified and sensitive people attended the meeting. A letter writing campaign was organized and four specialist doctors sent their psychological assessments to CIC and confirmed that Dr. Patan was not removable due to his vulnerability.

In 2002, Citizenship and Immigration Canada accepted Dr. Patan's *Humanitarian and Compassionate* application in principle. In April 2003, after suffering in limbo for more than four and a half years, he got his landed status. What follows are his remarks:

> "I owe my life to CCVT. I never forget the protection you offered to me when I was near my last breath. There are many people like me in Canada. I am a successful established person today after the horrible trauma of torture. I started building my life from my refugee shelter, Matthew House and The Salvation Army. I beg you all to protect the Canadian humanitarian and compassionate tradition like your eyes."

Concluding Remarks

THE CASES SHARED above are stories of real people. I have included only sixteen stories in this chapter but there are many other stories I have documented that could be told one day. From this tiny cross-section of non-citizens in limbo, various themes become apparent. One of the major themes, and indeed, the most tragic one, is the absence of human rights consideration in our Immigration system. There is a powerful bureaucracy with vested interests working behind closed doors and this prolongs the process. Non-citizens are considered and treated as objects, not human beings who are wives, husbands, daughters, sons, brothers and sisters. As non-governmental service agencies, we are referred to the Immigration Minister if we complain to a local Immigration official. When we approach the Minister, we are asked to go to the local authorities. It seems that the devil has no face in this abhorrent vicious circle.

With the prolongation of limbo, it becomes very difficult to help victims. With the lack of any person-to-person contact with Immigration officers, clients in limbo take us for them and blame us for their ongoing suffering. In fifteen out of the sixteen cases described in this chapter, my clients have blamed me for prolonging their limbo. There is a dilemma here: those who have decision-making power do not bother; those who bother do not have any decision-making power.

The plight of rejected refugees (as shown in the cases of Zhaleh and Mr. Didd) is one of the least recognized instances of the suffering of devastated human beings in limbo. Stateless persons (as seen in the stories of Ali, Daniela and Mostafa) suffer as well, due to no fault of their own. Some countries, including the US, regularize the status of people with no status from time to time. It is advantageous to both uprooted non-citizens and their host countries. The Canadian government has so far been very reluctant to even listen to NGOs about this option. Once upon a time, people who had lived underground in Canada for seven years could come forward to regularize their status. This provision has been dropped from the H&C guidelines.

The awkward condition of non-citizens in Immigration detention (as was seen in the cases of Rama and Farhad) is another area of grave concern. NGOs have frequently asked the government to consider detention as the last resort, to prepare a nationwide standard for detention, to appoint an independent ombudsperson to receive detainees' complaints, and not to keep people in detention for a long time. Following the implementation of the new *Immigration and Refugee Protection Act,* the Department of Immigration promised not to keep anybody in its detention for more than six months. This promise has thus far not gone beyond lip service.

One of the most tragic effects of limbo is the separation of families. In terms of a gender analysis of the phenomenon of family separation, there is double pressure on women, especially those with children. Women who flee with only their children lack the familial support system that is crucial for the children's well-being and for their own well-being and happiness. The impact of family separation (as was shown in the case of Jasmine) is so devastating that its consequences could continue years after the family separation is over.

In families separated due to limbo, children might step into the role of the absent parent and take on huge burdens and responsibilities and even sometimes replace the sole parent as the head of the household. The children may rebel and act out in the absence of the authority figure and in response to the frustration of having only one parent, who is emotionally fragile (as in the case of Jasmine's siblings). From the mother's perspective, the pressures of limbo can create an overwhelming feeling of helplessness that may lead to severe depression. Having uncertain prospects for the future tends to weaken the family's ability to adapt and adjust to its new situation.

When individuals are forced to escape and leave family members behind indefinitely, a series of traumatic problems arises. Mr. Ahmed's story illustrates the psychological stress of not having his children safe with him in Canada. To this is added the guilt of conscience and feeling of wretchedness that individuals like Mr. Ahmed carry with them when their families overseas put pressure on them to bring them to Canada. Their frustrations reach an agonizing point when they receive ongoing blame from their loved ones for their supposed inaction, when in fact their inaction is often out of necessity and not out of choice.

Limbo creates a situation that cripples the hopes of its victims. There is also the loneliness of living in limbo and the feeling of being excluded and rejected, which in turn can lead to feelings of apathy, hostility, and isolation, and the feeling of being a "nobody." It leaves a negative impact on refugees' endeavours to empower themselves.

The sixteen cases of non-citizens in limbo provide the reader with a glimpse into some different situations of this tormenting life condition. They are not, of course, fully representative of the multitude of experiences of the non-citizens falling between the cracks of the Immigration system. Limbo could affect individuals and families differently, depending on the complexity of socio-economic, political, cultural, psychological, and personal factors. We have, however, learned from our experiences at CCVT that limbo is particularly devastating for any family or individual who has experienced war and/or torture. As was shown in the chapter on "Limbo as a Technique of Torture," survivors of torture are forced to experience it all over again in a country that is celebrated as a Paradise on Earth. This makes the healing process from the traumas extremely difficult and in some cases virtually impossible.

Conclusion

WE HAVE ARRIVED at the end of our journey into the human inferno of torture. A question haunts the mind of every decent human being in this upturned world: will the day come when we rid ourselves of all man-made disasters and evils and embrace everlasting peace and prosperity, or will we be condemned to an eternity of suffering through war, tyranny and torture?

The hope for everlasting peace is connected to the clear perception of the essence of humans as social beings. There are two fundamentally conflicting views in this area. According to the first, humans are, by their very nature, aggressive, egotistical, savage and, ultimately, self-destructive. In his famous book *Leviathan*, 17th century British philosopher Thomas Hobbes issued the warning, "homo homini lupus est" (man is the wolf of man). We are trapped in a vicious circle with victims and victimizers exchanging positions constantly and every human being having the potential to be a torturer.

A lack of faith in the ultimate triumph of good and justice is abundant in the literature of every nation. The 19th century German philosopher Arthur Schopenhauer denied historical progress by referring to a "blind and irrational will" that rules the world. His compatriot, philosopher Eduard Von Hartmann believed in the futility of any effort towards self-reorganization and the improvement of human life. Our dream for a world free from tyranny, torture and injustice is an illusion. There is no hope and no future. As the Persian poet Omar Khayyam wrote in his *Rubaiyat* (tr. Edward Fitzgerald):

> The Worldly Hope men set their Hearts upon
> Turns Ashes – or it prospers; and anon,
> Like Snow upon the Desert's dusty Face
> Lighting a little Hour or two – is gone.

In one of his pieces, the celebrated American writer and satirist Mark Twain complains that "human history in all ages is red with blood, bitter with hate, and stained with cruelties" (Mark Twain, *Letters from the Earth*, Letter XI). There are thinkers who maintain that the abolition of war and torture is not feasible, because they are normal businesses of all sovereign states. Hegel, for instance, looked upon war as morally good for nations.

The butchers of humankind have always glorified war and found virtue in it. "War alone," said Mussolini in his *Political and Social Doctrine of Fascism*, "brings up to its highest tension all human energy and puts the stamp of nobility upon the people who have the courage to meet it." Hitler echoed this in *Mein Kampf*: "In eternal warfare mankind has become great; in eternal peace mankind would be ruined."

On the other side of the fence, there are philosophers, poets, artists and humanists who believe in the ultimate triumph of the human race. Rather than adhere to the rhetoric of the "savage nature of man," they focus on socio-economic, political and psychological evils that have ruined human lives. These evils can, of course, be removed through consistent efforts. Positive change will be enacted through public awareness and grass-roots consciousness.

We find promising words about the ultimate triumph of the human race in some religious texts. The prophet Isaiah, for instance, believed that humankind would one day attain a paradise on earth:

> And it shall come to pass in
> The last days, that
> The Mount of the Lord's House
> Shall stand firm above the mountains
> And shall be exalted above the hills;
> And all nations shall flow unto it.
> And they shall beat their swords into plowshares
> And their spears into pruning hooks:
> Nation shall not lift up
> Sword against nation;
> Neither shall they learn war anymore.
>
> (*Old Testament*, Isaiah 2:2)

Utopian thinkers like Plato, Thomas More, Francis Bacon, Gerrard Winstanley, James Harrington, Samuel Butler, William Morris, Edward Bellamy, and H.G. Wells provide us with a hopeful look at human nature and ultimate destiny. They believe that the human race is destined to live in peace, harmony, justice, freedom, equality, abundance, wisdom and beauty. Love will eventually overcome hate.

The 19th century socialists – Robert Owen, Charles Fourier, Saint Simon, Proudhon, Alexander Herzen, Nikolai Chernyshevsky, Nikolai Dobroliubov and Vissarion Belinskii – envisioned a social order in which the individual would achieve full development through collective collaboration. Marx and Engels provided us with the prospect of a free and egalitarian society with no tyranny of the state and in which people would contribute according to their capacity and receive according to their needs.

I too believe in the ultimate triumph of the human race. Otherwise, I would never have attempted to write this book. While I remain hopeful, I disagree with those extreme optimists that consider the existing world and the status quo to be optimum. This view, in my opinion, leads to the denial and ultimate justification of the social evils ruining our lives today. Furthermore, belief in the concept of utopianism brings with it the danger of making us captives of our illusions. I do not believe that viciousness is inherent in human nature, but I think that we have a long and wavering way to go in order to make this planet a better place in which to live. That will only be achieved through our collective and life-long endeavours.

Let us not forget that each and every phenomenon of life has multiple and, in most cases, opposing dimensions. Historical changes do not come overnight. We need to have a long-term approach. Those who claim that victims and victimizers are interchangeable are suffering from the epidemic of generalization. They see a contaminated drop but are blind to the vitality of the vast ocean; they see a diseased tree but ignore the vast jungle; they see a dying star but forget the ceaseless chain of birth and rebirth in the infinite cosmos. Only the small-minded counterpoise eternity with momentary fluctuations.

Time is pregnant with the seeds of progress and enlightenment. There is an inextinguishable flame in the hearts of our younger generation for new knowledge and the opportunity to take positive action. The German philosopher Immanuel Kant has reminded us that humankind is morally obligated to achieve peace. "There shall be no war," he reiterated. Torture and atrocities will be vanquished one day. Kant encourages humankind to work hard towards a world government of law and justice as the prerequisite for everlasting peace and progress.

In his speech at the annual banquet of the Royal Academy in London, on

May 5, 1883, the celebrated English biologist Thomas Huxley compared science to a monster that "if left alone ... is very debonair and gentle." Unscrupulous politicians, war lords and torturers have turned the gentle monster into a violent and destructive one. It has, however, not yet surrendered to complete barbarism.

The scientific and information revolution of our epoch has revealed tremendous potential for human prosperity and progress. Prophets of darkness and retrogression cannot stop the global movement towards freedom. We need hope, patience and consistent work to humanize our dehumanized world.

Let me end by quoting a Persian proverb:

> Whether a sphinx or a moth
> Thou who burn thyself
> For a cause,
> Swallow your tears
> And stand the ordeals
> With courage and steadfastness.

Acronyms

AI	Amnesty International
BNWLA	Bangladesh National Women Lawyers' Association
CAT	*Convention Against Torture*
CBSA	Canada Border Service Agency
CCIJ	Canadian Centre for International Justice
CCR	Canadian Council for Refugees
CCRA	*Corrections and Conditional Release Act*
CCVT	Canadian Centre for Victims of Torture
CIC	Citizenship and Immigration Canada
CRC	*Convention on the Rights of the Child*
CSIS	Canadian Security Intelligence Service
DRC	Democratic Republic of Congo
ECHR	*European Convention on Human Rights*
ECPT	European Committee for the Prevention of Torture and Inhuman or Degrading Treatment or Punishment
FACT	Federation of Associations of Canadian Tamils
H&C	Humanitarian and Compassionate
IACHR	Inter-American Commission on Human Rights
ICC	International Criminal Court
ICCPR	*International Covenant on Civil and Political Rights*
ICCR	Inter-Church Committee for Refugees
ICRC	The International Committee of the Red Cross
ICTR	International Criminal Tribunal for Rwanda
ICTY	International Criminal Tribunal for the former Yugoslavia
IHL	*International Humanitarian Law*
IRB	Immigration and Refugee Board
IRCT	International Rehabilitation Council for Torture Victims
IRPA	*Immigration and Refugee Protection Act*
JP	Jaya Prakash Narayan
LAW	Lawyers Against the War

LRA	Lord's Resistance Army
LTTE	Liberation Tigers of Tamil Eelam
NGO	Non-Governmental Organization
OAS	Organization of American States
OMCT	World Organization Against Torture
PDRCCC	Post-Determination Refugee Claim in Canada Class
PRAWA	Prisoners Rehabilitation and Welfare Action
PRRA	*Pre-Removal Risk Assessment*
PSEPC	Public Safety and Emergency Preparedness Canada
PTSD	Post-Traumatic Stress Disorder
RCMP	Royal Canadian Mounted Police
SAVAK	*Sazeman-e Ettea'at va Amniyat-e Keshvar* (in Farsi, the Iranian Intelligence under the Shah)
TRC	Truth and Reconciliation Commission
UCRCC	Undocumented Convention Refugee in Canada Class
UNCHR	UN Commission on Human Rights
UNHCR	United Nations High Commissioner for Refugees
UNICEF	The United Nations Children's Fund
UNMIBH	UN Mission in Bosnia and Herzegovina
USSR	Union of Soviet Socialist Republics
WMA	World Medical Association
WTM	World Tamil Movement

Acknowledgements

FIRST AND FOREMOST, I would like to thank the scores of CCVT clients whose struggle, resilience, and hope inspire me to continue with my work. Their stories assisted and motivated me to complete this book.

I would like to extend my full thanks and gratitude to everybody at the CCVT for contributing their ideas and research and for providing moral support: the Executive Director, each and every member of the Board, Committee members (especially the Legal Committee), former and present staff members, volunteers, and placement students.

I am particularly indebted to Paulina Wyrzykowski, Michele Millard, Stephanie Carmichael, Fred and Mara Herscovitch, Zorana Alimpic, Salima Andany, Ed Tarter, and Laryssa Carter for critically reviewing chapters of the book and providing me with their sagacious feedback. I am similarly grateful to my friends and colleagues Delfina Vega de Paiz, Allyssa Case, Darnace Torou, Joan Borja, Peri Matthew, Erin O'Hara, Yodit Wendim, Suham Khaledi, Indira Rodrigo, Kofi Adu-Parko, Minoo Homily, Giti Hedayat, Muneeba Karolia, Lindsay and Claudia, who helped me generously at different stages of this project.

I also wish to express my sincere thanks for the love and support I received from numerous friends and family members.

I am most grateful to Seraphim Editions and to those who helped bring this book to completion: Bernard Kelly, for the book design, and Allan Briesmaster, for his meticulous proofreading. Last but not least, I must acknowledge that without the ongoing help and crucial support from my editor, Tanya Nanavati, and my publisher, Maureen Whyte, this book would never have been published.

Finally, I would like to confirm that although I owe the book to the CCVT and the above-mentioned contributors, I bear sole responsibility for its contents.

Index

Abai, Mulugeta, 9, 49, 91, 98, 148, 283
absolute
    denial of torture, 41
    helplessness against torture, 69, 89
    impunity, 87
    loyalty, 38
    prohibition of torture, 12, 40, 49, 51, 54, 177, 183
    right of non-refoulement to torture, 54, 181-183, 246
    uncertainty, 205
Abu Zaida, Sufian, 73
admissibility
    criteria, 234
    hearing, 184
adversarial system, 178
Afghanistan, 16-18, 59, 69, 73, 79, 83, 168, 173, 235
African-Americans, 175
Al Dura, Jamal, 91
Albania, 69, 82, 187
Algeria, 38, 45, 84
Alighieri, Dante, 195
Al-Zakawi, Abu Mussa, 23
American Convention on Human Rights, 60, 176
American Declaration of Rights and Duties of Man, 60, 176
American Revolution, 175
amnesty, 128, 150, 166-167, 170, 229

Amnesty International, 8, 24, 27, 29, 62-64, 69, 73, 78, 93-96, 168, 171-173
Andric, Ivo, 30, 48
Angola, 43, 48, 69, 77, 82-83, 164, 173
Annan, Kofi, 18, 27, 67
anti-impunity measures, 187
Anti-Terrorist Act, 183-184, 189
Apartheid, 101, 157, 167, 170
Arar, Maher, 13, 185
Ardabil, 113, 115
Argentina, 69, 160, 164, 166, 217, 220, 222, 226
art therapy, 44, 140
Ashur, 16
Ashurbanipal, 15-16
asylum, 11, 16, 46, 76, 96, 192, 220, 228, 243-245, 249, 267, 275-276, 282
Athens, 51
atrocities, 47, 78, 80, 89-90, 146, 149-150, 172, 188, 190, 291
Atyam, Angelina, 81, 217
Australia, 18, 65, 76, 255
Awino, Charlotte, 81
Azerbaijan, Iran, 106, 113-114

backlog, 229-233
Balic, Smail, 171, 173
Bangladesh 31, 73, 75, 84, 163
Bangladesh National Women Lawyers' Association, 75

INDEX

Baradaran, Monireh, 37, 49, 99
Basijis (mobilized militia in Iran), 81
Basra, 78
Belgium, 161-162, 165
Benito, Elizabeth Odio, 65, 156
Beslan, Russia, the capture of a school, 19, 79
Bill C-44, 240-241
Bombay (Mumbai), 171
Book of Torture, The, 29, 48
Bosnia, 30, 90, 161, 170, 173
Bouzari, Houshang, 188, 192
Brazil, 47, 69, 74, 164, 226
Bruno, Giordano, 36, 48
Burundi, 82-83, 85
Bush, George, Sr., 25
Bush, George W., 11, 16-18, 24, 26, 159, 164, 168, 170

Cambodia, 81-83, 92, 164, 173, 228
Canada Border Service Agency, 184, 192
Canada,
    against torture, 175-192
    and ICC, 156, 169
    and motion on Armenian Genocide, 150
    and Optional Protocol to CAT, 65
    and universal jurisdiction, 158-159
    backlog, 224-233
    children in jail, 76
    current immigration limbo, 233-234
    immigration history, 224-229
    impunity, 186-189
    legal obligation, 175-179
    non-refoulement to torture, 181-184
    opposition to war, 24
    protection of citizens overseas, 185
    security concerns, 237-240
    service to torture survivors, 44
    torture practice, 179-181
Canadian Centre for International Justice (CCIJ), 8, 188
Canadian Centre for Victims of Torture (CCVT),
    art therapy, 140
    history and mandate, 44
    hope after horror, 142
    limbo project, 223
    protection of children, 69
Canadian Charter of Rights and Freedoms, 176, 180, 184, 188, 228
Canadian Council for Refugees (CCR), 233, 263, 284
Canadian Network for the Health of Survivors of Torture, 8
Canadian Security Intelligence Service (CSIS), 182, 185, 238-40, 263-264, 266
capital punishment,
    against children, 72
    and physicians, 58
    as a form of torture, 34-35
Caplan, Elinor, 236, 242, 283
Cecilia Rosana N. Chipana vs. Venezuela, 183, 191
Center for Constitutional Rights (CCR), 25
Center for Justice and Accountability, 169
Chahal v. the United Kingdom, 183, 191
Charkaoui, 184
Chechnya, 19
Children,
    alone in jail, 73-74
    and backlog, 232-233
    and family separation, 242
    Beslan, school, Russia, 19, 79
    child soldiers, 80-83
    death penalty, 35, 73

detention in Canada, 252
during Armenian genocide, 149
global plight, 67-68
impact of torture and war, 89
in jail with mothers, 74-76
in Nazi camps, 198
international instruments for, 86-87
Iraqi, 16, 21, 78, 80
Israeli, 22
kidnapped and disappeared, 78, 80-82, 88, 217, 220
limbo against, 216
types of torture against, 68-72
uprooted, 83-86
war-affected, 77-87, 89-93, 96-98, 217
Chile, 151, 162-164, 172-173, 187, 227
China, 65, 197, 226
Chinese immigrants, 225-226
Chomsky, Noam, 22-23, 27
Cicero 64, 220
circles of silence, 41-42
Citizenship and Immigration Canada, 178-89, 184, 233, 236, 238, 240, 246-247, 256, 263, 272, 285
Clinton, Bill, 25
collective trauma, 45, 89
Colombia, 60, 69, 80, 82, 84, 173
Colter, Irwin, 47
compensation, 55, 150, 188-189
Concerned Parents of Uganda, 81, 217
consecrated tortures, 56
Convention Against Torture, 31-32, 53, 56-57, 147, 150, 152, 154, 159, 175-177, 179, 181, 183, 185, 188, 190, 192, 245-246, 249, 268
Convention on the Rights of the Child (CRC), 53, 68, 72, 80, 86-87, 97, 176
Coomarasamy, Sudha, 231, 256
Copenhagen, Denmark, 49, 63

corporal punishment, 52
Corrections and Conditional Release Act (CCRA), 177
Costa Rica, 60, 65, 156
Court of Human Rights and Commission of Human Rights, 60-61
crimes against humanity, 12-13, 21, 23, 39, 47, 50, 54, 147, 151-152, 154, 157-158, 161, 169, 177, 186, 191-192
Crimes Against Humanity and War Crimes Act, 177, 186, 191
Criminal Code, 31, 159, 177, 190
cruel, inhuman treatment, 13, 31, 47-48, 52-53, 55-58, 60-61, 64-65, 70, 73, 76, 86, 175, 177-180, 185, 189, 192, 229, 231, 265, 268
Cuba, 53, 65, 227
Czechoslovakia, 224, 227

Darabi, Azargoshasb, 72
Darfur, Sudan, 78
death penalty, 34-35, 47-48, 58, 63, 72, 183, 212
against children, 58, 63, 72, 94, 191, 212
death row, 35, 103, 146, 203, 207, 212-213
Defoe, Daniel, 194, 221
Democratic Republic of Congo, 69, 72, 80, 83-84
deportation, 149, 152, 157, 182-183, 187, 225- 226, 228, 245-246, 254-255, 258, 266, 268-269, 275-276, 281, 284
detention, 13, 25, 37, 53, 55, 57-58, 61-63, 65, 69-70, 72, 76, 85-86, 89, 95-96, 160, 176, 178-180, 182, 187, 189, 200, 203, 215, 237, 246, 249-253, 256. 261, 268, 270, 274, 276-277, 279-281, 283-284, 286

Dittus, Pedro Fernandez, 151
domestic violence, 32, 75, 178

East Africa, 25
East Timor, 163, 166, 173
Eastern Europe, 73, 175
El Salvador, 49, 82, 166, 169, 173, 231, 233
enforcement measures, 184, 234
Erasmus of Rotterdam, 29, 48
European Committee for the Prevention of Torture, 61
European Convention on Human Rights (ECHR), 35, 61, 154
European Court of Human Rights, 182-183, 191
Evin jail, 36, 103, 109, 200-201, 203, 208, 222
exclusion, 184, 226
extradition, 159, 163, 165, 177, 183, 187-188, 191

Fallujah, 78
family separation, 232, 242, 271, 286
Fanon, Frantz Omar, 45, 50
Farah, Randa, 90, 97
Federation of Associations of Canadian Tamils, 182
female genital mutilation, 32, 56, 178
Fitzgerald, Edward, 193, 289
forgiveness, 115, 142, 170-174
France, 24, 152, 162, 164, 198, 221, 250, 255
freedom fighters, 21
Galeano, Eduardo, 20, 22, 26-27, 38, 47, 49-50, 219, 222
Gandhi, Mahatma, 48
gang rape, 43, 78, 117, 155
Ganjavi, Nezami, 218, 222
gender-related persecution, 24, 32, 63, 70, 109, 113, 155, 157, 178
Genefke, Dr. Inge, 63

Geneva Conventions, 52-62, 152, 157, 161, 227, 246, 249
Genghis Khan, 26
genocide, 11, 34, 45, 85, 148-150, 152, 155, 157-158, 160-164, 169, 172, 199
Germany, 24, 99, 150, 161, 198, 221-222, 226-227
Graça, Machel, 77, 96
Guantánamo Bay prison, 25, 59, 73, 159
Guatemala, 69, 82, 173, 233

Habré, Hissène, 162, 165, 173
Hafiz, Iranian poet, 194
Hamas, 78
Heinbecker, Paul, 169, 173
Helsinki Accords, 63
Helsinki Watch, 63
Helwig, Maggie, 151, 172-173
Hezbollah, 23, 78, 138
Hindu fundamentalism, 32
Hitler, Adolph, 26, 149, 152, 290
HIV/AIDS, 67-68, 73, 77, 94
holistic, 8, 12, 44, 90, 167, 257, 268, 273, 279
Holocaust, 149, 150, 175
Human Rights Watch, 63, 79, 173
Humanitarian and Compassionate (H&C), 224, 247, 250, 261, 266, 280, 284-286
Hungary, 65, 224, 227
Hussein, Saddam, 23

identification, 234-237, 246, 250-251, 256, 272, 281
Immigration and Refugee Board, 177-179, 192, 228, 236, 243-246, 249, 268-269, 276, 283, 286
Immigration and Refugee Protection Act, 177-181, 184, 234-237, 241, 245, 249, 254, 268-269, 276, 283-284, 286

Immigration backlog, 232
impunity,
    Canada, 158-159, 169, 172-173, 186-188
    definition, 147
    for torture against children, 69, 87
    forgiveness, 170-171, 174
    history of anti-impunity, 55, 151-158
    impact, 147-150
    international tribunals, 155-157
    role of the US, 168-170
    Rome Statute, 157-158, 172
    Truth Commissions, 165-168, 173
    universal jurisdiction, 158, 162-165, 173
    why impunity, 150-151
inadmissibility,
    and PRRA, 280
    certificate, 181-182, 189, 241
    decisions, 238
    medical, 243
    provisions, 181, 238
    Suresh, 182
India, 14, 25, 32, 34, 67, 74, 76, 84, 87, 89, 95-96, 137-138, 142-143, 145, 171, 183, 197, 228
Indonesia, 25, 79, 84, 163, 173
Inquisition, 51
Inter-American Commission on Human Rights, 60, 176
Inter-American Commission to Prevent and Punish Torture, 154
Inter-Church Committee for Refugees (ICCR), 8, 230, 233, 247, 255, 283
International Committee of the Red Cross (ICRC), 62
International Conference on War-affected Children, 81, 97, 217
International Covenant on Civil and Political Rights (ICCPR), 35, 52, 72, 86, 175, 256
International Criminal Court (ICC), 12, 54, 80, 87, 93, 155-157, 168, 173, 177, 186
International Criminal Tribunal for Rwanda, 155
International Criminal Tribunal for the former Yugoslavia, 155, 187
International Humanitarian Law (IHL), 52, 152, 157
International Rehabilitation Council for Torture Victims (IRCT), 49, 63-64
Intifada, 20, 73, 78, 91
Iran, 6, 12-14, 30-31, 36-37, 43, 48, 65, 69-70, 72, 81, 94, 99, 106-108, 110-111, 113, 116, 130-133, 136-138, 142-143, 146, 148, 185, 188, 192, 194, 200, 202, 204-219, 221-222, 235, 240, 276-279, 282-284
Iraq, 15-18, 20-21, 23-24, 26, 59, 78-81, 84, 159, 190, 209
Israel, 18, 20, 22, 25, 73, 78, 91, 95, 164, 168
Izidi, Bakhtiar, 72
Izidi, Jila, 72

Jackson, Derrick, 16, 26
Japan, 154
Jenkins, Simon, 22-23, 27
Jesuit Refugee Service, 85, 133, 231, 247, 255-256
Jewish refugees, 226-227
Jews, 150, 175, 226-227

Kazemi, Zahara, 13, 185, 192
Khadr, Omar, 73, 95
Khalkhali, Ayatollah, 72
Khomeini, Ayatollah, 26, 100, 204, 221
Kirsh, Phillippe, 156
Kissinger, Henry, 162-164, 172-173

INDEX

Kosovo, 69, 82, 187, 192
Kurdish refugees, 240
Kurdistan, 72, 221

Laden, Osama bin, 23, 27
landmines, 79, 81, 96
Law of *Taazir*, 119
Lawyers Against the War, 159
League of Nations, 51
Liberation Tigers of Tamil Eelam, 182
Liberia, 80, 82, 84, 173
limbo,
    A Planet with No Refuge, 280-285
    after release, 215-216
    after serving the sentence, 214-215
    against families, 216-220
    All Is Limbo, 257
    and incarceration, 274-280
    as a religious punishment, 195-196
    As a Technique of Torture, 193
    backlog, 229-233, 254-255
    current immigration limbo, 233-234
    due to security suspicion, 260-269
    during the act of torture, 199-202
    in jail, 202-207
    in literature, 193-195
    Limbo in Paradise, 223
    legal and bureaucratic backgrounds, 234-244
    non-citizens in limbo, 244-254
    of death row, 212-214
    outcasts, 257-260
    Towers of Forgetfulness, 196-199
    with the feeling of death, 207-211
Lord's Resistance Army, 80-81, 217
Loyalists, 175, 224

Madagascar, 75, 96
Malawi, 73
Malaysia, 18, 25
Maplehurst Correctional Centre, 180
Marivan, 72
Martin-Baro, Ignacio, 36, 41, 49
massacre, 16, 21, 43, 45, 78-79, 89, 187, 192, 208
Mastan, Haji, 171
Mauritania, 31
McDougall, Barbara, 229
Mexico, 85, 173
migrant workers, 225, 256
military occupation, 52
mock executions, 43, 211-212, 268
moksha, 195
Mozambique, 82
Multi-Country Demobilization and Reintegration Program, 83
Muslim, 21, 23, 73, 101-103, 108, 196, 282
Mussolini, Benito, 26, 290

Nabopolassar, 15, 26
Narayan, Jaya Prakash, 171
natural law, concept of, 51
Nazism, 47, 152
Nepal, 79, 173
Nero, 26
Netherlands, 161, 168
Nigeria, 31, 72, 173, 199, 251, 282
Nineveh, 15-26
nirvana, 195
nonconformity, 178
non-refoulement, 181, 183, 189, 246, 268
Nuremberg Trial, 152-153, 157, 172

Occupied Palestinian Territory, 79
Optional Protocols
    to CAT, 57, 65, 176, 190
    to CRC, 80, 86-87
    to ICCPR, 35, 52, 86
Organization of American States (OAS), 60, 176

Pakistan, 23, 31, 72, 75, 95, 163, 179-180
Palestine, 20, 23
Papua New Guinea, 79
Paris, Erma,168
Penitentiary Service Regulations, 177
Peru, 82, 173, 222
Philippines, 75, 82, 173
Pillay, Navanethem, 156
Pinochet, Augusto, 159, 162-164, 172-173, 187
police violence, 13, 69, 73, 89, 181
Post-Determination Refugee Claim of Canada Class, 259
Post-Traumatic Stress Disorder (PTSD), 42, 50, 91, 97, 270
Praise of Folly, The, 29, 48
Pre-Removal Risk Assessment (PRRA), 246, 276, 279-280
Principles of Medical Ethics, 53, 58-59, 65, 261
Prisoners Rehabilitation and Welfare Action, 199
prisoners of war, 52, 62, 216, 226
protection officers, 178
provincial governments of Canada, 176
Public Safety Act, 2002, 183, 189
Public Safety and Emergency Preparedness Canada, 184

Quran, 36, 117, 196, 221

racism, 11, 16, 224-226, 229
Ramaswamy, Anindita, 74, 95
rape, 32-33, 35, 43, 52, 70, 72, 75, 78, 80, 82-83, 85, 116-118, 124, 148-149, 155, 157, 178, 185, 216-217, 245
reconciliation, 12, 148, 165-167, 170, 173
rehabilitation, 12, 43, 49, 55, 62-64, 83, 86, 133, 135, 137, 139, 141-145, 167, 170, 179, 181, 189-190, 199, 222, 260, 268, 272-273
removal, 13, 179, 181, 184, 189, 237, 241, 246-247, 249, 251, 260, 276, 279, 280, 284
rendition, 48
reparation, 150, 166-167, 170, 195, 246, 266
retraumatization, 13, 34, 41, 44, 113, 149, 155, 178, 220, 231, 238, 244, 252, 261, 264, 266, 280, 283
Romania, 224
Rome Statute of the International Criminal Court (ICC), 54, 79-80, 87, 152, 155-158, 160, 169, 172, 177, 186
Royal Canadian Mounted Police (RCMP), 158, 177, 179, 185, 240
Royal Canadian Mounted Police Code of Conduct, 177
Russell Tribunal, 153-154, 172
Rwanda, 34, 82-83, 85, 148, 151, 155-156, 160-162, 168, 188

Saboori Jahromi, Farzaneh, 72
Saeideh, 113-132
Saint Mary's, 81-82
Sampson, William, 13, 185
sanctioned torture, 31, 36, 39, 56, 67
Saudi Arabia, 31, 65, 72, 185
SAVAK, 30, 133-137, 200, 202, 213, 214, 221
Scots, 175
secret trials, 184
Security certificate, 184, 189
Senegal, 162, 165
sexual abuse, 34, 68, 73, 75, 90-91, 117, 155
sexual enslavement, 82, 154-155, 157
sexual violence, 155, 157
Shah of Iran, 13, 30, 37, 70, 111, 133, 137, 204, 212-214, 221

Shakespeare, William, 15, 26
Sierra Leone, 34, 82-83, 173
Sinclair, Andrew, 22, 27
slavery, 68, 82, 131, 149, 154, 157, 175, 183
Slovo, Gillian, 170, 173
Social Darwinism, 36, 38
Somalia, 68, 69, 80, 186, 192, 235
South Africa, 18, 156, 167, 170, 173
Soyinka, Wole, 171, 174
Spain, 24, 49, 163
Sri Lanka, 25, 43, 69, 82-84, 161, 168, 173, 181, 228, 231, 235
Stalin, 26, 216
Stalinist, 175
state terrorism, 11, 17-20, 22, 35, 164, 175, 219
stateless children, 68
stateless people, 248-251, 256, 280-281, 283, 286
stoning, 34, 56, 72
Strasbourg, 61
Sudan, 31, 34, 69, 73, 76, 78, 81, 84, 96, 217, 251
suicide, 20, 22, 25, 43, 106, 172, 186, 283-284
Supreme Court of Israel, 25
Suresh, 181-183, 191
suttee, 31-32, 56
Swain, John, 29, 48
Sweden, 65, 160, 191, 222
Switzerland, 62, 160
Syria 24, 34, 84, 185, 242

Taazir, 119
Tabriz, 114
Tagore, Rabindranath, 67
terrorism, 16-20, 22, 24, 27, 35, 160, 164, 175, 180, 182, 189, 190, 219, 237
terrorists, 11, 16, 17, 19-23, 25, 39, 40, 49, 58, 78, 179, 180, 181-184, 189-190, 236-238, 264-265
Thailand, 25, 86
Timor-Leste, 82
Timur, 26
torture,
    absolute prohibition, 40, 49, 51, 54, 177
    acceptance of, 40-41
    against children, 67-98
    against women, 24, 29, 31-33, 53
    collective trauma, 45
    capital punishment, 34-35
    definition, 30-32
    denial and silence, 41-42
    helping survivors, 42-45
    humiliation, 20, 52, 57, 71, 109, 237, 252
    in Afghanistan, 59
    in Guantánamo Bay, 159
    in Iraq, 159
    International instruments against, 51-60
    limbo of torture, 137, 146, 199-202
    medical involvement in, 59
    methods, 32-34
    non-governmental instruments, 62-64
    Optional Protocol to CAT, 57
    purpose, 35-37
    regional instruments against, 60-61
    UN Convention Against, 53-57
transitional justice, 12, 167
Truth and Reconciliation Commissions (TRC), 12, 165-167, 170, 173
Turkey, 23, 34, 69, 82, 84, 138, 150, 240
Tutu, Archbishop Desmond, 83

Uganda, 80-84, 173, 217, 227
UN Commission on Human Rights, 54, 57, 95

UN Committee Against Torture, 54, 56-57, 182, 184-185, 188, 191
UN Committee on the Rights of the Child, 87, 93
UN *Convention Against Torture*, See Convention Against Torture
UN *Declaration of Human Rights*, 52, 60, 175
UN Human Rights Committee, 52, 230
UN Mission in Bosnia and Herzegovina, 170
UN Special Rapporteur Against Torture, 54
UN Special Rapporteur on Violence Against Children, 93
UN Voluntary Fund for Victims of Torture, 55, 65
Undocumented Convention Refugees in Canada Class (UCRCC), 235, 236
United Kingdom (UK), 11, 74, 76, 152, 159, 162-164, 183, 191
United Nations Children's Fund, 94, 96
United Nations High Commissioner for Refugees, 228, 258, 259, 263, 270
United States, 18, 22, 39, 44, 68, 72, 76, 137, 159, 169, 173, 186, 191-192, 224, 245, 255
Universal Jurisdiction, 60, 150, 154, 158-165, 173, 186, 188
US war resisters, 227
USSR, 63, 152, 175, 227

vicarious retraumatization, 46
Vietnam, 44, 153, 164, 227-228

Wall Street Journal Europe, 25, 27
war crimes, 12, 21, 47, 79, 87, 147, 148, 152-158, 160, 161, 169, 172, 177, 186-188, 191

War on Terror, 16, 24
West Bank, 18, 78, 91
women, 12, 16, 21, 24, 29, 31-33, 39, 48, 52, 53, 68, 73-78, 83-85, 90, 95-97, 100, 109-110, 113, 117, 149, 154-156, 198, 213, 222, 252, 286
World Bank, 83
World Medical Association, 58, 65
world military expenditure, 17, 26
World Organization Against Torture, 69, 173
World Tamil Movement, 181
World War II, 77, 152, 175, 187, 224, 226

xenophobia, 11, 16, 224-226, 229, 243

Yeats, William Butler, 20, 27
Yemen, 72
Yusuf, Mohammed Abu, 91